CACHE Level 2 Award/Certificate/Diploma in

Child Care and Education

CACHE Level 2 Award/Certificate/Diploma in

Child Care and Education

Carolyn Meggitt

HODDER
EDUCATION
PART OF HACHETTE LIVRE UK

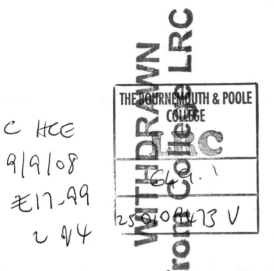

Orders: please contact Bookpoint Ltd, 130 Milton Park, Abingdon, Oxon OX14 4SB.
Telephone: (44) 01235 827720. Fax: (44) 01235 400454.
Lines are open from 9.00–5.00, Monday to Saturday, with a 24-hour message answering service.
You can also order through our website www.hoddereducation.co.uk.

British Library Cataloguing in Publication Data
A catalogue record for this title is available from the British Library.

ISBN: 978 0 340 97159 8

First Published 2008
Impression number   10 9 8 7 6 5 4 3 2 1
Year   2012 2011 2010 2009 2008

Hachette Livre UK's policy is to use papers that are natural, renewable and recyclable products and made from wood grown in sustainable forests. The logging and manufacturing processes are expected to conform to the environmental regulations of the country of origin.

Cover photo © Rana Faure/Getty Images.
Artwork by Barking Dog Art.
Typeset by Servis Filmsetting Ltd, Stockport, Cheshire.

Printed in Italy for Hodder Education, part of Hachette Livre UK, 338 Euston Road, London NW1 3BH.

Contents

Acknowledgements

The authors and publishers would like to thank the following people for the specially commissioned photographs in this book:

David Meggitt for his photography; all the staff, children and their parents at Bushy Park Nursery; Gabriel and his parents; Augusta and her parents; Liz Allen for photos of Jack; Jack and Issey and their parents; and the Shooting Star Children's Hospice for permission to photograph the sensory room and for the loan of percussion instruments.

The author would like to thank the editorial team at Hodder Education for their help and support – in particular, Kate Short, desk editor.

Every effort has been made to acknowledge ownership of copyright. The publishers will be pleased to make suitable arrangements with copyright holders whom it has not been possible to contact.

Foreword

This is the third edition of the popular text *An Introduction to Child Care and Education*. The book has developed and changed its form in each edition, but the important messages are still there, and it is relevant and up to date.

In the first edition, I wrote the chapter on play, and it is good to see that this has been incorporated into the second and third editions. The book continues to value the principles which ensure that practitioners working with young children and their families strive to offer quality experiences. This is important in group care situations and also home learning environments.

This book gives an easy-to-read introduction to the more advanced studies found in the Level 3 text book which Carolyn and I have written together (now in its 5th edition). It gives those new to working with young children and their families a firm foundation on which to build their knowledge and understanding.

Observation is key to working with young children, and knowing how babies, toddlers and young children develop and learn is part of that. The physical development is of great importance, and so is play. The intellectual life of the child, or what we might call mindful learning, is given a balanced emphasis. The feelings, thoughts and ideas of children are valued, and the emotional and social aspects of development are at the centre. Children need to spend time with adults who love them, and who respect their feelings and ideas.

Many children nowadays are spending time in the care of people other than their families. The updated edition of this book will help practitioners to give their best when working with other people's children, so that the children may flourish.

Professor Tina Bruce
Roehampton University

Introduction

The **CACHE Level 2 Award/Certificate/Diploma in Child Care and Education** is an excellent foundation, or starter, course for anyone wanting to work with young children. The course usually runs for one-year full-time in schools or colleges of further education. Institutions – schools and colleges – that offer the course are called **study centres** and the way training is provided can vary. Some may organise training programmes on a part-time basis to meet local needs. This qualification is split into three levels: Award, Certificate and Diploma, with the Award and Certificate building towards the Diploma. It is expected that most people will progress through the Award and Certificate to complete the Diploma in order to be able to practise as an early years practitioner.

You must be at least 16 years old to begin the course. In practice, the course often attracts some older students, who find it an ideal programme for them to ease back into an education environment and to provide a recognised qualification.

CACHE does not state any prescribed entry qualifications, but individual study centres are likely to have their own guidelines. Although the course is vocational rather than academic, the amount of written work involved usually leads centres to ask for some evidence of your ability to communicate well both orally and in writing. When discussing your suitability for this course (and its suitability for you!) they will also be looking for personal qualities that are essential for a career in this field (more about these later!). They may expect you to have completed a period of 'work experience' involving children, or to have helped with children's holiday activities or clubs. This would show that you have some idea of what to expect and that you already know that you enjoy being with children. You may also have had experience through babysitting. Remember: working with children as a professional involves much more than looking after them.

HOW THE COURSE IS STRUCTURED

There are different elements in the course; each one is important and supports the others. The 'theory' part – what you are taught in the classroom – is often referred to as 'underpinning knowledge'. The 'practical' part – what you actually do in your training placements – is detailed in **practice evidence records (PERs)** and is discussed in the overview of Unit 6.

The 'content' – what you have to know, understand and be able to do – is divided into units. You must complete Units 1 and 2 to achieve the Award, Units 1–5 for the Certificate and, for the Diploma, Units 1–6 plus one optional unit chosen by your study centre from Units 7–11.

As a vocational course it is multi-disciplinary (i.e. it covers a wide range of subject areas) and includes health-related units, education-related units and some dealing with social studies. As part of these units you should get the opportunity to carry out practical activities in the classroom as well as in your training placements. You are likely to be taught two, or even three, modules at the same time, so personal organisation – of your time and your paperwork – is important.

Patterns of study vary and while some students will have alternate weeks in placement and school/college, others will have set days (usually two or three) each week, so there is a weekly mix of school/college and placement. The recommended number of training placement days for the course is 65: 30 with children aged 1 to 3 years 11 months; 20 with children aged 4 to 7 years 11 months; and 15 to cover whichever option module is taken.

HOW YOUR WORK WILL BE ASSESSED

* **Attendance record:** this is the form that is perhaps most easily overlooked. CACHE recommends that you achieve 80 per cent attendance at your study centre for each and every taught module. A lower level of attendance suggests that you are unlikely to have gained sufficient understanding and knowledge across the whole course. (Attendance at your training placement is also recorded to ensure that you fulfil the practical requirements of the course.)
* **Assessment of your learning:** unit assessments (see Table 1).

Award	**Certificate**	**Diploma**	Unit 1	An Introduction to Working with Children	Introductory assignment
			Unit 2	The Developing Child	MCQ paper
			Unit 3	Safe, Healthy and Nurturing Environments for Children	Assessment task
			Unit 4	Children and Play	Assessment task
			Unit 5	Communication and Professional Skills within Child Care and Education	Portfolio of work
			External assessment: short answer test based on a seen case study		
			Unit 6	The Child Care Practitioner in the Work place (Practical Unit)	Practice evidence records Professional development profiles
			Units 7–11	Optional Units	Assessment task
			External assessment: short answer test		

Table 1: Unit assessments

HOW THIS BOOK WILL HELP YOU GAIN YOUR QUALIFICATION: YOUR PATHWAY TO SUCCESS

This book is a comprehensive textbook which contains all the underpinning knowledge required to gain the Level 2 Award/Certificate/Diploma in Child Care and Education. It covers all six Mandatory Units and all five Optional Units, and aims to set the standard for progression to Level 3 qualifications in child care and education.

Throughout the book there are suggested activities, shown in boxes, many of which can be carried out during your practical placements. They can also be used as evidence in your portfolio of work.

Unit 2 is assessed by a multiple-choice question paper. Your teacher or tutor will ensure that you have MCQ papers with which to practise before the final paper. Twenty multiple-choice questions (**MCQs**) relating to Unit 2 – and their answers – can be found in the Appendix on pages 296–299.

There is also a useful **Glossary** of terms and a **Bibliography** (which also includes a list of useful websites) to help you complete your written assignments.

I hope you enjoy using this book and wish you well in your work with children!

Carolyn Meggitt

Unit 1

An Introduction to Working with Children

Contents

Unit 1 is divided into four sections:

Section 1: The types of setting providing care for children

Section 2: Preparing for your placement: roles and responsibilities

Section 3: Children's individual needs

Section 4: Study skills

Section 1

The types of setting providing care for children

A wide range of organisations exists to provide services for young children and their families. These include statutory services, voluntary services and private services.

Many of the settings provide both care and education for children. Parents can choose child care from the following settings:

* **crèches** – provide occasional care for children under 8
* **toddler groups** – informal groups of parents and carers that meet locally with their children on a regular basis, usually including children who are under 5
* **pre-schools and playgroups** – provide play time and, often, early education to under 5s
* **day nurseries** – provide care for children from birth to 4 or 5 and beyond, often integrated with early education and other services

THE TYPES OF SETTING PROVIDING CARE FOR CHILDREN

STATUTORY SERVICES

Statutory services are those that are funded by government and that have to be provided by law (or statute). Some services are provided by *central* government departments – for example:

* the National Health Service (NHS)
* the new Department for Children, Schools and Families (DCSF)
* the Department for Education and Skills (DfES).

These large departments are funded directly from **taxation** – income tax, VAT and National Insurance.

Other **statutory services** are provided by *local* government – for example:

* Housing Department
* Local Education Authority
* Social Services Department.

These are largely funded through **local taxation** (Council Tax) and from grants made by central government.

VOLUNTARY SERVICES

These are health, education and social care services that are set up by **charities** to provide services that local authorities can buy in and so benefit from their expertise. Voluntary organisations are:

* non-profit making
* non-statutory
* dependent on donations, fundraising and government grants.

Example: The **National Council of Voluntary Child Care Organisations (NCVCCO)** is an organisation whose members are all registered charities that work with children, young people and their families. They range from very large national organisations (such as Barnardo's) to small, locally based charities.

PRIVATE SECTOR

The private sector consists of organisations set up to provide health, education and social care services 'at a price'. They are income-generating and profit-making services, which include:

* 'public' and independent or private schools
* private care homes and hostels
* complementary and alternative medicine and therapies, some hospitals and private health screening services
* child care providers (e.g. private nurseries and crèches; workplace nurseries).

* **Sure Start Children's Centres** – offer early learning, child care, health advice and family support for families with children up to age 5
* **out-of-school or kids' clubs** – open before and after school and all day long during school holidays, giving 3 to 14 year olds (and up to 16 for children with special needs) a safe and enjoyable place to play, meet and sometimes catch up on homework
* **holiday play schemes** are often run by voluntary organisations, local authorities or charities, in local parks, community centres, leisure centres or schools; they offer a wide range of activities to keep children busy – such as sports or drama, arts and crafts or music; they also offer opportunities for children to meet and make friends
* **childminders** – usually look after children under 12 in the childminder's own home, and often collect school-aged children from a nearby school
* **nannies** – provide child care in the child's own home and can look after children of any age.

SOCIAL SERVICES FOR CHILDREN

Social Services departments are a statutory service, organised at a local level; they provide a range of care and support for children and families, including:

* families where children are assessed as being **in need** (including disabled children)
* children who may be suffering **'significant harm'**
* children who require looking after by the local authority (through **fostering** or **residential care**), and
* children who are placed for **adoption**.

Looked-after children

Children who are in the care of local authorities are described as 'looked-after children'. They are one of the most vulnerable groups in society. The majority of children who remain in care are there because they have suffered abuse or neglect.

There are two main reasons for children being in local authority care.

1. Children who are subject to a **care order** made by the courts under Section 31 of the Children Act 1989 (about 65 per cent of all looked-after children) – for the courts to grant a care order they have to be satisfied that a child is suffering or would suffer 'significant harm' without one.
2. Children who are accommodated by the local authority on a voluntary basis under Section 20 of the Children Act 1989 (about a third of all looked-after children).

At any one time, around 60,000 children are looked after in England, although some 90,000 pass through the care system in any year. A total of 42 per cent of looked-after children return home within six months. The system aims to support rehabilitation back into families where possible.

Foster care

Children are generally looked after in foster care. A minority will be cared for in **children's homes** and some by prospective adoptive parents. Irrespective of the setting in which children are accommodated, all looked-after children will have a social worker and carers (e.g. foster carers, residential care staff) responsible for their day-to-day care, who should be involved in making plans or decisions about the child.

EDUCATION SERVICES FOR CHILDREN

Since 1972, schooling has been compulsory for all children between the ages of 5 and 16. A very small number of children are home-schooled. There are strict regulations to ensure that they receive appropriate education. The Department for Education and Skills (DfES) is headed by the Secretary of State for Education, and is responsible for deciding the policies of and the funding granted to the local education authorities.

All 3 and 4 year olds are now entitled to free early education for 12.5 hours per week for 38 weeks of the year. Many children under 5 attend:

* **maintained (or state) nursery schools**
* **nursery classes** attached to primary schools
* **playgroups or pre-schools** in the voluntary sector
* **privately run nurseries**
* **children's centres**
* **Home Learning Environment (HLE)** – many young children are cared for by childminders (in the childminder's home) or by nannies or grandparents.

From the age of 5, children attend:

* **infant schools** (for children aged 5–7 years)
* **primary schools** (for children aged 5–11 years)
* **preparatory and independent schools** (private sector)
* **after-school clubs**.

INTEGRATED PROVISION FOR CHILDREN

Children's centres serve children and their families from the antenatal period through until children start in reception or Year 1 at primary school. Each centre offers to families with babies and/or pre-school children the services listed in Table 1.1.

Children's centres act as a 'service hub' within the community, offering not only a base for childminder networks, but also a link to other day care provision, out-of-school clubs and extended schools, for example. Centres may also offer other services, such as training for parents (e.g. parenting classes, basic skills, English as an additional language), benefits advice, child care services for older children, and toy libraries.

Within any local authority in the UK there are child care and education settings that come into the category of **voluntary provision**. Two examples are described below.

1. **Community nurseries:** community nurseries exist to provide a service to

Good-quality early learning integrated with full day care provision (a minimum of ten hours a day, five days a week, 48 weeks a year)	Good-quality teacher input to lead the development of learning within the centre
Parental outreach	Family support services
A base for a childminder network	Child and family health services, including antenatal services
Support for children and parents with special needs	Effective links with Jobcentre Plus, local training providers, and further and higher education institutions

Table 1.1: Services offered by children's centres

local children and their families. They are run by local community organisations – often with financial assistance from the local authority – or by charities such as Barnardo's and Save the Children. Most of these nurseries are open long enough to suit working parents or those at college. Many centres also provide, or act as a venue for, other services, including parent and toddler groups, drop-in crèches, toy libraries and after-school clubs.

2. **Pre-School Learning Alliance Community Pre-Schools:** Pre-School Learning Alliance Community Pre-Schools (playgroups) offer children aged between 3 and 5 years an opportunity to learn through play.

   * They usually operate on a part-time sessional basis. Sessions are normally two and a half hours each morning or afternoon.
   * Staff plan a varied curriculum that takes into account children's previous experiences and developing needs.
   * The nationally set Foundation Stage curriculum framework, approved by the Department for Education and Skills (DfES), is adapted by each group to meet the needs of their own children and to allow them to make the most of a variety of learning opportunities that arise spontaneously through play.
   * At many pre-school playgroups, parents and carers are encouraged to be involved, and there are often parent and toddler groups meeting at the same sites.

LEISURE ACTIVITIES AND RECREATION SERVICES

These services provide children and their families with activities and opportunities for recreation and sport. Some of these are provided by the local authority and are either provided free or at a subsidised cost; others are privately owned and run. They include:

* sports centres, children's gyms
* music groups
* parks
* adventure playgrounds and soft play areas
* holiday schemes and activities
* lessons, e.g. dance and drama
* clubs, e.g. Beavers, Cubs and Scouts; Rainbows, Brownies and Guides, Woodcraft Folk
* libraries.

LOCAL PROVISION FOR CHILDREN

Most local authorities have a special department to coordinate all the services to children within their locality. These departments are often called Early Years Services, and deal exclusively with the needs of young children and their families. The range of services provided varies greatly from one local authority to another, but typically will include the following services (those marked ★ must be provided by law).

* **Housing:** children and their families in need, e.g. homeless families and those seeking refuge are a priority. Services include providing bed and breakfast accommodation or council housing.★
* **After-school clubs:** these offer supervised play opportunities in a safe, supportive and friendly environment. They usually cater for children from 5 to 11 years, but some centres have facilities for under 5s.★
* **Nursery education:** most authorities are not able to offer full nursery education to all children within the borough. Nursery classes are usually

attached to maintained primary schools. Nursery schools are separate.

* **Community places for families with low incomes:** most local authorities keep a number of full day nursery places at Children's Centres, specifically for children in families with low incomes.
* **Regulation and registration of services:** such as childminders, private fostering and private or voluntarily run day care and family centres.★
* **Social workers:** work with families where children are assessed as being 'in need'; they give practical support and advice on a wide range of issues including adoption and foster care.★
* **Infant or primary education:** children must attend full-time school from the age of 5, and must follow the National Curriculum.★
* **Residential holidays:** provide opportunities for children to develop self-reliance, as well as providing a break for many children who otherwise would not have the chance of a holiday.
* **Holiday play schemes:** full-day programmes of activities during the school holidays.

* **Advice, information and counselling:** local authorities have a duty to provide information and counselling to families where there is a child in need.★
* **Children's centres:** these include early learning, parent information services, and support for children and parents with special needs.★
* **Respite care:** families where a child has special needs may be offered a residential holiday for their child so that they can have a break – or respite – from caring for them full-time.★

These services are usually listed and coordinated by a local **Council for Voluntary Service**. Voluntary organisations sometimes also provide some of the statutory services and will receive payment from the local authority or government for these services – for example, after-school clubs.

SOURCES OF INFORMATION AND GUIDANCE

Some useful sources of information about early years services are listed opposite.

ACTIVITY: FINDING OUT ABOUT YOUR AREA

1. Design a booklet that you could give to a family who are new to your area to inform them about the following sources of information.

Where to find information on:
* support groups for parents
* mother and toddler groups
* pre-school groups (playgroups)
* nursery schools and infant schools.

How to access information on:
* health care for their family – hospitals and accident & emergency departments
* location of health clinics, GP centres
* Community Health Councils – these are

independent bodies that represent the views of patients and users of the Health Service.

Where to find out what benefits and allowances they may be entitled to receive – for example:
* child benefit
* lone-parent benefit
* housing benefit.

2. List some useful general voluntary organisations that exist to support families with young children, with addresses, telephone numbers and, where possible, their website addresses.

* *Charities Digest*: available in the reference section of public libraries and most college libraries.
* www.charitynet.org.uk.
* Citizens Advice Bureau: trained staff provide free, impartial advice and help on legal, social and financial matters to anyone who contacts them.
* Public library: for information on all local voluntary groups, often on computer link.
* *Yellow Pages*/phone book: usually listed under 'Charitable & Voluntary Organisations'.
* Local Authority (Council) Information Service: useful addresses of voluntary organisations.
* Post Offices and Benefit Agency Offices (DSS): for leaflets explaining the benefits and allowances available for families with young children.

Section 2

Preparing for your placement: roles and responsibilities

During the course, you will be allocated a range of placements, which may include nurseries, schools and families. These are arranged by your study centre and should enable you to carry out all the requirements set out in your Course Handbook. The variety of placements available will depend on where you are studying and the local structure of early years care and education provision.

Every work setting will be different depending on staff, premises, function, attitude, outlook and, of course, the children! There is plenty to learn from those who have experience and are willing to share their expertise with you and offer advice. You will have the opportunity to decide if you have a preferred age range, which may be useful when you seek employment. Similarly, you may feel more comfortable and confident in some staff teams than others. This may be because of organisational factors or attitudes – try to analyse what makes the difference.

If you are following the career path that is right for you, then it is probable (and preferable) that you enjoy your training placement time more than your study centre time! If this is not the case, think carefully about your choices for now and the future. Child care and education is one field in which you cannot achieve through written work alone. Students who show little initiative, have poor communication and display little interest in placement are unlikely to receive satisfactory PDPs (personal development profiles) and so will not succeed, whereas those who are very good in their placements can usually be given the necessary support to complete written tasks successfully to achieve the award.

BEFORE STARTING YOUR PLACEMENT

Many students are nervous when starting in a new placement, and staff will be aware of their concerns. The information that follows will help you to feel more confident and to feel settled more quickly.

Before you start: making contact

Find out exactly where the placement is – practise the route beforehand so that you allow enough time; make sure you have the telephone number and that you know who to report to. (Many placements will be happy to show you around prior to starting work.) At this first visit you could ask the following questions.

* What hours will I be working?
* What should I wear?
* What sort of things will I have to do?
* What shall I do if I am ill or cannot attend?
* What shall I do at lunchtime?
* What happens at the end of a placement period?

What are the placement responsibilities?

Many training placements have a wealth of experience in helping students on a number of courses and may have a designated person (e.g. a placement supervisor) to liaise with the study centre.

* They welcome well-motivated students and will afford time and advice for those willing and keen to accept it.
* They understand that there are course requirements that you need to be able to implement, but they will also expect you to carry out tasks they have planned and arranged, and to follow the policies and procedures laid down in their setting.

Take advantage of any extra opportunities you may have to attend special events or outings as these provide valuable experience in seeing children in a range of situations and environments.

What are your responsibilities as a student in the placement?

Your responsibilities are as follows:

* attendance
* appearance

* paperwork
* cooperation and teamwork
* confidentiality.

Attendance

Check attendance times

Make sure you have checked the following with your supervisor: your starting time, break and lunch times, and finishing time. There is sometimes some flexibility if you have limited transport choices or have unavoidable appointments.

Be flexible

Always offer to make up missed time, and be prepared to stay longer on some occasions, if possible, to help complete a job and prepare for the following day (for example, when displays are being changed – much easier to do without children around!).

Reliability and punctuality

These are very important and poor performance in these aspects can lead to tensions between you and staff. Their main concern must be the children in their care and they will be less likely to cooperate with you and to give responsibility for tasks if you cannot be relied upon to arrive on time and be prepared.

Absence from placement

If, for some good reason, you cannot attend then you must contact your placement and inform them as soon as possible (preferably before the children arrive) so alternative arrangements can be made, indicating whether you are likely to be able to attend on the next scheduled date. You should also inform your study centre to avoid a visiting tutor making an unnecessary journey. Whenever possible, missed days should be 'made up'.

Appearance

Your study centre will give guidance for appearance, particularly if there is a dress code or uniform (often a sweatshirt over dark trousers).

✳ Choose clothing carefully, bearing in mind the types of activity you are likely to be involved in.
✳ Footwear should be comfortable and not too heavy.
✳ Hair should be tied back if long; young children in group settings often have **head lice** – you can help to avoid getting them yourself by ensuring you keep your hair well brushed and by tying it back.
✳ Avoid long fingernails and don't wear nail varnish – flakes chipping off into the snack you are preparing is neither appetising nor hygienic!
✳ Similarly, avoid all jewellery other than a watch – small children pull on chains and dangly earrings, and heavy rings and bracelets are inappropriate for dealing with play dough or paint, or for changing nappies.

Paperwork

Although time is always precious, try to identify a time each week or fortnight when you can sit down with your supervisor and discuss your progress. You should talk about:

✳ what competencies you feel you have achieved
✳ how you might achieve those that do not occur during the normal daily routine
✳ what activities you have planned and need to carry out
✳ forthcoming plans and events that involve you.

Keeping a log or diary

This will help you to recall things you have done and match them to the competencies in the practice evidence record (PER) (see below). It is *your* responsibility to do this, not your supervisor's. Try to become familiar with the requirements and make a pencil mark next to each one you believe you have carried out competently – if you can show a date, or dates, and refer to your log, then your supervisor is more likely to remember it and may sign it off.

Remember that your **PER** is your record of achievement in placement and is vital evidence for you to earn the Certificate.

✳ **Do not lose it!** It is important to keep a record of signed competencies throughout the course and check it regularly with your tutor in case the worst should happen.
✳ **Keep your PER in a safe place:** try to avoid leaving your PER with your supervisor – this may seem sensible but often leads to disaster if you or he/she is absent, the book gets mislaid or damaged, or the placement comes to an end followed by a long holiday.
✳ **Attendance record:** your study centre may require you to keep an attendance sheet that logs the times and dates of placement attendance. This needs to be signed regularly by your supervisor and kept by you.
✳ **Getting signatures:** in addition to your attendance record and PER competencies you will also need to obtain your supervisor's signature to authenticate (i.e. show that they are genuine) displays, observations and portfolio activities.

Cooperation and teamwork

No two training placements, nor supervisors, will be the same. It is important, therefore, to settle as quickly as possible into new and different routines and practices. Gathering the placement information, as suggested on pages 7–8, should speed up this process.

Cooperating with other professionals and recognising their contributions are areas that are assessed through the PDP at the end of each placement. If you are a student who attends for one or two days a week it can be difficult to pick up the threads of what has happened on the days you have been at your study centre. The opportunity to attend your placement for a block week will give you the chance to experience the full range of activities, including PE, music, cookery and other topic work that you may otherwise be missing.

As you are attending on the same days each week it may seem that you are always given the same jobs to do – Fridays usually involve washing paint pots! These have to be done and, if they are carried out by other staff members or helpers on other occasions, then it is not unreasonable for you to be expected to do them too as part of your training.

It only becomes a problem if you are given tasks that are always – or often – away from the children, and you are not having the opportunity to carry out the requirements of the course. If this is the case you need to speak to your tutor, who may visit and discuss these issues with your supervisor.

Confidentiality

Anyone working with young children, whether in a nursery setting, a school or in the family home, will need to practise confidentiality.

* Confidentiality is respect for the privacy of any information about a child and his or her family. In most instances you will be working under the supervision of others and it is likely that parents will pass confidential information directly to a staff member. However, there may be occasions on which *you* are given information and asked to pass it on, or that you may hear or be told confidential information in the course of the daily routine.

* You may be entrusted with personal information about children, parents and staff, either directly (being told or being given written information) or indirectly (hearing staffroom discussions, parental comments or children's conversations) and it is important that you do not repeat any of it at home or to friends.

* There have been embarrassing – not to say unpleasant – incidents, sometimes resulting in students' placements being cancelled, through thoughtlessness. In small communities, such as schools or nurseries, it is easy for a parent or family member to overhear confidential information relating to daily events (e.g. an incident involving aggressive behaviour or swearing) or individual children (personal or family difficulties affecting the child concerned) if it is mentioned to a neighbour or the person you baby-sit for, even if it is through concern. The incidents may be discussed in your teaching sessions among your student group, but you should not identify the children concerned, and it must be agreed that they are not talked about beyond the group.

As long as you follow the guidelines, procedures and practices that apply to the work setting you will not go far wrong.

Practising confidentiality

Children and their parents and carers need to feel confident that:

* you will not interfere in their private lives and that any information you are privileged to hold will not become a

source of gossip; breaches of confidentiality can occur when you are travelling on public transport, for example, and discussing the events of your day; always remember that using the names of children in your care can cause a serious breach of confidentiality if overheard by a friend or relative of the family

* you will ensure that any child or family's personal information is restricted to those who have a real *need to know* – for example, when a child's family or health circumstances are affecting their development

* you will not write anything down about a child that you would feel concerned about showing their parents or carers

* you understand when the safety or health needs of the child override the need for confidentiality; parents need to be reassured that you will always put the safety and well-being of each child before any other considerations.

TIME MANAGEMENT

There are often conflicting pressures on your time when working in early years settings. However well prepared a timetable is, something can always occur that upsets the smooth running of the day. Even when you are caring for one young baby in the parent's home, you will find it useful to follow these guidelines.

* **Prioritise your tasks:** it is a good idea to make a written list of the various tasks you have to complete in a particular session; then you can divide the tasks into essential and non-essential (but desirable) tasks.

* **Set targets:** try to set deadlines for completing certain tasks; you may be able to fit in a simple task – such as organising the creative play area – between other tasks. Be realistic in what you hope to achieve. Be aware that you may be interrupted in what you are doing and will need to return to it later.

* **Try not to become overwhelmed:** there will be some days when you wonder if you will ever complete any one task. Take a deep breath and try to put it all into perspective. As long as you are doing your best and have the children's welfare as your primary concern, try not to panic if you are running late!

* **Share your concerns:** your colleagues will understand the pressures (and the rewards) of working with children, and about the unpredictability of such work. By sharing your worries you can learn how to manage your time and routines more effectively.

Fig 1.1. Talking at the child's level

WHAT QUALITIES MAKE A GOOD CHILD CARE PRACTITIONER?

Above all else, you need to like children and to enjoy being with them. The main qualities needed when working with young children are as follows.

- **Listening:** attentive listening is a vital part of the caring relationship. Sometimes a child's real needs are communicated more by what is left unsaid than what is actually spoken. You need to be aware of the different forms of non-verbal communication; when you are listening closely to a child, watch out also for the way they stand or sit and their facial expressions, as these give vital clues to a child's feelings.

- **Comforting:** this has both a physical and an emotional meaning. Physical comfort may be provided by hugging a child who appears distressed. Touching, listening and talking can all provide emotional comfort as well.

- **Empathy:** this should not be confused with sympathy. Some people find it easy to appreciate how someone else is feeling by imagining themselves in that person's position. A good way of imagining how a strange environment appears to a young child is to kneel on the floor and try to view it from a child's perspective.

- **Sensitivity:** you need to be able to be aware of, and to respond to, the feelings and needs of another person. Being sensitive to others' needs means you can anticipate their feelings; for example, when a child's mother has been admitted to hospital or their pet dog has just died, you may need to be ready with a friendly hug or a few words to show that you understand and that you really care.

- **Patience:** you need to be patient and tolerant of other people's methods of dealing with problems, even when you feel that your own way is better – for example, letting a child develop independence by dressing himself even when you need to hurry.

- **Respect:** you need to be aware of a child's personal rights, dignity and privacy, and must show this at all times. Every child is unique, so your approach will need to take account of each child's individual needs.

- **Interpersonal skills:** a caring relationship is a two-way process. You do not have to like the child you are caring for, but being able to show warmth and friendliness helps to create a positive atmosphere and to break down barriers. Acceptance is important; you should always look beyond any disability or disruptive behaviour to recognise and accept the person.

- **Self-awareness:** you can become a better early years worker if you can judge what effect your behaviour has on other people, and be willing to adapt. When you are working as part of a team, you need to be aware of how others see you and to be prepared to change your behaviour to help the team to function well.

- **Coping with stress:** you need a great deal of energy when you are working in a caring profession; you need to be aware of the possibility of professional burnout. In order to help others we must first help ourselves; the carer who never relaxes or develops any outside interests is more likely to suffer 'burnout' than the carer who finds his own time and space.

- **Knowledge and understanding:** you need to have an understanding of child development and basic child care in order to promote children's all-round development.

- **Learning from experience:** it is important to continue to learn and grow as professionals; observing babies and children helps you to avoid making assumptions about a child and helps you to identify any special need a child may have.

VALUES AND POSITIVE ATTITUDES

Our values and attitudes towards others develop from early childhood. The way in which we are brought up and the behaviour we see around us will help us to form opinions and to make choices about every aspect of our lives. The first values we absorb into our learning come from our early childhood experiences, particularly from:

* our parents or primary carers and our family
* our friends and their families
* our early experiences in playgroup, nursery and school.

Children learn moral values by example and by imitation. If a child is made to feel secure and loved within their family, they will develop confidence and self-esteem, and find it easier to form close relationships with others. Children whose early life involves unhappy or very weak relationships with others often find it difficult to form close, lasting relationships when they are older. Attitudes are the opinions and ways of thinking that we have towards others and their beliefs. These attitudes are shaped by our values.

Examples of moral values are:

* truth
* right conduct
* love
* non-violence
* peace
* justice.

Our attitudes towards others are based on our beliefs and feelings about the world. Negative attitudes towards others may result from assumptions about people and their way of life, which may be very different from our own. Travellers, for example, have often been discriminated against within care settings because of these differences.

Positive attitudes towards children enable them:

* to feel good about themselves
* to feel that they are valued
* to develop high self-esteem.

It is not our task to try to change the values and attitudes of others, but we should challenge others if their behaviour shows discrimination. What is most important is that we act as **good role models** through our work with children, so that they can learn to imitate our behaviour and express positive attitudes towards others.

ACTIVITY: EXPLORING YOUR ATTITUDES AND VALUES

Consider the following moral questions.
1 Should women go out to work when they have young children?
2 Should the armed forces accept gay men and women into their ranks?
3 Should it be against the law to smack a child? Should childminders and teachers have the right to smack a child if the parents consent?

4 Should gay couples (male or female) be allowed to adopt a child?
5 Should men take an equal share with women in bringing up their children?

In pairs, discuss each question in turn, making brief notes on the arguments for and against each question. Then, in the whole group, consider how each answer could affect your attitudes towards parents and children in the work setting.

The poem in the box below by Dorothy Law Nolte describes the effect our values have on children's development.

BEING A GOOD ROLE MODEL

Children learn more from how they *see us act* than they do from anything we may tell them. Children directly copy what adults do, so it is important that we nurture an environment that is free from any bias and that encourages equality of opportunity. Being a good role model involves the following aspects.

* **Non-verbal communication:** children pick up signals about how we think, feel and act from our body language, facial expressions, gestures, pauses etc. When listening to children, make sure that your eyes are at their eye level, and give them time to express themselves, making encouraging sounds and smiling.

* **Using appropriate language:** how you talk to children and respond to them is very important. You need to be able to adapt your language to the individual child and to be aware of any communication difficulties.

* **Cooperating with others:** children need to see that you are pleasant and that you can get along with parents and other adults. Any conflicts between members of staff, for example, should be aired when in the staff room.

CHILDREN LEARN WHAT THEY LIVE

If children live with criticism, they learn to condemn.
If children live with hostility, they learn to fight.
If children live with fear, they learn to be apprehensive.
If children live with pity, they learn to feel sorry for themselves.
If children live with ridicule, they learn to be shy.
If children live with jealousy, they learn to feel envy.
If children live with shame, they learn to feel guilty.
If children live with encouragement, they learn confidence.
If children live with tolerance, they learn patience.
If children live with praise, they learn appreciation.
If children live with acceptance, they learn to love.
If children live with approval, they learn to like themselves.
If children live with recognition, they learn it is good to have a goal.
If children live with sharing, they learn generosity
If children live with honesty, they learn truthfulness.
If children live with fairness, they learn justice.
If children live with kindness and consideration, they learn respect.
If children live with security, they learn to have faith in themselves and in those about them.
If children live with friendliness, they learn the world is a nice place in which to live.

ACTIVITY: EXPLORING MORAL VALUES

Working in pairs or small groups, identify and list five moral values within the poem above and, for each value, discuss how it can be promoted within the care and education setting. (One example could be the value of appreciation; by praising children every time they have achieved something, however small that thing may be, you are demonstrating your appreciation for them as individuals and promoting their self-concept – or feelings of self-worth.)

* **Showing respect:** learning how to pronounce difficult names and listening to other people's opinions are important in showing your respect for others.
* **Avoiding stereotypes and labels:** avoid using labels that result in children being stereotyped (e.g. 'the boy with glasses', 'the Asian girl' or 'the girl with the pretty dress'). Such labels devalue children, restricting their sense of self-worth. Always use the child's name.
* **Challenging discrimination:** children pick on weaker children or 'different' children. If you see a child teasing, insulting or hitting another child, explain that such behaviour is hurtful. Criticise the behaviour rather than the child; for example, you could say: 'Kicking hurts. Carla is very upset because it hurt', rather than 'You're very naughty. Don't do that, I'm very cross with you.' This avoids children feeling that you don't like them or that they are worthless.

Knowing your responsibilities and the limits of your role

You need to practise your skills with regard to certain responsibilities; these responsibilities include the following.

Respect for the principles of confidentiality

Confidentiality is about trust and sensitivity to the needs and the rights of others. You should always treat all the information you are privileged to receive within the work setting as confidential; avoid gossip and stereotyping.

Commitment to meeting the needs of the children

All children should be treated with respect and dignity, and their needs must be considered as paramount. This means working within the guidelines of an equal opportunities code of practice, and not allowing any personal preferences or prejudices to influence the way you treat children.

Responsibility and accountability in the workplace

The supervisor, line manager, teacher or parent will have certain expectations about your role, and your responsibilities should be detailed in your job contract. (As a student, you should always consult your tutor if you are uncertain about anything, as you will not have a job contract.) As a child care practitioner, you need to carry out all your duties willingly and be answerable (or accountable) to others for your work. You need to know about the lines of reporting within a work setting and how to find out about your own particular responsibilities. If you are unsure what is expected of you – or if you do not feel confident in carrying out a particular task – then you should ask your line manager or your immediate supervisor for guidance.

Respect for parents and other adults

You need to respect the wishes and views of parents and other carers, even when you disagree with those views. You should also recognise that parents are usually the people who know their children best. In all your dealings with parents and other adults, you must show that you respect their cultural values and religious beliefs.

Communicate effectively with team members and other professionals

Being able to communicate effectively with team members, other professionals and with parents is a very important part of your role as a child care practitioner. You should always:

* be considerate of others and polite towards them
* recognise the contributions made by other team members; we all like to feel we are valued for the work we do; you can help others to feel valued by being aware of their role and how it has helped you fulfil your own role
* explain clearly to the relevant person any changes in routine or any actions you have taken; for example –
  * as a nanny, always informing a parent when a child you are caring for has refused a meal or been distressed in any way, or
  * reporting any behaviour problem or incident to your line manager in a nursery setting.

To meet the needs of all the children in a setting, the staff members must work effectively together as a team. The roles and responsibilities of individual team members will depend on the organisation of the work setting.

In your role as a nursery assistant you will be supporting the work of others. You will usually work under the direction, sometimes under the supervision, of a nursery nurse or teacher, depending on the setting. There may also be professionals from other disciplines (e.g. medicine, social services, dentistry) who are involved with the families and children you work with. A special school or nursery that cares for children with physical disabilities will have a 'multidisciplinary' team; this may include teachers, nursery nurses and assistants, trained special care assistants, physiotherapists, paediatricians and, possibly, social workers.

Effective teamwork is vital in such settings to ensure that:

* all concerned know their individual roles and responsibilities
* parents and primary carers know which team member can deal with any specific concerns.

Knowing the limits of your role

Children are likely to treat you as any other adult on the staff – assuming that you can help them and are there to care for them as well as discipline them. This means that, by your behaviour, language and attitudes, you set an example for the children you are working with and caring for.

Being a good role model involves:

* showing consideration for others
* taking care over hygiene and appearance
* using appropriate language (you must address the children and adults politely and using the correct terms – avoid referring to the children as kids!)
* supporting other staff and parents, and following set procedures and policies.

Use of initiative is one of the aspects some students struggle with. It involves trying to anticipate (see in advance) situations and taking appropriate action.

* **Have confidence:** using initiative effectively requires confidence on your part and reassurance from your supervisor that you can (and should) deal with many incidents yourself if you happen to be the nearest adult.
* **Safety issues:** it is vital that you take steps on your own initiative when matters of safety are concerned (e.g. spilt sand or water, a child who is choking, a blocked fire exit).

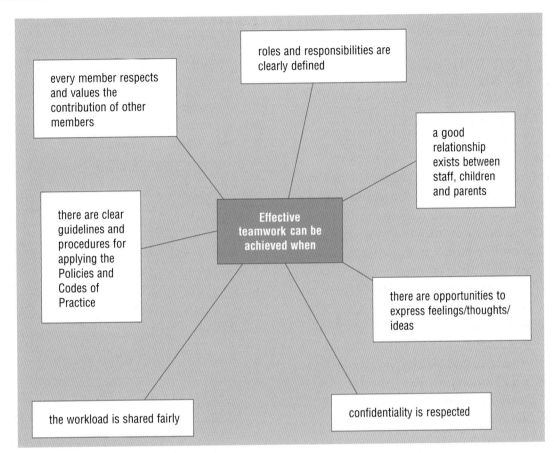

Fig 1.2. Achieving effective teamwork

* **Handling disputes:** additionally, you will be expected to deal with children's disputes and maintain behaviour according to your placement guidelines when you are supervising groups.

Being friendly – but not friends: it is important to remember that your relationship with the children in your care is a professional one. You should always be friendly and approachable – but not try to take the place of the child's parents. At the same time, you should communicate with each child at a level that is appropriate to their stage of development and to their needs; you should not act as a child would when interacting with them. The same

principle applies when you are communicating with parents. If the child of one of your friends attends your placement, you will both have to appreciate that there are then two different relationships – the 'friends' one and the workplace one.

REMEMBER
Nobody will expect you to know everything at first. Staff are there to help you to get the most out of each placement and your tutor will discuss any concerns you may have. If you are unsure about any aspect of care, or how to speak with a parent, don't be afraid to ask your supervisor or college tutor.

Children's individual needs

Children's needs vary greatly. Apart from the basic needs that every child has, each child will have **individual needs**; these include the following.

* **Short-term needs:**
  * a child may have been unwell and have a short-term need for extra rest and attention to physical needs
  * a child who has recently joined the setting will need more attention from his or key person while settling in.
* **Long-term needs:**
  * a child who has visual or hearing difficulties may have several needs; for example, a child getting used to wearing glasses or using a hearing aid may need help and encouragement with managing the situation
  * a child who has asthma may become frightened when breathless and will need reassurance and access to an inhaler at all times.

FAIRNESS AND INCLUSIVE PRACTICE

It is important that you recognise the differences between children and that you *value* those differences. Children should be encouraged not to feel anxious about people who are different from them. Many of the traditions practised within families from ethnic minorities are now adopted by western societies (e.g. baby massage with natural oils and the carrying of babies in fabric slings). We all have a great deal to learn from one another.

Children may feel themselves to be different in other ways too, not simply by having a different cultural heritage. Children with special needs often feel that they are the odd ones out in a group setting – for example, if a child:

* wears glasses or a hearing aid
* has frequent bouts of asthma
* has a mobility problem
* has learning difficulties.

AVOIDING STEREOTYPING AND LABELLING

It is important to avoid labelling or stereotyping people. A stereotype is a way of thinking that assumes that all people who share one characteristic also share another set of characteristics. Some examples are listed below.

* **Racism:** racism is the belief that some 'races' are superior to others – based on the false idea that different physical characteristics (like skin colour) or ethnic background make some people better than others.
* **Sexism:** sexism occurs when people of one gender (or biological sex) believe that they are superior to the other.
* **Ageism:** this occurs when negative feelings are expressed towards a person or group because of their age; in western society it is usually directed towards older people.
* **Disablism:** this occurs when disabled people are seen in terms of their disability, rather than as unique individuals who happen to have special needs.

There are many other stereotypes, such as those concerning gay and lesbian groups, people from low socio-economic groups and those who practise a minority religion.

Stereotyped thinking can prevent you from seeing someone as an individual with particular life experiences and interests, and so lead to negative attitudes and to prejudice and discrimination.

Case studies: Making assumptions

Sam, Jason, Laura and Fatima are playing in the home corner. The nursery teacher asks Sam and Jason to tidy away the train set and trucks, and asks Laura and Fatima to put the dolls and cooking pots away, as it is nearly story time.

The assumption here is that dolls and cooking utensils are 'girl' playthings, whereas trains and trucks are 'boy' playthings. The teacher is reinforcing this stereotype by separating the tasks by gender.

Paul's mother arrives at the school open day. She is in a wheelchair, being pushed by Paul's father. The teacher welcomes the parents and then asks Paul's father if his wife would like a drink and a biscuit.

This is a common feature of daily life for people who use wheelchairs. They are often ignored and questions are addressed to their companion, often because the other person is embarrassed by the unusual situation and fearful of making a mistake. The assumption here is that the person in the wheelchair would not be able to understand and reply to what is said to them.

Members of staff are having a tea break and discussing a new child who has just started at their school. Julie says: 'I can't stand the way these travellers think they can just turn up at school whenever they feel like it – they don't pay taxes you know and they live practically on top of rubbish dumps . . . poor little mite, he doesn't know any different.'

An assumption has been made that is based on prejudice and stereotyped thinking; in this case, travellers are assumed to be 'scroungers' and to live in unhygienic conditions. Such attitudes will be noticed by all the children in the class and may result in the individual child being treated differently, damaging his self-esteem and leading to feelings of rejection.

Harry's mother is a registered heroin addict who has been attending a drug rehabilitation programme for the last few months. Whenever Harry behaves in an aggressive way to other children or to staff, one staff member always makes a jibe about his home life: 'Harry, you may get away with that sort of thing where you come from, but it won't work here. We know all about you.'

This is an extreme and very unkind form of stereotyping. It is assuming that, because his mother is a drug user, Harry is somehow less worthy of consideration and respect. By drawing attention to his home life, the member of staff is guilty of prejudice and discriminatory behaviour. There is also a breach of the policy of confidentiality.

Section 4
Study skills

*I hear – I forget ♪
I see – I remember ♪
I do – I understand.
(Confucius c.551–479 BC)*

LEARNING STYLES AND STRATEGIES

We all have our own particular way of learning new information – our own preferred **learning style**. It doesn't have anything to do with how intelligent we are or what skills we have learned. It has to do with how the brain works most efficiently to learn new information. There are many different theories about learning styles.

19

What works best for *you* will not necessarily be the same as the approach used by other students, even those studying the same course. We are all unique as learners, although there are some patterns that emerge in any group of students. It is important to explore a whole range of approaches because that will enable you to find out what works best for you.

Your approach to learning may change as you develop new study skills, and many of us use different styles depending on the problem or task at hand. It is now widely accepted that the capacity to learn can be improved by:

* analysing how you do things
* being willing to try new things, and
* recognising what works best for you.

Finding out about your learning style

Experts have identified three basic learning styles: **auditory**, **visual** and **tactile**.

1. **Auditory** learners prefer to learn and remember by:
* talking out loud, and
* having things explained orally.

They may have trouble with written instructions; auditory learners may talk to themselves when learning something new.

Motto: If you hear it, you remember it.

If you are an auditory learner, you benefit:

* when information is presented in an oral language format
* from listening to lectures and participating in group discussions
* from obtaining information from audio tape
* when interacting with others in a listening/speaking exchange
* from talking aloud, when studying alone, to aid recall.

2. **Visual** learners prefer to learn and remember by:
* seeing what they are learning (visual details)
* writing down instructions; they may have trouble following lectures with no visual props, and
* studying alone in a quiet room.

Motto: You have to see it to believe it.

If you are a visual learner, you benefit from:

* teachers who use the whiteboard (or overhead projector) to list the essential points of a lecture, or who provide you with an outline to follow along with during the lecture
* information obtained from textbooks and class notes.

3. **Tactile (kinaesthetic)** learners prefer to learn and remember by:
* doing activities that allow them to practise what they are learning about
* touching things in order to learn about them, and
* being physically active in the learning environment.

Motto: If you can touch it with your hands, you will remember it.

If you are a tactile learner, you benefit from:

* teachers who encourage demonstrations
* 'hands on' student learning experiences
* jotting down key words, drawing pictures or making charts to help remember the information in the classroom.

WHAT SORT OF LEARNER ARE YOU?

You probably won't fit neatly into any one category; most people have a mixture of learning styles.

Example

Try thinking about the way in which you remember a phone number.

✳ Can you visualise (or see, in your mind's eye), how the numbers look on the phone? Or can you visualise the number on a piece of paper, 'seeing' it exactly as you wrote it down? (**visual learning style**)

✳ Can you 'hear' the number in the way that someone recited it to you? (**auditory learning style**)

✳ Do you 'let your fingers do the walking' on the phone? That is, your fingers dial the number without looking at the phone? (**tactile learning style**)

LEARNING STRATEGIES

While it is useful to know about personal learning styles, it is really our understanding of our learning *strategies* that makes us effective learners. The easiest way to think

about learning strategies is to explore how you actually tackle a learning task (see Table 1.2).

Organising and planning your time: getting the balance right

Any activity can seem preferable to working on an assignment or settling down to revision: tidying your room, staring at the wall, fetching 'just one more' small snack, or even doing the washing up!

However, when work is postponed regularly, deadlines and examination dates can increase feelings of disorganisation and panic, and can trigger a 'flight' response. It can become tempting to produce the minimum work possible, or even to abandon assignments completely. Excuses have to be invented, deadlines renegotiated, further assignments become due before the last ones are completed and, before long, the course begins to feel overwhelming and

Visual learners	Auditory learners	Tactile learners
• Use visual materials such as pictures, charts, and maps • Use colour to highlight texts and own notes • Take notes or use handouts; look carefully at headings and patterns of topics • Brainstorm using illustrations, mind maps and models • Use multimedia where possible (computers, mind maps) • Study in a quiet place away from visual disturbances • Visualise information as a picture • Skim-read to get an overview before reading in detail	• Participate frequently in discussions and debates • Make speeches and presentations • Use a tape recorder if possible instead of (or as well as) making notes • Read text aloud • Create musical jingles and **mnemonics*** to aid memory • Discuss your ideas verbally • Dictate to someone else while they write your ideas down • Speak on to an audio tape and listen to your own ideas played back	• Take frequent study breaks • Move around to learn new things (e.g. read while using an exercise bike; model in clay to learn a new concept) • Stand up to work • Use bright colours to highlight reading material and turn it into posters or models • Skim-read before reading in detail

Table 1.2: Strategies for learning

* 'Mnemonic' is another word for a memory tool. Mnemonics are techniques for remembering information that is otherwise quite difficult to recall. A simple example is the '30 days hath September ...' rhyme for remembering the number of days in each calendar month.

ACTIVITY: DISCOVERING YOUR LEARNING STYLE

Answer the questions below, and then compare your answers with those of other students.

	Yes	No
Do you do best in classes when teachers do a lot of writing at the whiteboard, provide clear handouts, and make extensive use of an overhead projector?	V	
Does listening to audio tapes help you learn better?	A	
Do you try to remember information by creating pictures in your mind?	V	
Do you learn better when you have an actual object in your hands rather than a picture of the object or a verbal or written description of it?	T	
Do you seem to learn best in classes where there are class discussions?	A	
When trying to study, do you become distracted by activity around you?	T	
Do you forget names but remember faces, or remember where you met?	V	
In class, do you talk little but also dislike listening for too long?	V	
Do you do generally do well in classes in which there is a practical (task) component?	T	
When trying to study, do you become distracted by untidiness or movement?	V	
Do you learn best when you can move about and handle things?	T	
Do you find yourself reading aloud or talking things out to gain better understanding?	A	
In class, do you enjoy listening but are impatient to talk?	A	
When trying to study, do you become distracted by sounds or noises?	A	
In class, do you use a lot of body language (i.e. gestures and expressive movements)?	T	
Do you take detailed written notes from your textbooks and in class?	V	
When having problems on the computer, do you call the help desk or ask someone else?	A	
When having problems on the computer, do you keep trying to do it or try it on another computer?	T	

Key: A = auditory learner;   V = visual learner;   T = tactile learner

If you answered Yes mostly to the questions with **V** in the column, you are probably a visual learner; if you answered Yes mostly to the questions with **A** in the column, you are probably an auditory learner; if you answered Yes mostly to the questions with **T** in the column, you are probably a tactile learner. You may find you answered Yes to a mixture of learning styles, which means you respond to a variety of teaching methods.

unmanageable. Of course, people can have very good reasons for finding their workload difficult to manage: child care or other family responsibilities, the need to earn money through part-time work, and unexpected traumas or illnesses can all increase pressure on students. However, if you are generally enjoying your course and finding the work stimulating and interesting, you are likely to want to find a way of organising your time so that you can keep a balance between your work, your social life and your other interests and commitments.

Planning time

There are only so many hours in a week. Although keeping rigidly to a 'weekly planner' or timetable will not always be easy or desirable, it should help you to focus on what free time you have in a week, and which 'chunks' of it can be used for course work and revision.

Motivation during study periods

It is important to find a place where you can work without interruptions and distractions. Even if you have the luxury of a room and a desk of your own at home, you will probably need to consider using your school, college or public library for some study periods. Settling down to a period of study is easier if you:

* remove all distractions of hunger, noise, cold – and sociable friends!
* try not to study if you are feeling angry or upset
* keep a pad of paper or a jotter next to you as you work; when ideas or other things occur to you, you can note them down before you forget them
* give yourself realistic targets and decide for how long you will study before you start; try not to work for more than an hour without a short break; reward yourself for completing what you planned to do
* try to give yourself a variety of activities to work on

ACTIVITY: PLANNING YOUR TIME

1. Draw up a table, or print one out from a calendar program on a computer, showing the seven days of the week as headings and hourly blocks of time down the left-hand side (for example 8–9 a.m., 9–10 a.m. through to 9–10 p.m.).

2. Now mark on:
   * your college or school timetabled commitments (i.e. your lectures and lessons)
   * any paid work, housework or child care/family commitments
   * travelling time
   * time you normally spend with friends/sports activities/other leisure pursuits

   * any 'unmissable' TV programmes (not too many!).

3. What 'chunks' of time have you left for studying?
   * In the day?
   * In the evening?
   * At weekends?

Don't forget that the half-term or end of term holidays can be a good time to catch up on assignments and revision. Remember to include these in your long-term calculations. However, having completed your planner, will you need to readjust any commitments to give you enough time to complete course work? How important will it be for you to spend some time studying in the day as well as in the evening?

* have the phone number of someone else from your class or group handy in case you need to check what you need to do or want to discuss the best way to go about a task.

Compiling a portfolio

A portfolio is a collection of the different types of evidence that can be used to show successful completion of the course. Examples of evidence include:

* completed assignments, projects or case studies, including action plans and evaluations; these can be in written form or word-processed, although work in the form of video recordings, audio tape recordings, photographs, logbooks or diaries may also be acceptable where they contain evidence of the practical demonstration of skills – check with your teacher or tutor
* past records of achievement, qualifications, work experience or other evidence of 'prior learning'
* samples of relevant class or lecture notes, lists, personal reading records or copies of letters written (perhaps regarding work experience, to request information or advice, or related to job or higher education applications).

Equipment and materials

As soon as you know how many mandatory and optional units you will be taking for the course, it will be worthwhile taking advantage of any cheap stationery offers at high-street stores and equipping yourself with:

* A4 files, with subject dividers
* a hole punch
* file paper (plain and lined)
* plastic pockets or report files; these are not essential but you may feel better if finished assignments are presented neatly

in a binder or pocket of some sort; however, do not enclose each individual sheet of an assignment within a plastic pocket – this is expensive, ecologically unsound and drives your teachers and assessors crazy when they have to remove sheets to make comments on your work!
* post-it index stickers can be useful to help 'flag up' important pieces of work in your completed portfolio
* small exercise books or notebooks, to act as logbooks or diaries.

If you are dyslexic or have another disability that prevents or makes it difficult for you to take notes in lectures, you might consider acquiring a small tape recorder and supply of cassettes, to enable you to record lectures and play them back at another time.

Reading, note taking and using a library

Textbooks such as this can offer you a basic framework for the ideas and information you need for the different subject areas covered in the course: CACHE Level 2 Child Care and Education. Your lectures and classes will supply you with additional material. However, you will need to carry out your own reading and research, making your own notes and updating information in areas where there is constant change (such as child care legislation). It will be useful for you to find out how the national organisation of care and education services works in the area and in the community in which you live.

You cannot do this successfully without making full use of libraries (including their computers), newspapers and journals, television and film, and information produced by a range of national, local and voluntary organisations. If you have personal access to the internet, you may find such research decidedly easier, and this book contains many references to websites worth exploring. Make sure that you are shown how to use all the relevant facilities of your library, whether school, college or public.

Using the internet

Think before reaching for the mouse. Using the internet can be highly productive but it can also take up a lot of your time. Before you start, work out:

* what you need to know
* how much you need to know
* when you need the information by
* whether you have a sensible search strategy – do you have a list of recommended sites or know the best way to use a 'search engine' such as Google or Yahoo!
* could you find the information you need more easily in books or a journal?

Strategies for reading and note taking

We have all had the experience of reading a sentence, paragraph, or even a whole page, without being able to remember what we have just read. To be of most use to you, reading will often need to be combined with note taking.

Taking notes is time-consuming and requires *active* concentration. Students often worry if:

* they are spending too much time taking endless, detailed notes without really understanding what they will be used for
* they give up note taking because they cannot seem to work out what to write down and what not; this can be a particular problem when taking notes in lessons and lectures.

Essentially, note taking is a strategy for helping you to:

* **think, understand** and **remember**.

There are many situations in life when it is important to focus on the **key issues** or points being communicated.

Example: You may have to know exactly what to do if a child in your care has an asthma attack or needs adrenalin for a peanut allergy. You may have to explain these things quickly to another person, summarising essential information.

Deciding what to write down when you take notes is easier if you think about *why* you are taking notes. You may need to take different types of notes for different reasons. You will get better at working out methods of note taking that suit you, the more you try out different approaches. It also helps to think about ways to store your notes so that they are easily accessible to you when you need them. If they are written or designed in such a way that you can make use of them again, you will be more likely to come back to them.

Mind mapping

If you work better visually or spatially rather than in writing, you can make graphic 'notes': flow charts, block designs, family trees, spider plans or other forms of **mind map**. These can be used for:

* generating ideas
* planning your work (e.g. for an observation or report)
* note taking and – later on – revising.

1. In the centre of your page draw a picture of, or name in words, your main topic or theme.
2. Draw branches from this main topic in thick lines (use different colours or patterns). Label your branches with key words and/or images.
3. Draw sub-branches from the main branches to represent sub-topics or to elaborate and extend your ideas. Again,

use key words, phrases, images, pictures and colour. Use italics, underlining and capitals to highlight your work.

Let your ideas flow and develop. Add more detail to your mind map as ideas occur to you. However, the mind map is not meant to be an art form or elaborate doodle – more a way to focus your attention on the essential components of a piece of work, topic or report.

Underlining and highlighting

If you own the book or article you are taking notes from, highlighting, underlining and marking the margin with asterisks or other symbols can be a quick and effective method of skim-reading a text, focusing your attention on it and getting to grips with the material as a whole. Again, the most

important part of this activity is that you are *concentrating* on what you are doing.

Writing assignments, observations and reports

Much of your *written* course work is set in the form of assignments and projects – although some are assessed through multiple-choice question papers (MCQs) and short answer tests.

Planning and prioritising tasks

If you use a planner regularly (see page 23) it is easier to break up assignments, plans and observations into a series of smaller tasks, each of which you could aim to complete within a manageable time, such as an hour or two. Sub-dividing your course work in this

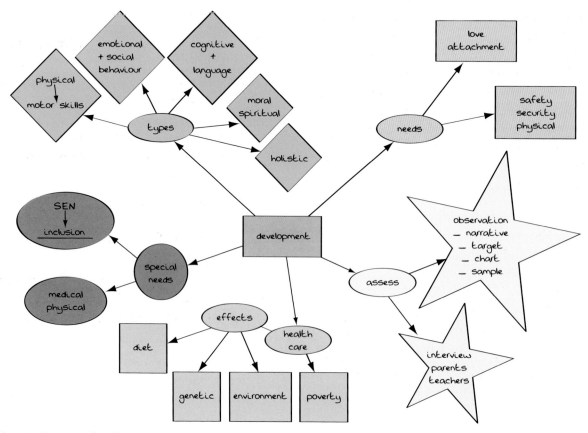

Fig 1.3. An example of a mind map

way also allows you to **prioritise** the tasks. In what order are they best done? Which really need to be done straight away? Make a list of small tasks in order of priority, with the time you estimate they will take and target dates for completion. Leave room on your action plan to amend these dates when and if your plan is modified.

Monitoring and revising your work

There are likely to be many points during the completion of a piece of course work when you will change direction or modify your original plan in some way. On your action plan, keep a note of:

* the reasons for changing your plans
* what new plans you have for the work.

Writing a bibliography

You will be expected to write a bibliography (a list of books, articles and other resources used) for each assignment or observation you submit. To do this properly, you need to make a note of the materials and references you use as you study. There is nothing worse than finishing an assignment and then spending valuable time hunting down the name of a book you read in the library but did not note the details of. As a general rule, you need to note:

* the title of the book or article (or website address)
* the author(s)
* the publisher
* the date of publication
* the place of publication.

Here are some examples.

* **Book:** Bruce, T. (2005) *Early Childhood Education* (3rd edn). London: Hodder Education.

* **Article:** Bruner, J., Wood, D. and Ross, G. (1976) The role of tutoring in problem-solving. *Journal of Child Psychology and Psychiatry*, **17**, pp. 89–100.

The **Harvard system of referencing** is most often used. The **references** *within* your text use the author's name and the date of publication. Then the full details of the book or article are listed – alphabetically – in the 'Bibliography' and/or 'References' list at the end of the assignment. Other sources of information or references in your work may come from the internet (give the website address and the date you accessed the site), workplace (acknowledge the source), television programmes, video or film (give the title and date) or friends, family and teachers (attribute information as accurately as you can).

When you need to take a test or MCQ paper

When the day of a test arrives, give yourself plenty of time to check everything; check equipment, have breakfast, arrive on time but not too early. Try not to talk about the test with friends before you start. Have a last look at any brief notes or summaries you have made. As soon as you are allowed to, read the questions.

* Make sure you understand the test instructions.
* Ask for help if necessary.
* Take your time.

Highlight key words and note down any key facts you know you will have to use at some point but may forget as the test proceeds.

Unit 2

The Developing Child

Contents

Unit 2 is divided into five sections:

Section 1

The stages and sequence of child development

It is important to keep in mind that every child is unique. By looking at the holistic – or integrated – development of children, we can view the child as a whole person: physically, emotionally, intellectually, morally, culturally and spiritually.

THE EXPECTED PATTERN OF DEVELOPMENT

Physical **growth** is different from physical **development**. Physical growth means that children grow in height and weight, whereas physical development means that children gain **skills** through being able to control their own bodies.

STUDYING CHILD DEVELOPMENT

The whole child may be looked at under six headings. You can remember these as together they make up the acronym **PILESS**:

* **P**hysical development
* **I**ntellectual development
* **L**anguage development
* **E**motional development
* **S**ocial development
* **S**piritual development.

Physical development

Physical development is the way in which the body increases in skill and becomes more complex in its performance. There are two main areas:

1. **Gross motor skills:** these use the large muscles in the body and include walking, squatting, running, climbing, and so on.
2. **Fine motor skills:** these include *gross manipulative skills*, which involve single limb movements, usually of the arm (for example, throwing, catching and sweeping arm movements); and *fine manipulative skills*, which involve precise use of the hands and fingers for pointing, drawing, using a knife and fork, writing, doing up shoelaces, and so on.

Intellectual development

Cognitive, or **intellectual**, development is development of the mind – the part of the brain that is used for recognising, reasoning, knowing and understanding.

Psychologists have tried for many years to find out how children learn. The area of

---

THE PATTERN OF PHYSICAL DEVELOPMENT

Children's development follows a pattern:
* from simple to complex – a child will stand before he can walk, and walk before he can skip or hop
* from head to toe – physical control and coordination begins with a child's head, and works down the body through the arms, hands and back, and finally to the legs and feet
* from inner to outer – a child can

coordinate his arms using gross motor skills to reach for an object before he has learned the fine motor skills necessary to pick it up
* from general to specific – a young baby shows pleasure by a massive general response (e.g. eyes widen, legs and arms move vigorously); an older child shows pleasure by smiling or using appropriate words or gestures.

development connected with knowledge, understanding and reasoning is referred to as intellectual or cognitive development.

Intellectual or cognitive development involves:

* what a person knows, and the ability to reason, understand and problem-solve
* memory, concentration, attention and perception
* imagination and creativity.

Language development is very closely linked with cognitive development and a delay in one area usually affects progress in the other.

There is an ongoing debate about how children develop and learn, often referred to as the nature/nurture debate. It centres on this question:

* **Nature or nurture?** Is our ability to learn determined by our inherited genes and characteristics (i.e. NATURE)? *Or* is our ability to learn determined by our upbringing (i.e. NURTURE)?

The illustration below shows features important for intellectual development.

Language development

Language development is the development of **communication** skills. This includes skills in:

* **receptive speech** – what a person understands
* **expressive speech** – the words the person produces
* **articulation** – the person's actual pronunciation of words.

Emotional, social and behavioural development

Emotional development involves the development of feelings:

* the growth of feelings about, and awareness of, oneself
* the development of feelings towards other people
* the development of **self-esteem** and a **self-concept**.

Social development

Social development includes the growth of the child's relationships with other people. **Socialisation** is the process of learning the skills and attitudes that enable the child to live easily with other members of the community.

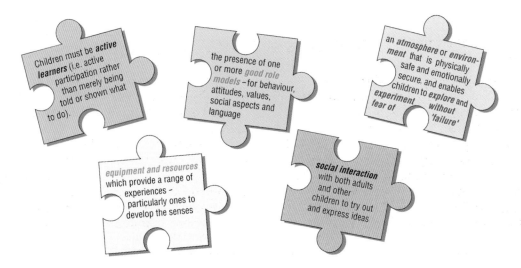

Children must be **active learners** (i.e. active participation rather than merely being told or shown what to do).

the presence of one or more *good role models* – for behaviour, attitudes, values, social aspects and language

an *atmosphere* or *environment* that is physically safe and emotionally secure, and enables children to *explore* and *experiment without* fear of *'failure'*

equipment and resources which provide a range of experiences – particularly ones to develop the senses

social interaction with both adults and other children to try out and express ideas

Behaviour is the way we act, speak and treat other people and our environment; it is closely linked to emotional and social aspects of development.

Moral and spiritual development

Moral and spiritual development consists of a developing awareness of how to relate to others – ethically, morally and humanely. It involves understanding values such as honesty and respect, and acquiring **concepts** such as right and wrong, and responsibility for the consequences of one's actions.

THE STAGES AND SEQUENCE OF PHYSICAL DEVELOPMENT FROM BIRTH TO 16 YEARS

There are wide variations in the ages at which children acquire physical skills, such as sitting, standing and walking. The rate at which children develop these skills will have an effect on all the other areas of development – for example, on the development of language, understanding, self-confidence and social skills. Once a child has learnt to crawl, to shuffle on her bottom, or to be mobile in other ways, she will be more independent and able to explore things that were previously out of reach. Adults will make changes to the child's environment now that she is mobile, by putting reachable objects out of her way, and making clear rules and boundaries.

Table 2.1, on the following pages, outlines the main features of **holistic** child development, the ages shown being those at which the *average* child performs the specific tasks. Remember, however, that children develop at different rates and some may be faster or slower than others to learn certain skills.

Age	Gross motor skills	Fine motor skills (and sensory development)
Birth to 4 weeks	*Babies:* • lie **supine** (on their backs) with head to one side • when placed on their front (the **prone position**), lie with the head turned to one side and their knees tucked under the abdomen • if pulled to sitting position, the head will lag, the back curves over and the head falls forward.	*Babies:* • usually hold their hands tightly closed • often hold their thumbs tucked in under their fingers • react to loud sounds but, by 1 month, may be soothed by particular music • turn their head towards the light and stare at bright, shiny objects • are fascinated by human faces and gaze attentively at carer's face when fed or held.
4 to 8 weeks	• can now turn from side to back • can lift their head briefly from prone position	• will open their hands to grasp an adult's finger • turn their head towards the light and stare at bright, shiny objects

	• arm and leg movements are jerky and uncontrolled • have head lag when pulled to sitting position.	• will show interest and excitement by facial expression, and will gaze attentively at carer's face while being fed.
8 to 12 weeks	• keep their head in a central position when lying supine • can now lift head and chest off bed in prone position, supported on forearms • have almost no head lag in sitting position • can kick their legs vigorously, both separately and together • can wave their arms and bring their hands together over the body.	• move their head to follow adult movements • watch their hands and play with their fingers • can hold a rattle for a brief time before dropping it.
4 to 5 months	• are starting to use a **palmar grasp** and can transfer objects from hand to hand • are very interested in all activity • take everything to their mouth • move their head around to follow people and objects.	• now have good head control and are beginning to sit with support • roll over from back to side and are beginning to reach for objects • when supine, play with their own feet • hold the head up when pulled to sitting position.
6 to 9 months	• can roll from front to back • may attempt to crawl but will often end up sliding backwards • may grasp feet and place in own mouth • can sit without support for longer periods of time • may 'cruise' around furniture and may even stand or walk alone.	• are very alert to people and objects • are beginning to use a pincer grasp with thumb and index finger to transfer toys from one hand to the other and look for fallen objects • explore objects by putting them in their mouth.
9 to 12 months	• will now be mobile – may be crawling, bear-walking, bottom- shuffling or even walking • can sit up on their own and lean forward to pick things up	• have a well-developed **pincer grasp** and can pick things up and pull towards themselves • can poke with one finger and will point to desired objects • can clasp hands and imitate adults' actions

	• may crawl upstairs and on to low items of furniture • may bounce in rhythm to music.	• can throw toys deliberately • can manage spoons and finger foods well.
15 months	• probably walk alone, with feet wide apart and arms raised to maintain balance • are likely to fall over and sit down suddenly a lot • can probably manage stairs and steps, but will need supervision • can get to standing without help from furniture or people, and kneel without support.	• can build with a few bricks and arrange toys on the floor • can hold crayon in **palmar grasp** and turn several pages of a book at once • can point to desired objects • show a preference for one hand, but use either.
18 months	Children: • walk confidently and are able to stop without falling • can kneel, squat, climb and carry things around with them • can climb on to an adult chair forwards and then turn round to sit • can come downstairs, usually by creeping backwards on their tummy.	Children: • can thread large beads • use pincer grasp to pick up small objects • can build a tower of several cubes • can scribble to and fro on paper.
2 years	• are very mobile – can run safely • can climb up on to the furniture • can walk up and down stairs, usually two feet to a step • try to kick a ball with some success – cannot yet catch ball.	• can draw circles, lines and dots, using preferred hand • can pick up tiny objects using a fine pincer grasp • can build tower of six or more blocks (bricks) with longer concentration span • enjoy picture books and turn pages singly.

3 years	• can jump from a low step • can walk backwards and sideways • can stand and walk on tiptoe, and stand on one foot • have good spatial awareness • ride tricycle using pedals • can climb stairs with one foot on each step – downwards with two feet per step.	• can build tall towers of bricks or blocks • can control a pencil using thumb and first two fingers – the **dynamic tripod grasp** • enjoy painting with large brush • can use scissors to cut paper • can copy shapes, such as a circle.
4 years	• are developing a sense of balance – may be able to walk along a line • can catch, kick, throw and bounce a ball • can bend at the waist to pick up objects from the floor • enjoy climbing trees and frames • can run up and down stairs, one foot per step.	• can build a tower of bricks, and other constructions too • can draw a recognisable person on request, showing head, legs and trunk • can thread small beads on a lace.
5 years	• can use a variety of play equipment – slides, swings, climbing frames • can play ball games	• may be able to thread a large-eyed needle and sew large stitches • can draw a person with head, trunk, legs, nose, mouth and eyes

	• can hop and run lightly on toes – can move rhythmically to music • have a well-developed sense of balance • can skip.	• have good control over pencils and paintbrushes • copy shapes, such as a square.
6 and 7 years	• have increased agility, muscle coordination and balance • develop competence in riding a two-wheeled bicycle • hop easily, with good balance • can jump off apparatus at school.	• can build a tall, straight tower with blocks, and other constructions too • can draw a person with detail, e.g. clothes and eyebrows • can write letters of alphabet with similar writing grip to an adult • can catch a ball thrown from 1 metre with one hand.
8 and 9 years	• can ride a bicycle easily • have increased strength and coordination • play energetic games and sports	• can control their small muscles well; improved writing and drawing skills • draw people with details of clothing and facial features • are starting to join letters together in handwriting
10 and 11 years	• differ in physical maturity; because girls experience puberty earlier they are often as much as 2 years ahead of boys • have body proportions becoming more similar to adults	• tackle more detailed tasks such as woodwork or needlework • are usually writing with an established style – using joined-up letters.

From 12–16 years

Physical development during adolescence is known as **puberty**. The age at which puberty starts varies from person to person but on average it begins between 9–13 in girls and 10–15 in boys. Many physical changes occur during puberty.

- **Growth** accelerates rapidly – often called a **growth spurt**. This usually happens in a particular order from outer to inner:
  - the head, feet and hands grow to adult size first, then
  - the arms and legs grow in length and strength, and finally
  - the trunk (the main part of the body from shoulder to hip) grows to full adult size and shape.

  This sequence of growth means that, for a brief period, adolescents may feel gawky and clumsy, as they appear to be 'out of proportion'. The average boy grows fastest between 14 and 15. Girls start earlier, growing fastest when 12 and 13. Girls also finish their growth spurt earlier, at 18, while boys need another two years before they finish growing aged 20.

- **Secondary sex characteristics** develop; these are external traits that distinguish the two sexes, but are not directly part of the **reproductive system**; for example, the growth of pubic hair in both sexes, facial hair and deepened voice for males, and breasts and widened hips for females.

- Primary sex characteristics develop; these are the penis and sperm in males and the vagina and ovaries in females. During puberty, hormonal changes cause a boy's penis and testicles to grow and the body to produce sperm. Girls start to menstruate or have their monthly period. Both these events signal **sexual maturity** – the ability to reproduce.

The main features of physical development in puberty	
In girls	In boys
The first *external* sign of puberty in most girls is usually breast development – often accompanied by a growth spurt. **Breasts develop:** at first, the nipples start to stick out from the chest (often called 'budding'). Behind the nipple, milk ducts begin to grow. Next, the flat, circular part of the nipple, the areola, rises and starts to expand. Glands that make sweat and scent develop beneath it. The breast begins to fill out, as fat is deposited around the nipple. Some girls feel a tingling sensation or have tender breasts. Initially the breasts stick out in a conical shape. As growth continues they gradually round off into an adult shape. **Body size and shape:** grows taller. Hips widen as the pelvic bones grow. Fat develops on the hips, thighs and buttocks, and the ratio of fat to muscle increases. The waist gets smaller and the body develops a more curved shape. **Menstruation:** menstruation – having periods – is part of the female reproductive cycle that starts when girls become sexually mature during puberty. During a menstrual period, a woman bleeds from her uterus (womb) via the vagina. This lasts anything from three to seven days. Each period begins approximately every 28 days if the woman does not become pregnant during a given cycle. The onset of menstruation is called the menarche; it can occur at any time between the ages of 9 and 16, most commonly around the age	The first *external* sign of puberty in most boys is an increase in the size of the testicles and then the penis. This is followed by the growth of pubic and underarm hair. At the same time, the voice deepens and muscles develop. Lastly, boys grow facial hair. **Voice breaking:** testosterone causes the voice box – or larynx – to enlarge and the vocal cords to become longer. Sometimes, as the voice changes to become deeper, it may change pitch abruptly, or 'break', at times; the voice box tilts and often protrudes at the neck – as an 'Adam's apple'. (Many boys start to develop breasts in their teenage years, but this disappears as the testosterone levels increase.) **Body size and shape:** grows taller. Body takes on a new, more muscular shape as the shoulders and chest become broader and the neck becomes more muscular. **Chest hair** may appear during puberty – or some years later. **Penile erections:** these occur spontaneously, even from infancy, but during puberty they become more frequent. Erections can occur with or without any physical or sexual stimulation and can cause acute embarrassment.

of 12–13. It means that the body is capable of **reproduction**.	**Sperm:** once the testicles begin to grow they also develop their adult function – producing sperm. Mature sperm is present in the male body towards the end of puberty (most commonly between the ages of 13 and 15) and means that the body is capable of **reproduction**.

In both girls and boys
Pubic hair starts to grow around the genitals, and becomes coarse, dark and curly. In girls, pubic hair forms an upside-down triangle shape; in boys, the hair grows between the legs and extends up from the penis to the abdomen
Hair grows in the armpits and on the legs
Sweat: a different kind of sweat is now produced in response to stress, emotion and sexual excitement. It is produced by the apocrine glands, and occurs only in the armpits, the belly button, the groin area, the ears and the nipples. As bacteria break down the sweat it starts to smell strongly – known as BO (body odour).
Oil glands: oil-secreting glands in the skin can become over-active – this can cause skin to become greasier and can also cause acne.

Table 2.1: Normative physical development: from birth to 16 years

COMMUNICATION AND LANGUAGE DEVELOPMENT CHARTS

During the first 3 months	Babies need to share language experiences and cooperate with others from birth onwards. From the start babies need other people. Babies listen to people's voices. Babies 'call out' for company. When adults close to them talk to them in **motherese** (a high-pitched tone referring to what is around and going on) babies dance, listen, and reply in babble and coo. Babies cry with anger to show they are tired or hungry, and to say they need to be changed. A hearing-impaired baby babbles and cries too. Babies are comforted by the voices of those who are close to them and they will turn especially to the voices of their family.
From birth to 4 weeks	Babies: • respond to sounds, especially familiar voices • quieten when picked up • make eye contact • cry to indicate need • may move the eyes towards the direction of sound.
4 to 8 weeks	• recognise carer and familiar objects • make non-crying noises, such as cooing and gurgling • become more expressive in their cries • look for sounds.
8 to 12 weeks	• are still distressed by sudden loud noises • often suck or lick lips when they hear sound of food preparation • show excitement at sound of approaching footsteps or voices.

3 to 6 months	• become more aware of others so they communicate more and more; as they listen, they imitate sounds they can hear, and they react to the tone of someone's voice – for example, they might become upset by an angry tone, or cheered by a happy tone • begin to use vowels, consonants and syllable sounds, e.g. 'ah', 'ee aw' • begin to laugh and squeal with pleasure • continue to do everything they did in the first 3 months.
6 to 9 months	• babble becomes tuneful like the lilt of the language they can hear (except in hearing-impaired babies) • begin to understand words like 'up' and 'down', raising their arms to be lifted up, using appropriate gestures • repeat sounds; babies continue to do everything they did in the first 6 months.
9 to 12 months	• cooperation develops further from the early proto-conversations of early motherese – for example, when adults wave 'bye-bye', or say 'show me your shoes' the babies enjoy pointing and waving • can follow simple instructions, e.g. 'kiss teddy' • word approximations appear, e.g. 'hee haw' = donkey, or more typically 'mumma' and 'dadda', and 'bye-bye' in English-speaking contexts • the tuneful babble develops into 'jargon', and babies make their voices go up and down just as people do when they talk to each other – 'Really? Do you? No!' – the babble is very expressive. Children are already experienced and capable communicators by this time; they are using emergent language/protolanguage. It is nothing short of amazing that all this happens within 1 year. They know about: • facial expressions • combined sounds (e.g. 'hee-haw') • gestures • shared meanings • persuading, negotiating, cooperating, turn-taking • interest in others, their ideas, their feelings, what they do. They know that words stand for people, objects, what they do and what happens. They are taking part in the language of their culture.
From 1 to 2 years	Children begin to talk with words or sign language. They add more and more layers to everything they know about language and communication in the first year.
By 18 months	• They enjoy trying to sing, as well as to listen to songs and rhymes. Action songs (for example, 'pat-a-cake') are much loved. • Books with pictures are of great interest. They point at and often name parts of their body, objects, people and pictures in books. • They echo the last part of what others say (echolalia). One word or sign can have several meanings (holophrases). For example, C-A-T = all animals, not just cats. This is sometimes called 'extension'. • They begin waving their arms up and down, which might mean start again, or I like it, or more. • Gestures develop alongside words. Gesture is used in some cultures more than in others.

By 2 years	Researchers used to say that children are using a vocabulary of 50 or so words but they understand more. Modern researchers do not use vocabulary counts so much and they simply stress that children are rapidly becoming competent speakers of the languages they experience. • They over-extend the use of a word (e.g. all animals are called 'doggie'). • They talk about an absent object when reminded of it (e.g. seeing an empty plate, they say 'biscuit'). • They use phrases (telegraphese) (e.g. 'doggie-gone'), they call themselves by their name – for example, 'Tom'. • They spend a great deal of energy naming things and what they do. For example, chair; and as they go up a step they might say 'up' • They can follow a simple instruction or request – for example, 'Could you bring me the spoon?' They are wanting to share songs, dance, conversations, finger rhymes, etc. more and more.
From 2 to 3 years	During this period, language and the ability to communicate develop so rapidly that they almost seem to explode. The development is stunning. Children begin to: • use plurals, pronouns, adjectives, possessives, time words, tenses and sentences • make what are called 'virtuous errors' in the way that they pronounce (articulate) things; this is also true of the way they use grammar (syntax) – they might say 'two times' instead of 'twice'; they might say 'I goed there' instead of 'I went there' • love to converse and chat, and ask questions (what, where and who) • enjoy much more complicated stories and ask about their favourite ones over and over again. It is not unusual for children to stutter because they are trying so hard to tell adults things and to talk. Their thinking goes faster than the pace at which they can say what they want to say. They can quickly become frustrated.
From 3 to 4 years	During this time children: • ask why, when and how questions as they become more and more fascinated with the reasons for things and how things work (cause and effect) • wonder what will happen 'if' (problem solving and hypothesis making) • can think back and they can think forward much more easily than before • can also think about things from somebody else's point of view, but only fleetingly; past, present and future tenses are used more often • can be taught to say their name, address and age. As they become more accurate in the way they pronounce words, and begin to use grammar, they delight in nonsense words that they make up, and jokes using words. This is called metalinguistics. They swear if they hear swearing.
From 4 to 8 years	Children: • try to understand the meaning of words; they use adverbs and prepositions; they talk confidently, and with more and more fluency; as they become more and more part of their culture they become aware of the roles of the language(s) they speak; they use language creatively • add vocabulary all the time; their articulation becomes conventional; they are explorers and communicators • begin to be able to define objects by their function (e.g. 'What is a ball?' 'You bounce it'). Young children do not learn anything in isolation from other children and adults. They: • begin to share as they learn; sharing sharpens and broadens their thinking; this helps them to learn better – for example, they begin to understand book language, and that stories have characters and a plot (the narrative)

	• begin to realise that different situations require different ways of talking. They establish a sense of audience (who they are talking to).
From 8 to 9 years	Children: • use and understand complex sentences • are increasingly verbal; they enjoy making up stories and telling jokes • use reference books with increasing skill.
From 10 to 11 years	Children: • can write fairly lengthy essays • write stories that show imagination, and are increasingly legible and grammatically correct.
From 12 to 16 years	During this period, young people become increasingly independent and spend much of their day outside the home – at school or at after-school activities and with peers. Young people: • have a fast, legible style of handwriting • communicate in an adult manner, with increasing maturity. • comprehend abstract language, such as idioms, figurative language and metaphors. • are able to process texts and abstract meaning, relate word meanings and contexts, understand punctuation, and form complex syntactic structures.

Table 2.2: Normative communication and language development: from birth to 16 years

INTELLECTUAL OR COGNITIVE DEVELOPMENT CHARTS

From birth to 4 weeks	Concepts (ideas) are beginning to develop already. Concepts are based in the senses and in what is perceived (i.e. the baby is aware of a sensation). Babies explore through their senses and through their own activity and movement.
	• Touch and movement (kinaesthetic)
	  – From the beginning babies feel pain.
	  – Their faces, abdomens, hands and the soles of their feet are also very sensitive to touch.
	  – They perceive the movements that they themselves make, and the way that other people move them about through their senses.
	  – For example, they give a 'startle' response if they are moved suddenly; this is called the Moro response.
	• Sound
	Even a newborn baby will turn to a sound. Babies might become still and listen to a low sound, or quicken their movements when they hear a high sound. A baby often stops crying and listens to a human voice by 2 weeks of age.
	• Taste
	Babies like sweet tastes – for example, breast milk.
	• Smell
	Babies turn to the smell of the breast.
	• Sight
	  – Babies can focus on objects 20 cm (a few inches) away.
	  – They are sensitive to light.
	  – Babies like to look at human faces – eye contact.
	  – They can track the movements of people and objects.
	  – They will scan the edges of objects.

	– They will imitate facial expressions (for example, they will put out their tongue if you do). If you know any newborn or very young babies, try it and see! – Psychologists think that babies may not see in colour during the early stages of development.
From 4 to 16 weeks	They recognise (have a concept of) differing speech sounds. By 3 months they can even imitate low- or high-pitched sounds. By four months they link objects they know with the sound – for example, mother's voice and her face. They know the smell of their mother from that of other mothers.
4 to 5 months	By 4 months babies reach for objects, which suggests they recognise and judge the distance in relation to the size of the object. This is called **depth perception**, but it also suggests that the baby is linking the immediate perception with previous ones and predicting the future, which is an early concept of dimensional objects.
5 to 6 months	Babies prefer complicated things to look at from 5 to 6 months. They enjoy bright colours. They know that they have one mother. Babies are disturbed if they are shown several images of their mother at the same time. They realise that *people* are **permanent** before they realise that *objects* are. Babies can coordinate more (e.g. they can see a rattle, grasp the rattle, put the rattle in their mouths – they coordinate tracking, reaching, grasping and sucking). They can develop favourite tastes in food and recognise differences by 5 months.
6 to 9 months	The baby understands **signs** (e.g. the bib means that food is coming). Soon this understanding of signs will lead into **symbolic** behaviour. From 8 to 9 months babies show they know objects exist when they have gone out of sight, even under test conditions. This is called the concept of object constancy, or the **object permanence test** (as described by **Piaget**). They are also fascinated by the way in which objects move.
9 months to 1 year	Babies are beginning to develop images. **Memory** develops. They can remember the past. They can anticipate the future. This gives them some understanding of routine daily sequences (e.g. after a feed, changing and a sleep with teddy). They imitate actions, sounds, gestures and moods after an event is finished (e.g. imitate a temper tantrum they saw a friend have the previous day, wave bye-bye remembering grandma has gone to the shops). They catch the moods and feelings of other people (e.g. sadness or joy). This **emotional contagion** is the beginning of sympathy for others.
From 1 to 4 years	Children develop **symbolic behaviour**. This means that they: • talk • pretend play – often talking to themselves as they do so • take part in simple non-competitive games • represent events in drawings, models, etc. Personal images dominate, rather than conventions used in the culture (e.g. writing is 'pretend' writing). Children tend to focus on one aspect of a situation. It is difficult for them to see things from different points of view. The way people react to what they do helps them to work out what hurts and what helps other people.

	This is an important time for moral development.
	They often enjoy music and playing sturdy instruments, and join in groups singing and dancing.
From 4 to 8 years	Children begin to move into deeper and deeper layers of symbolic behaviour.
	Language is well established, and opens the way into literacy (talking, listening, writing and reading).
	Personal symbols still dominate until 6 or 7 years of age.
	Thinking becomes increasingly coordinated as children are able to hold in mind more than one point of view at a time.
	Concepts – of matter, length, measurement, distance, area, time, volume, capacity and weight – develop steadily.
	They enjoy chanting and counting (beginning to understand number). They can use their voice in different ways to play different characters in their pretend play. They develop play narratives (stories), which they return to over time. They help younger children into the play. They are interested in their own development – from babies to now.
	They are beginning to establish differences between what is real and unreal/fantasy. This is not yet always certain, and so they can easily be frightened by supernatural characters.
	They begin to try and work out right and wrong (e.g. hurting people physically or their own feelings as language develops and deeper discussion of issues becomes more possible).
From 8 to 9 years	Children:
	• have an increased ability to remember and pay attention, and to speak and express their ideas
	• are learning to plan ahead and evaluate what they do
	• have an increased ability to think and to reason
	• can deal with abstract ideas
	• enjoy different types of activities – such as joining clubs, playing games with rules, and collecting things
	• enjoy projects that are task-orientated, such as sewing and woodwork.
From 10 to 11 years	Children:
	• begin to understand the motives behind the actions of another
	• can concentrate on tasks for increasing periods
	• begin to devise memory strategies
	• may be curious about drugs, alcohol and tobacco
	• may develop special talents, showing particular skills in writing, maths, art, music or woodwork.
From 12 to 16 years	Around this time, young people experience a major shift in thinking from **concrete** to **abstract** – an adult way of thinking: Piaget described this as the **formal operational stage** of cognitive development. This involves:
	• *thinking about possibilities* – younger children rely heavily on their senses to apply reasoning, whereas adolescents think about possibilities that are not directly observable
	• *thinking ahead* – young people start to plan ahead, often in a systematic way; for example, younger children may look forward to a holiday, but they are unlikely to focus on the preparation involved
	• *thinking through hypotheses* – this gives them the ability to make and test hypotheses, and to think about situations that are contrary to fact
	• *thinking about their own thought processes* – this is known as metacognition; a subcategory of **metacognition** is **metamemory**, which is having knowledge about your

	memory processes – being able to explain what strategies you use when trying to remember things (e.g. for an exam) • *thinking beyond conventional limits* – thinking about issues that generally preoccupy human beings in adulthood, such as morality, religion and politics. They approach a problem in a systematic fashion and also use their imagination when solving problems.

Table 2.3: Normative intellectual/cognitive development: from birth to 16 years

EMOTIONAL AND SOCIAL DEVELOPMENT CHARTS

From birth to 4 weeks	Babies: • first smile in definite response to carer is usually around 5–6 weeks • often imitate certain facial expressions • use total body movements to express pleasure at bath time or when being fed • enjoy feeding and cuddling • are learning where they begin and end (e.g. a hand is part of them but their mother's hand is not).
From 4 to 8 weeks	Babies: • will smile in response to adult • enjoy sucking • turn to regard nearby speaker's face • turn to preferred person's voice • recognise face and hands of preferred adult • may stop crying when they hear, see or feel their own carer.
From 8 to 12 weeks	Babies: • show enjoyment at caring routines such as bath time • respond with obvious pleasure to loving attention and cuddles • fix the eyes unblinkingly on the carer's face when feeding • stay awake for longer periods of time.
4 to 5 months	Babies: • enjoy attention and being with others • show trust and security • have recognisable sleep patterns. By 5 months babies have learnt that they have only one mother. They are disturbed when shown several images of their mother at the same time.
6 to 9 months	Babies: • manage to feed self with fingers • are now more wary of strangers, showing stranger fear • offer toys to others • show distress when the mother leaves • begin to crawl; this means they can do more for themselves, reach for objects and get to places and people • are now more aware of other people's feelings (e.g. they cry if a sibling cries); they love an audience to laugh with them; they cry and laugh with others – this is called recognition of an emotion; it does not mean they are really laughing or crying, though.

9 to 12 months	Babies: • enjoy songs and action rhymes • still like to be near to a familiar adult • can drink from a cup with help • will play alone for long periods • have and show definite likes and dislikes at mealtimes and bedtimes • thoroughly enjoy peek-a-boo games • like to look at themselves in a mirror (plastic safety mirror) • imitate other people (e.g. clapping hands, waving bye-bye), but there is often a time lapse so that they wave after the person has gone.
1 to 2 years	Children: • cooperate when being dressed • begin to have a longer memory • develop a **sense of identity** (I am me) • express their needs in words and gestures • enjoy being able to walk, and are eager to try to get dressed – 'Me do it!' • are aware when others are fearful or anxious for them as they climb on and off chairs, etc.
2 to 3 years	Children: • begin to be able to say how they are feeling • can dress self and go to the lavatory independently, but need sensitive support in order to feel success rather than frustration. **Pretend play** develops rapidly when adults foster it.
3 to 4 years	Children: • are beginning to develop a gender role as they become aware of being male or female • make friends and are interested in having friends • learn to negotiate, give-and-take through experimenting with feeling powerful, having a sense of control, and through quarrels with other children • are easily afraid – for example, of the dark – as they become capable of pretending; they imagine all sorts of things. Pretend play helps children to decentre. (This means they begin to be able to understand how someone else might feel.)
4 to 8 years	Children: • have developed a stable self concept • have internalised the rules of their culture • can hide their feelings once they can begin to control them • can think of the feelings of others • can take responsibility (e.g. in helping younger children).
8 to 12 years	At 8 or 9 years old, children: • may become discouraged easily • take pride in their competence • can be argumentative and bossy, but can equally be generous and responsive • are beginning to see things from another child's point of view, but still have trouble understanding the feelings and needs of other people. At 11 or 12 years old, children: • may be experiencing sudden, dramatic, emotional changes associated with puberty (especially girls, who experience puberty earlier than boys)

	• tend to be particularly sensitive to criticism • prefer to spend leisure time with friends and continue to participate in small groups of the same sex, but are acutely aware of the opposite sex • succumb to peer pressure more readily and want to talk, dress, and act just like friends.
12 to 16 years	Young people: • may become self-conscious or worried about physical changes (e.g. too short, too tall, too fat, too thin) • develop a sexual identity; self-labelling as gay or lesbian tends to occur around the age of 15 for boys and 15½ for girls, although first disclosure does not normally take place until after the age of 16½ years for both sexes • often feel misunderstood • can experience wide emotional swings (e.g. fluctuate between emotional peaks of excitement and depths of moodiness) • want to become accepted and liked • tend to identify more with friends and begin to separate from parents; they are less dependent on family for affection and emotional support

Table 2.4: Normative emotional and social development: from birth to 16 years

MORAL AND SPIRITUAL ASPECTS OF DEVELOPMENT

Birth to 1 year	Even a tiny baby experiences a sense of awe and wonder, and values people who are loved by them. Worship is about a sense of worthship. People, and loved teddy bears, a daisy on the grass grasped, looked at (put in the mouth!) all help to build the child's spiritual experiences. These have nothing to do with worship of a god or gods. Spirituality is about the developing sense of relating to others – ethically, morally and humanely.
1 to 3 years	Judy Dunn's work suggests that, during this period, children already have a strongly developed moral sense. They know what hurts and upsets their family (adults and children). They know what delights them and brings warm, pleased responses. Through their pretend play, and the conversations in the family about how people behave, hurt and help each other, they learn how other people feel. They learn to think beyond themselves.
3 to 8 years	With the help and support of their family, early childhood workers and the wider community, children develop further concepts like being helpful, forgiving and fairness. By the age of 7 years, they have a clear sense of right and wrong – for example, they realise that it is wrong to hurt other people physically.
8 to 12 years	By 8 or 9 years, children continue to think that rules are permanent and unchangeable because they are made up by adults, who must be obeyed and respected. They have a clear idea of the difference between reality and fantasy, and are highly concerned about fairness. By 10 and 11 years, children understand that certain rules can be changed by mutual negotiation; often, they do not accept rules that they did not help make. They may begin to experience conflict between parents' values and those of their peers.
12 to 16 years	Young people are able to think beyond themselves more and to understand the perspective of another. They are developing their own ideas and values, which often challenge those of home; they may deliberately flout rules or keep to them only if there is otherwise a risk of being caught.

Table 2.5: Normative moral and spiritual aspects of development: from birth to 16 years

Section 2

Using observations to support the development of children

WHY OBSERVE CHILDREN?

Parents, babysitters and child care workers automatically watch the children in their care. They want to know that the children are safe, happy, healthy and developing well. Watching or observing closely can often reassure all concerned that everything is all right, but may also alert them to problems or illness. Any discussion about a child usually relates to what has been seen, heard or experienced, and leads to conclusions about his/her personality, likes and dislikes, difficulties, etc.

Anyone who works with children needs to develop the skill of observing them (sometimes to be written/recorded) to check that a child is:

*   **safe** – not in any physical danger from the environment, from itself or from others
*   **contented** – there are many reasons why a child might be miserable, some may relate to physical comfort (e.g. wet nappy, hunger, thirst) or emotional comfort (e.g. main carer is absent, comfort object is lost) or lack of attention and stimulation
*   **healthy** – eats and sleeps well and is physically active (concerns about any of these aspects may indicate that the child is unwell)
*   **developing normally** – in line with general expectations for his/her age in all areas; there will be individual

differences but delays in any (e.g. crawling/walking or speaking) may show a need for careful monitoring and, perhaps, specialist help; any particular strength or talent may also be identified and encouraged.

A series of observations – particularly if they are written or recorded in some way (e.g. photos) – can provide an ongoing record of progress, which can be very useful to parents and other professionals who may be involved with a child's care and education.

The importance of careful observations

Observations can provide valuable information about:

*   individual children – their progress and how they behave in particular situations
*   groups of children – the differences between individuals in the same situations
*   adults – how they communicate with children and how they deal with behaviour
*   what activities are successful and enjoyed by children.

What should be recorded?

There is some information that should be included in any observation, but other aspects will depend on the purpose of the observation. If it is to consider the child's fine motor skills then the detail will probably be different from one that is to find out about his/her social development – even if the same activity or situation is being observed. You should also record some *introductory* information (see below).

When you carry out a written observation it is usually because you want to find out something about an individual child or a group of children. This provides an **aim**, which should be identified at the start of your work. For example:

* **Aim:** 'To see what gross motor skills Child R uses in a PE lesson and consider how confident he is on the apparatus.'

A clear aim explains what you want to find out and the activity or context that you have decided will best show you. This is better than saying you will watch Child R in a PE lesson. The aim you identify should affect what information you write in your introduction and in the actual observation.

As well as an aim, your observation should also have the following:

* date carried out
* start and finish times
* who gave permission
* where it took place (setting)
* number of children present
* number of adults present
* age of child/ages of children
* names or identification of children (remember confidentiality)
* method used (brief reason for choice)
* signature of supervisor or tutor.

How should it be recorded?

Your tutors will have their own preferences for how they want you to present your work but, generally, each observation should include the following sections:
Introduction; **Actual observation**; **Evaluation**; **Bibliography**.

Introduction

In this section you must state where the observation is taking place (e.g. At the sand tray in a reception class) and give some information about what is happening (e.g. the children had just returned to the classroom from assembly . . .). If there is any relevant information about the child you might include it here (e.g. Child R has been ill recently and has missed two weeks of school). Include information that is relevant to your aim – it may be important to know whether he is of average build if you are dealing with physical skills, but not particularly relevant if you are dealing with imaginative play.

Actual observation

There are many different methods of recording and your tutors will help you decide which one is best – perhaps a 'chart' format, a checklist, or a written record describing what you see as it happens. Remember only to write what you see and, if appropriate, hear. **Do not write your judgements, opinions, assessments, and so on.** Make sure you include information about other children or adults involved, if it is relevant.

When recording your observation remember to maintain **confidentiality** by only using a child's first name or initial, or some other form of identification (e.g. Child R). You may use 'T' or 'A' for 'teacher' or 'adult'.

Evaluation

An evaluation is an assessment of what you have observed. This section can be dealt with in two parts.

1. You need to look back at your recorded information and summarise what you have discovered. Example: 'Child R was looking around the classroom and fidgeting with his shoelaces during the story, and appeared bored and uninterested. However, he was able to answer questions when asked so he must have been listening for at least part of the time.' This is a *review* of what you saw.

2. You then need to consider what you have summarised, and compare your findings to the 'norm' or 'average' or 'expected' for a child of this age and at this stage of development. What have you, yourself, learnt about this particular child/group of children, and how has this helped you to understand children's development more widely? Use relevant books to help you and make reference to them – or quote directly if you can find a statement or section that relates to what you are saying or the point you are making. Your tutor or assessor wants to know what you understand, not information s/he could read in a book, so use references carefully.

As observation of children can help carers to plan for individual needs, try to suggest what activity or caring strategy might be needed next. You may also, in this section, give your opinion as to reasons for the behaviour, and so on – take care not to jump to conclusions about the role of the child's background, and never make judgements about the child or the child's family.

Bibliography

The bibliography is a list of the books you have used when reading and researching for information relating to your observation. See page 27 for information on referencing.

TECHNIQUES FOR OBSERVATIONS

There are six different types of observation.

1. **Narrative:** perhaps the most common is the narrative or descriptive observation. This type attempts to record everything that happens, as it happens, with plenty of detail. Methods that fit into the 'narrative' framework are:

   * descriptive/running record
   * detailed
   * target child
   * diary description
   * anecdotal record
   * tape and transcript (may be considered to fit into this category so long as the section focused upon and used for evaluation purposes is continuous and not a series of edited extracts)
   * video recording (as for tape and transcript).

2. **Time sampling:** this is specific, selected information recorded at chosen time intervals. A chart format is most often used.

3. **Event sampling:** this involves specific actions, incidents or behaviour observed whenever they occur. A chart format is most often used.

4. **Diagrammatic:** these provide a visual and accessible display of collected information or, in the case or growth charts, information plotted in the context of identified 'norms'. They could take the form of:

   * pie charts
   * bar graphs
   * flow diagrams
   * sociograms
   * growth charts.

5. **Checklists:** this type of observation is carried out with a pre-prepared list of skills or competencies that are being assessed and is often used for 'can do' checks in the context of a structured activity.

6. **Longitudinal study:** usually a collection of observations and measurements taken over a period of time using a variety of recording methods.

SHARING OF INFORMATION

Most settings provide clear guidance (sometimes in a booklet or sheet written especially for students) about working with children. Some settings now also have an Observations Policy. As a student, you should also be given information that will help you understand what a particular setting is trying to achieve and how it goes about it. You will always need to gain **permission** to carry out an observation and your placement supervisor may well wish to read your work. This is not only to check it through, but also out of interest, to find out more about the children, activity or safety aspects that you observed. Remember, information accurately observed by you can be just as valuable to the setting as that gathered by staff.

Cooperation between professionals requires sharing of information. However, in a work setting observations and records must be kept confidentially and access given only to certain people – these may include the individual child's parents or legal guardian, supervisor, teacher or key worker and other involved professionals (e.g. the health visitor).

REMEMBER

Any information about a child may be shared only if the parent or legal guardian gives consent.

THE IMPORTANCE OF CONFIDENTIALITY AND OBJECTIVITY

Maintaining confidentiality is an important aspect of your role, but it is particularly important when carrying out observations, especially those that are written and recorded. For your own training and assessment purposes, the identity of the child and setting is not important. They must, therefore, be protected (see below). You are developing your observational and record-keeping skills as you learn more about children in general, children as individuals and the various work settings.

OBJECTIVITY IN OBSERVATIONS

When you record your observational findings you need to be as objective as possible. This means that you must record **factual information** – what you actually see and hear – rather than information you have already begun to interpret.

By including plenty of detail to describe what you see, you are providing yourself (and any reader) with a lot of information for analysis. For example, the first extract in the activity that follows presents a much fuller picture of the situation than the second, and may lead you to a different conclusion about G's interest and attention.

It is often difficult to describe facial expressions and actions accurately, which is why many students produce work in the style of Observation B rather than in the style of A.

Section 3

The influences affecting children's development

There are very many factors that affect the healthy growth and development of children. These work in combination, so it is often difficult to estimate the impact of any single

GUIDELINES FOR MAINTAINING CONFIDENTIALITY IN YOUR OBSERVATION

- Ensure you have permission for making an observation – from your supervisor and the parent/main carer (this is confirmed by an authorising signature).
- Use codes rather than names to refer to the individuals involved – you should never use a child's first name. An initial or some other form of identification (e.g. Child 1) is sufficient. (You may use 'T' or 'A' for 'teacher' or 'adult'.)
- Understand and abide by policies and procedures in the setting.
- Remember that photographic and taped evidence can reveal identity, and should only be used with appropriate authority.
- Take extra care when sharing observations with fellow students – they may have friends or family involved in a work setting and could easily identify individuals.
- Never discuss children or staff from your work setting in a public place (e.g. when sitting on a bus or in a café).
- Never identify individuals when talking at home about your daily experiences (e.g. they could be neighbours' children).

ACTIVITY: OBSERVATIONS

Read the two brief examples below and identify where the observer has substituted a conclusion or interpretation for what was actually seen.

Observation A

. . . G is sitting on the floor with her legs crossed and her left hand in her lap. She is twiddling her hair with her right hand and staring at a picture on the wall display behind the teacher's head. She is smiling. The teacher says 'G, what do you think will happen to the cat next?' G stops fiddling with her hair and looks at the teacher. 'I think it will hide,' she says and laughs as she turns to N next to her . . .

Observation B

. . . G is sitting cross-legged on the floor in front of the teacher. She is fiddling with her hair and looking bored. The teacher asks her a question, 'G, what do you think will happen to the cat next?' G says, 'I think it will hide.' . . .

factor on holistic child development. Factors include:

- diet
- infection
- poverty and social disadvantage
- housing
- accidents
- environmental factors
- emotional and social factors
- parental health and lifestyle.

DIET

There are various conditions that may occur in childhood that are directly related to a poor or unbalanced diet:

- **failure to thrive** (or faltering growth) – poor growth and physical development
- **dental caries** or tooth decay – associated with high consumption of sugar in snacks and fizzy drinks
- **obesity** – children who are overweight are more likely to become obese adults

* **nutritional anaemia** – due to an insufficient intake of iron, folic acid and vitamin B12
* **increased susceptibility to infections** – particularly upper respiratory infections, such as colds and bronchitis.

INFECTION

During childhood there are many infectious illnesses which can affect children's health and development. Some of these infections can be controlled by childhood immunisations; these are diphtheria, tetanus, polio, whooping cough, measles, meningitis, mumps and rubella. Other infections can also have long-lasting effects on children's health.

POVERTY AND SOCIAL DISADVANTAGE

Poverty is the single greatest threat to the healthy development of children in the UK. Growing up in poverty can affect every area of a child's development: physical, intellectual, emotional, social and spiritual, as outlined below.

* **Accident and illness:** children from the bottom social class are four times more likely to die in an accident, and have nearly twice the rate of long-standing illness than those living in households with high incomes.
* **Quality of life:** a third of children in poverty go without the meals, or toys, or the clothes that they need.
* **Poor nutrition:** living on a low income means that children's diet and health can suffer.
* **Space to live and play:** poorer children are more likely to live in sub-standard housing and in areas with few

shops or amenities, where children have little or no space to play safely.
* **Growth:** they are also more likely to be smaller at birth and shorter in height.
* **Education:** children who grow up in poverty are less likely to do well at school, and have poorer school attendance records.
* **Long-term effects:** as adults they are more likely to suffer ill health, be unemployed or homeless. They are more likely to become involved in offending, drug and alcohol abuse. They are more likely to become involved in abusive relationships.

HOUSING

Poor housing is another factor that puts people at a social disadvantage. Low-income families are more likely to live in:

* **homes that are damp and/or unheated** – this increases the risk of infection, particularly respiratory illnesses
* **neighbourhoods that are unattractive and densely populated,** with few communal areas and amenities – children without access to a safe garden or play area may suffer emotional and social problems
* **overcrowded conditions** – homeless families who are housed in 'hotels' or bed and breakfast accommodation often have poor access to cooking facilities and have to share bathrooms with several other families; often, children's education is badly disrupted when families are moved from one place to another.

ACCIDENTS

Some childhood accidents have lasting effects on a child's healthy growth and development, and many are preventable (see Unit 3).

ENVIRONMENTAL FACTORS

Pollution of the environment can have a marked effect on children's health and development. The three main threats to health are *water pollution*, *air pollution* and *noise pollution*. Children are particularly vulnerable to air pollution. This is partly because they have a large lung surface area in relation to their small body size; this means that they absorb toxic substances quicker than adults do and are slower to get rid of them. The effects of air pollution from factory chimneys, the use of chemical insecticides and car exhausts include:

* **lead poisoning** – children are particularly susceptible to lead poisoning, mostly caused by vehicle exhaust fumes; even very low levels of lead in the blood can affect children's ability to learn
* **asthma** – air pollution can act as a trigger for asthma and can make an existing condition worse; the incidence of asthma is much higher in traffic-polluted areas
* **cancer** – the use of insecticides and fertilisers by farmers has been linked with various childhood cancers; radioactivity from nuclear power stations has also been found to cause cancer.

EMOTIONAL AND SOCIAL FACTORS

A child who is miserable and unhappy is not healthy, although he or she may appear *physically* healthy. Children need to feel secure and to receive unconditional love from their primary carers. Child abuse, although not common, is bound to affect a child's health and well-being, and can have long-lasting health implications. (See Unit 3 for information about child abuse.)

PARENTAL HEALTH AND LIFESTYLE

There are a number of factors that have an impact – directly or indirectly – on the child's health and well-being. Children who live with one or both parents who have a mental health problem, such as **depression**, may suffer from a lack of good parenting; also some older children may find themselves in the role of carer for younger children.

Children with parents with a **substance misuse** problem – alcohol or other substances – may be affected by the following factors.

* **Parents not available to their children:** the addiction may mean that parents are often absent both physically (because they are out looking for drugs) and emotionally (because they are intoxicated). Either way, they are not available to the child.
* **Poor parenting skills:** substance misuse is often, but not always, associated with poor or inadequate parenting. This can show itself in a number of ways:
    - **physical neglect** – children are not kept clean, warm or fed, and there is a lack of care for the child's safety
    - **emotional neglect** – the parent shows little or no affection or nurture
    - **unpredictable parental behaviour** – for example, lurching between 'too much' or 'not enough' discipline and mood swings – being very affectionate or very remote; this leads to inconsistent parenting, which can be confusing and damaging to the child
* **Living conditions:** the child may be living in an unsafe environment because of the substance use – for example, through the people that come to the

house, being left alone for long periods, either because the parent is intoxicated or out, or being taken out late at night to seek drugs or alcohol. Domestic abuse may be a factor in both circumstances, although research shows that it is more often associated with *alcohol* misuse.

Section 4

The care needs of individual children

To achieve and maintain healthy growth and development (that is, physical, intellectual and emotional), certain basic needs must be fulfilled. Whenever you are caring for children, you should always treat each child as an individual. This means that you should be aware of their individual needs at all times. Sometimes a child may have special or additional needs. (For further information, see Unit 9.)

MEETING THE PHYSICAL AND HEALTH NEEDS OF CHILDREN

This includes:

* planning a healthy diet for children
* the importance of rest and sleep

* hygiene – caring for children's skin, hair and teeth
* the development of bowel and bladder control
* clothing and footwear.

Planning a healthy diet for children

During childhood we develop food habits that will affect us for life. By the time we are adults most of us will suffer from some disorder that is related to our diet – for example, tooth decay, heart disease or cancer. Establishing healthy eating patterns in children will help to promote normal growth and development, and will protect against later disease. As an early years practitioner, you need to know what constitutes a good diet and how it can be provided.

A healthy diet consists of a wide variety of foods to help the body to grow and to provide energy. It must include enough of these **nutrients** – proteins, fats, carbohydrates, vitamins, minerals, and fibre – as well as **water**, to fuel and maintain the body's vital functions.

Children need a varied **energy-rich** diet for good health and growth. For balance and variety, choose from the five main food groups (see Table 2.6).

Food groups	Main nutrients	Types to choose	Portions per day	Suggestions for meals and snacks
1. Bread, other cereals and potatoes All types of bread, rice, breakfast cereals, pasta, noodles, and potatoes (beans and lentils can be eaten as part of this group)	Carbohydrates (starch), fibre, some calcium and iron, B-group vitamins	Wholemeal, brown Wholegrain or high-fibre versions of bread; avoid fried foods too often (e.g. chips). Use butter and other spreads sparingly	FIVE All meals of the day should include foods from this group	One portion = • 1 bowl of breakfast cereal • 2 tabsp pasta or rice • 1 small potato Snack meals include bread or pizza base

2. Fruit and vegetables Fresh, frozen and canned fruit and vegetables, dried fruit, fruit juice (beans and lentils can be eaten as part of this group)	Vitamin C, carotenes, iron, calcium folate, fibre and some carbohydrate	Eat a wide variety of fruit and vegetables; avoid adding rich sauces to vegetables, and sugar to fruit	FOUR/FIVE Include 1 fruit or vegetable daily high in Vitamin C, e.g. tomato, sweet pepper, orange or kiwi fruit	One portion = • 1 glass of pure fruit juice • 1 piece of fruit • 1 sliced tomato • 2 tabsp of cooked vegetables • 1 tabsp of dried fruit – e.g. raisins.
3. Milk and dairy foods Milk, cheese, yoghurt and fromage frais (this group does not contain butter, eggs and cream)	Calcium, protein, B-group vitamins (particularly B12), vitamins A and D	Milk is a very good source of calcium, but calcium can also be obtained from cheese, flavoured or plain yogurts and fromage frais	THREE Children require the equivalent of one pint of milk each day to ensure an adequate intake of calcium	One portion = • 1 glass of milk • 1 pot of yogurt or fromage frais • 1 tabsp of grated cheese, e.g. on a pizza Under 2s – do not give reduced-fat milks, e.g. semi-skimmed – they do not supply enough energy
4. Meat, fish and alternatives Lean meat, poultry, fish, eggs, tofu, quorn, pulses – peas, beans, lentils, nuts and seeds	Iron, protein, B-group vitamins (particularly B12), zinc and magnesium	Lower-fat versions – meat with fat cut off, chicken without skin etc. Beans and lentils are good alternatives, being low in fat and high in fibre	TWO Vegetarians will need to have grains, pulses and seeds; vegans avoid all food associated with animals	One portion = • 2 fish fingers (for a 3 year old) • 4 fish fingers (for a 7 year old) • baked beans • chicken nuggets or a small piece of chicken
5. Fatty and sugary foods Margarine, low-fat spread, butter, ghee, cream, chocolate, crisps, biscuits, sweets & sugar, fizzy soft drinks, puddings	Vitamins and essential fatty acids, but also a lot of fat, sugar and salt	Only offer small amounts of sugary and fatty foods. Fats and oils are found in all the other food groups	NONE Only eat fatty and sugary foods sparingly, e.g. crisps, sweets and chocolate	Children may be offered foods with extra fat or sugar – biscuits, cakes or chocolate – as long as they are not replacing food from the four main food groups

Table 2.6: Food groups

How much food should children be given?

Children's appetites vary enormously, so common sense is a good guide to how big a portion should be. Always be guided by the individual child:

* do not force them to eat when they no longer wish to, but
* do not refuse to give more if they really are hungry.

Some children always feel hungry at one particular mealtime. Others require food little and often. You should always offer food that is nourishing as well as satisfying their hunger (see Table 2.7).

Meals and snacks

Some children really do need to eat between meals. Their stomachs are relatively small and so they fill up and empty faster than adult stomachs. Sugary foods should not be given as a snack, because sugar is an appetite depressant and may spoil the child's appetite for the main meal to follow. Healthy snack foods include:

* pieces of fruit – banana, orange, pear, kiwi fruit, apple or satsuma
* fruit bread or wholemeal bread with a slice of cheese
* milk or home-made milk shake
* sticks of carrot, celeriac, parsnip, red pepper, cauliflower
* dried fruit and diluted fruit juices
* wholegrain biscuits, oatcakes or sesame seed crackers.

Iron, calcium and vitamin D in children's diets

Iron

Iron is essential for children's health. Lack of iron often leads to **anaemia**, which can hold back both physical and mental development. Children most at risk are those who are poor eaters or on restricted diets.

Iron comes in two forms, either:

1. found in foods from animal sources (especially meat), which is easily absorbed by the body, or
2. found in plant foods, which is not quite so easy for the body to absorb.

If possible, children should be given a portion of meat or fish every day, and kidney or liver once a week. Even a small portion of meat or fish is useful because it also helps the body to absorb iron from other food sources.

If children do not eat meat or fish, they must be offered plenty of iron-rich alternatives, such as egg yolks, dried fruit, beans and lentils, and green leafy vegetables. It is also a good idea to give foods or drinks that are high in vitamin C at mealtimes, as this helps the absorption of iron from non-meat sources.

Calcium and vitamin D

Children need calcium for maintaining and repairing bones and teeth. Calcium is:

* found in milk, cheese, yoghurt and other dairy products
* absorbed by the body only if it is taken with vitamin D.

The skin can make all the vitamin D that a body needs when it is exposed to gentle sunlight. Sources of vitamin D include:

* milk
* fortified breakfast cereals
* oily fish
* meat
* fortified margarine
* soya mince, soya drink
* tahini paste★
* tofu.

Breakfast	Orange juice Weetabix + milk 1 slice of buttered toast	Milk Cereal, e.g. corn or wheat flakes Toast and jam	Apple juice 1 slice of toast with butter or jam	Milk Cereal with slice of banana, or scrambled egg on toast	Yoghurt Porridge Slices of apple
Morning snack	Diluted apple juice 1 packet raisins	Blackcurrant and apple drink Cheese straws	1 glass fruit squash 1 biscuit	Peeled apple slices Wholemeal toast fingers with cheese spread	Diluted apple juice Chapatti or pitta bread fingers
Lunch	Chicken nuggets or macaroni cheese Broccoli Fruit yoghurt Water	Thick bean soup or chicken salad sandwich Green beans Fresh fruit salad Water	Vegetable soup or fish fingers/cakes Sticks of raw carrot Kiwi fruit Water	Sweet potato casserole Sweetcorn Spinach leaves Chocolate mousse Water	Bean casserole (or chicken drumstick) with noodles Peas or broad beans Fruit yoghurt Water
Afternoon snack	Diluted fruit juice Cubes of cheese with savoury biscuit	Milk shake Fruit cake or chocolate biscuit	Diluted fruit juice Thin-cut sandwiches cut into small pieces	Hot or cold chocolate drink 1 small packed dried fruit mix, e.g. apricots, sultanas	Lassi (yoghurt drink) 1 banana 1 small biscuit
Tea or supper	Baked beans on toast or ham and cheese pasta Lemon pancakes Milk or yoghurt	Fish stew or fish fingers Mashed potato Fruit mousse or fromage frais Milk or yoghurt	Baked potatoes with a choice of fillings Steamed broccoli Ice cream	Home-made beefburger or pizza Green salad Pancakes Milk	Lentil and rice soup Pitta or wholegrain bread Rice salad Milk

Table 2.7: Providing a balanced diet

(★ Tahini is made from sesame seeds; these may cause an allergic reaction in a small number of children.)

Vitamin drops provide vitamins A, C and D. Children under the age of 5 should be given vitamin drops as a safeguard only when their diets may be insufficient.

Providing drinks for children

You need to offer children drinks several times during the day. The best drinks for young children are water and milk.

* **Water** is a very underrated drink for the whole family as it quenches thirst

ACTIVITY: THE BALANCED DAILY DIET

1. Look at the following daily diet.
   - Breakfast: a glass of milk + scrambled egg and toast
   - Mid-morning: a packet of crisps + a glass of blackcurrant squash
   - Lunch: a cheese and egg flan + chips + baked beans; apple fritters and ice cream + apple juice
   - Snack: chocolate mini-roll and orange squash

   - Tea: fish fingers + mashed potatoes + peas + strawberry milk shake

2. Arrange the portions or servings as shown in the example presented in Table 2.6 (i.e. the four food groups and one extra row for extra fat and sugar) and assess the nutritional content of the diet.

3. How could you improve the menu to ensure a healthy balanced diet?

without spoiling the appetite; if bottled water is used it should be still, not carbonated (fizzy), which is acidic. More water should be given in hot weather in order to prevent dehydration.

* **Milk** is an excellent, nourishing drink. Reduced-fat milks should not normally be given to children under the age of 5 because of their lower energy and fat-soluble content; however semi-skimmed milk may be offered from 2 years of age, provided that the child's overall diet is adequate.

Other drinks

All drinks which contain sugar can be harmful to teeth and can also take the edge off children's appetites. Examples are: flavoured milks, flavoured fizzy drinks, fruit squashes and fruit juices (containing natural sugar).

Unsweetened diluted fruit juice is the best drink – other than water or milk – for children, but should ideally be offered only at mealtimes. Low-sugar or diet fruit drinks contain artificial sweeteners and are best avoided.

Tea and coffee should not be given to children under 5, as they prevent the absorption of iron from foods. They also fill children easily without providing nourishment.

Establishing healthy eating habits

Some children can be choosy about the food they eat; this can be a source of anxiety for parents and for those who work with children. However, as long as children eat some food from each of the five food groups – even if they are the same old favourites – there is no cause for worry.

As an early years practitioner, you are ideally placed to ensure that **stereotyping** in relation to eating habits is not practised. Mealtimes and the choice of food can be used in a positive sense to affirm a feeling of cultural identity.

Special diets

Most children on special diets are not ill. Often they simply require a therapeutic diet that replaces or eliminates some particular nutrient in order to prevent illness. The diets listed in Table 2.8 are followed by children with specific needs.

Children on vegetarian diets

Children who are on a vegetarian diet need an alternative to meat, fish and chicken as the main sources of **protein**. These could include:

* milk, cheese and eggs, pulses (lentils and beans).

GUIDELINES: PROVIDING A HEALTHY DIET

- **Offer a wide variety of different foods:** give babies and young children a chance to try a new food more than once; any refusal on first tasting may be due to dislike of the *new* rather than of the food itself.
- **Set an example**: children will imitate both what you eat and how you eat it. Be relaxed, patient and friendly. It will be easier to encourage a child to eat a stick of raw celery if you eat one too! If you show disgust at certain foods, young children will notice and copy you.
- **Be prepared for messy mealtimes!** Present the food in a form that is fairly easy for children to manage by themselves (e.g. not difficult to chew).
- **Don't use food as a punishment, reward, bribe or threat:** for example, don't give sweets or chocolates as a reward for finishing savoury foods. To a child this is like saying, 'Here's something nice after eating those nasty greens.' Reward them instead with a trip to the park or a story session.
- **Give healthy foods as treats:** for example, raisins and raw carrots, rather than sweets or cakes.
- **Allow children to follow their own individual appetites** when deciding how much they want to eat. If a child rejects a food, never force-feed him. Simply remove the food without comment. Give smaller portions next time and praise the child for eating even a little.
- **Encourage children to feed themselves,** either using a spoon or by offering suitable finger foods.
- **Introduce new foods in stages:** for example, if switching to wholemeal bread, try a soft-grain white bread first. Involve the children in making choices as much as possible.
- **Teach children to eat mainly at mealtimes,** and avoid giving them high-calorie snacks (e.g. biscuits and sugary drinks) that might take the edge off their appetite for more nutritious food. Most young children need three small meals and three snacks a day.
- **Be imaginative with presentation:** for example, cut slices of pizza into interesting shapes. Use ideas from children's food manufacturers. Using these tactics can make mealtimes more fun.
- **Avoid adding salt to any food:** too much salt can cause dehydration in babies and may predispose certain people to hypertension (high blood pressure) if taken over a lifetime.
- **Never give a young child whole nuts to eat – particularly peanuts:** children can very easily choke on a small piece of the nut or even inhale it, which can cause a severe type of pneumonia. Rarely, a child may have a serious **allergic reaction** to nuts.
- **Respect individual preferences:** some families prefer to eat with their fingers, while others use chopsticks or cutlery. Whatever tool is preferred, be patient – as children need time to get used to them.

They also need enough **iron**. As iron is more difficult to absorb from vegetable sources than from meat, a young child needs to obtain iron from sources such as:

- leafy green vegetables, such as spinach and watercress
- pulses (beans, lentils and chickpeas)
- dried fruit (such as apricots, raisins and sultanas)
- some breakfast cereals.

It is easier to absorb iron from our food if it is eaten *with* foods containing vitamin C

Diabetes mellitus: diabetes mellitus occurs in 1 in every 500 children under the age of about 16 years, and results in difficulty in converting carbohydrate into energy due to underproduction of insulin. Insulin is usually given by daily injection and a diet sheet will be devised by the hospital dietician. It is important that mealtimes be *regular* and that some **carbohydrate** be included at every meal. Children with diabetes should be advised to carry **glucose** sweets whenever they are away from home in case of **hypoglycaemia** (low blood sugar).	**Cystic fibrosis:** the majority of children with cystic fibrosis have difficulty in absorbing fats; they need to eat 20 per cent more protein and more calories than children without the disease, and so require a diet high in fats and carbohydrates. They are also given daily vitamin supplements and pancreatic enzymes.
Coeliac disease: treatment for coeliac disease is by gluten-free diet and has to be for the rest of the person's life. All formula milks available in the UK are gluten-free, and many manufactured baby foods are also gluten-free. Any cakes, bread and biscuits should be made from gluten-free flour, and labels on processed foods should be read carefully to ensure that there is no 'hidden' wheat product in the ingredients list.	**Galactosaemia:** the child with galactosaemia cannot digest or use galactose – which, together with glucose, forms lactose, the natural sugar of milk. A list of 'safe foods' with a low galactose content will be issued by the dietician, and food labels should be checked for the presence of milk solids and powdered lactose, which contain large amounts of this sugar.
Obesity: a child who is diagnosed as being overweight will usually be prescribed a diet low in fat and sugar; high-fibre carbohydrates are encouraged (e.g. wholemeal bread and other cereals). The child who has to go without crisps, chips and snacks between meals will need a lot of support and encouragement from carers.	**Children who have difficulties with chewing and swallowing:** children with cerebral palsy can experience difficulties with either or both of these aspects of eating. Food has to be liquidised, but this should be done in separate batches so that the end result is not a pool of greyish sludge. Presentation should be imaginative. Try to follow the general principle of making the difference in the meal as unobtrusive as possible.

Table 2.8: Special diets

foods such as fruit and vegetables, or diluted fruit juices, at mealtimes; these make it easier to absorb the iron.

The vegan diet

A vegan diet completely excludes all foods of animal origin – that is, animal flesh, milk and milk products, eggs, honey and all additives that may be of animal origin. A vegan diet is based on cereals and cereal products, pulses, fruits, vegetables, nuts and seeds. Human breast milk is acceptable for vegan babies.

Variations in children's diets

Parents have a right to bring up their children according to their own beliefs and cultural practices. Sometimes, however, these preferences are difficult to accommodate within a group setting. Early years practitioners need to ensure that each child has their dietary needs and preferences recorded, and that every staff member knows how to follow these wishes. This is particularly important if a child has a **food allergy** or **intolerance**. Some nurseries have developed a system of personalised table placemats, which include the child's name and photo along with their specific dietary requirements.

Occasionally, children may arrive at the setting with sweets and packets of crisps. Both staff and parents need to work together to formulate a policy that gives consistent guidelines about what is allowed in the setting – and to ensure that every child is offered a healthy and nutritious diet when away from home.

Providing food in a multicultural society

The UK is the home of a multicultural and multi-ethnic society. Food is an important part of the heritage of any culture. Providing food from a wide range of cultures is an important way of celebrating this heritage. Children learn to enjoy different tastes, and to respect the customs and beliefs of people different from themselves.

The largest ethnic minority group in the UK belongs to the Asian community – about 1.25 million people. Asian dietary customs are mainly based on three religious groups: Muslims (or Moslems), Hindus and Sikhs.

Hindus

Orthodox Hindus are strict vegetarians as they believe in *Ahimsa* – non-violence towards all living beings – and a few of them are vegans. Some will eat dairy products and eggs, while others will refuse eggs on the grounds that they are a potential source of life. Even non-vegetarians do not eat beef as the cow is considered a sacred animal. It is also unusual for pork to be eaten, as the pig is considered unclean. Wheat is the main staple food eaten by Hindus in the UK; it is used to make chapattis, puris and parathas. Ghee (clarified butter) and vegetable oil are used in cooking. Three festivals in the Hindu calendar are observed as days of fasting; these last from sunrise to sunset, during which Hindus eat only 'pure' foods such as fruit and yoghurt:

1. Mahshivrati – the birthday of Lord Shiva (March)
2. Ram Naumi – the birthday of Lord Rama (April)

3. Jan Mash Tami – the birthday of Lord Krishna (late August).

Muslims

Muslims practise the Islamic religion, and their holy book, the Koran, provides them with their food laws. Unlawful foods (called **haram**) include pork, all meat that has not been rendered lawful (halal), alcohol and fish without scales. **Halal** meat has been killed in a certain approved way and must be bought from a halal butcher. Wheat, in the form of chapattis, and rice are the staple foods. During the lunar month of **Ramadan**, Muslims fast between sunrise and sunset. Children under 12 and elderly people are exempt from fasting.

Sikhs

Most Sikhs will not eat pork or beef. Some Sikhs are vegetarian, but many eat chicken, lamb and fish. Wheat and rice are staple foods. Devout Sikhs will fast once or twice a week, and most will fast on the first day of the Punjabi month or when there is a full moon.

African-Caribbean diets

The African-Caribbean community is the second largest ethnic minority group in the UK. Dietary customs vary widely. Many people include a variety of European foods in their diet alongside the traditional foods of cornmeal, coconut, green banana, plantain, okra and yam. Although African-Caribbean people are generally Christian, a minority are Rastafarians.

Rastafarians

Rastafarians' dietary customs are based on laws, laid down by Moses in the Bible, which state that certain types of meat should be avoided. The majority of followers will eat only '**Ital**' foods, which are considered to be in a whole or natural state. Most Rastafarians are vegetarians and will not eat processed or preserved foods.

Jewish diets

Jewish people observe dietary laws which state that animals and birds must be killed by the Jewish method to render them **kosher** (acceptable). Milk and meat must never be cooked or eaten together, and pork in any form is forbidden. Shellfish are not allowed as they are thought to harbour disease. The most holy day of the Jewish calendar is Yom Kippur (the Day of Atonement) when Jewish people fast for 25 hours.

Food and festivals

There are often particular foods that are associated with religious festivals (e.g. mince pies at Christmas and pancakes on Shrove Tuesday). Providing foods from different cultures within an early childhood setting is a very good way of celebrating these festivals. Parents of children from minority ethnic groups are usually very pleased to be asked for advice on how to celebrate festivals with food, and may even be prepared to contribute some samples.

The social and educational role of food and mealtimes

Promotes:

* hand–eye coordination – using cutlery and other tools
* sensory development – taste, touch, sight and smell
* language development – increased vocabulary
* development of concepts of shape and size, using different foods as examples
* learning through linked activities (e.g. cookery, weighing food, stories about food, where food comes from)

* independence – skills of serving food and taking responsibility
* listening skills
* courtesy towards others, and turn-taking
* sharing experience – a social focus in the child's day
* self-esteem – child's family and cultural background are valued
* self-confidence – through learning social skills, taking turns and saying 'please' and 'thank you'.

Sharing information with families

When parents register their child at nursery or school they are asked to detail any special dietary requirements that their child may have. Some children may need special diets because of an underlying medical condition; others may require a vegetarian or vegan diet. It is important that all child care and education settings are aware of any particular allergies or problems with eating that a child may have. If a parent or carer expresses any concern to you about the food provided within your nursery or school, refer them to the person in charge, or the child's key person, for guidance.

Fig 2.1. Eating as a social activity

The nutritional needs of babies

The way babies and children are fed is much more than simply providing enough food to meet nutritional requirements; for the newborn baby, sucking milk is a great source of pleasure, and is also rewarding and enjoyable for the mother. The ideal food for babies to start life with is breast milk, and breast-feeding should always be encouraged as the first choice in infant feeding. However, mothers should not be made to feel guilty or inadequate if they choose not to, or are unable to, breast-feed their babies.

Advantages of breast-feeding

* Human milk provides food constituents in the correct balance for human growth. There is no trial and error to find the right formula to suit the baby.
* The milk is sterile and at the correct temperature; there is no need for bottles and sterilising equipment.
* Breast milk initially provides the infant with maternal antibodies and helps protect the child from infection.
* The child is less likely to become overweight as overfeeding by concentrating the formula is not possible, and the infant has more freedom of choice as to how much milk she will suckle.
* Generally breast milk is considered cheaper despite the extra calorific requirement of the mother.
* Sometimes it is easier to promote mother–infant bonding by breast-feeding, although this is certainly not always the case.
* Some babies have an intolerance to the protein in cows' milk.
* The uterus returns to its pre-pregnancy state more quickly, by the action of oxytocin released when the baby suckles.

The advantages of bottle-feeding

* The mother knows exactly how much milk the baby has taken.
* The milk is in no way affected by the mother's state of health, whereas anxiety, tiredness, illness or menstruation may reduce the quantity of breast milk.
* The infant is unaffected by such factors as maternal medication. Laxatives, antibiotics, alcohol and drugs affecting the central nervous system can affect the quality of breast milk.
* Other members of the family can feed the infant. In this way the father can feel equally involved with the child's care and, during the night, could take over one of the feeds so that the mother can get more sleep.
* There is no fear of embarrassment while feeding.
* The mother is physically unaffected by feeding the infant, avoiding such problems as sore nipples.

How to support a mother who is breast-feeding

* Many mothers give up breast-feeding when they return to full-time work. Others continue to breast-feed their baby fully by expressing their own milk and bringing it to the nursery or crèche for it to be given by bottle. This involves a considerable amount of planning and organisational skill. The baby's key worker should reassure the mother that her wishes will be respected, and that every effort will be made to support her in her preference for breast-feeding. As with bottle-fed babies in your care, you should ensure that you record the amount of feed taken, and note any changes or problems in feeding.

Bottle-feeding

Types of milk

Only commercially modified baby milks – known as formula milks – should be used for bottle-feeding babies from birth to 1 year old. The main types of formula milk for babies under 6 months are as follows.

* **First-stage formula milk:** normally used for babies from birth; the protein content has more whey in it than casein, which reflects the balance of whey and casein in breast milk.
* **Second-stage formula milk:** suitable for babies from birth, although usually promoted as being for 'hungrier' babies as it has a greater casein content, which is less easily digestible and is intended to keep the baby feeling fuller for longer this is sometimes called 'follow-on' milk.
* **Soya formula:** made from soya beans, which, like cows' milk, are modified for use in formula with added vitamins, minerals and nutrients. This is used for babies who are unable to tolerate cows' milk formula or whose parents are vegans. Babies should be given soya-based formula only on the advice of a health professional, such as a health visitor, GP or dietician.

Some other specialist formula milks are used for babies who have other special needs – for instance, pre-term babies.

Preparation of feeds

A day's supply of bottles may be made and stored in the fridge for up to 24 hours. The following equipment will be needed:

* a container for sterilising bottles, large enough to submerge everything completely; or use a steam steriliser and follow the instructions
* wide-necked feeding bottles and teats designed for newborn babies
* a large plastic or Pyrex measuring jug and a plastic stirrer – or feeds can be made directly in bottles and shaken to mix
* sterilising liquid or tablets – check the manufacturer's instructions for length of time and correct dilution.

How to make up a feed

1. Wash hands and nails thoroughly.
2. Boil some fresh water and allow it to cool.
3. Take bottles from the steriliser.
4. Shake but **do not rinse** because this would desterilise them.
5. Pour the correct amount of boiled water into each bottle (check quantity at eye level on a firm surface).
6. Measure the exact amount of formula milk powder using the scoop provided; level with a plastic knife but do not pack down; add powder to each bottle.
7. Take teats from steriliser, taking care to handle by the edges, and fit into the bottles upside down; put caps, rings and tops on.
8. Shake each bottle vigorously until any lumps have dissolved.
9. If not using immediately, cool quickly and put bottles in the fridge.

Sterilising feeding equipment

It is very important that all bottles and equipment are thoroughly sterilised.

Note: Ordinary cows' milk, condensed milk, dried milk, goats' milk, evaporated milk, or any other type of milk should never be given to a baby under 12 months old.

1. After use, scrub all the bottles, caps and covers, using hot soapy water and a special bottle brush. Rinse thoroughly in clean running water.
2. Teats may be cleaned using a special teat cleaner; turn teat inside out to ensure all milk deposits are removed, and wash as the bottles.
3. Submerge bottles, teats and all other equipment needed for bottle-feeding in the sterilising solution, checking that no bubbles are trapped inside bottles and that teats are completely immersed.

Giving a bottle-feed

1. Collect all the necessary equipment before picking up the baby. The bottle may be warmed in a jug of hot water; have a muslin square or bib and tissues to hand.
2. Check the temperature and flow of the milk by dripping it on to the inside of your wrist (it should feel warm, not hot or cold).
3. Make yourself comfortable with the baby. Do not rush the feed – babies always sense if you are not relaxed and it can make them edgy too.

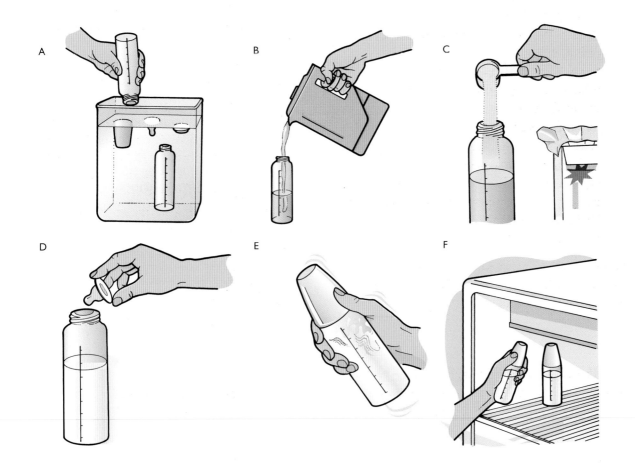

Fig 2.2. Preparing a bottle feed

4. Try to hold the baby in a similar position to that for breast-feeding and maintain eye contact; this is a time for cuddling and talking to the baby.

5. Stimulate the rooting reflex by placing the teat at the corner of the baby's mouth; then put the teat fully into the mouth and feed by tilting the bottle so that the hole in the teat is always covered with milk.

6. After about ten minutes, the baby may need to be helped to bring up wind; this can be done by leaning the child forwards on your lap and gently rubbing the back, or by holding the baby against your shoulder. Unless the baby is showing discomfort, do not insist on trying to produce a 'burp' – the baby may pass it out in the nappy.

Dummies

Babies are born with a strong sucking reflex and some babies are more 'sucky' than others. If a dummy is used before the baby is weaned, it should be sterilised in the same way as teats are sterilised. For older babies careful washing and rinsing is sufficient.

> **Safety point:** To prevent accidental strangulation, *never* hang a dummy from a ribbon or string around the baby's neck, nor from a cot rail.

Feeding problems

Babies often regurgitate small amounts of milk after a feed; this is known as **posseting** and is nothing to worry about. However, you should always inform the baby's parents if you are in a home setting, and your supervisor if you are in a group setting if you notice the following problems.

* **Vomiting:** if the baby brings up large quantities of the feed, this could be due to trapped wind but there could also be an underlying illness.
* **Refusal of a feed:** the baby may cry and draw her knees up to her chest – a sign of colic – or she may be hungry but unable to feed because of a problem with, for example, a blocked teat.

Always seek help if the baby you are caring for gives you cause for concern.

Weaning a baby – or starting on solid foods

Weaning is the gradual introduction of solid food to the baby's diet. The reasons for weaning are:

* to meet the baby's nutritional needs – from about 6 months of age, milk alone will not satisfy the baby's increased nutritional requirements, especially for iron
* to develop the chewing mechanism; the muscular movement of the mouth and jaw also aids the development of speech

GOOD PRACTICE WHEN BOTTLE-FEEDING A BABY

The National Children's Bureau states that babies who are bottle-fed should be held and have warm physical contact with an attentive adult while being fed. It is strongly recommended that a baby in a child care setting is fed by the same staff member at each feed. Babies should never be left propped up with bottles as this is dangerous and inappropriate to their emotional needs.

GUIDELINES ON FEEDING A BABY SAFELY

- Always wash hands thoroughly when preparing feeds for babies.
- Never add sugar or salt to the milk, and never make the feed stronger than the instructions state – this could result in too high a salt intake, which can lead to severe illness.
- Always check the temperature of the milk before giving it to a baby. Try a few drops on your wrist; it should feel neither hot nor cold to the touch – in other words, you should not really feel it at all as it will be at body temperature.
- Do not use a microwave oven to warm the bottle as this may produce isolated hot spots. Expressed breast milk should not be microwaved because this breaks down the natural chemistry.
- Always check that the teat has a hole the right size and that it is not blocked.
- **Never prop up a baby with a bottle** – choking is a real danger.
- Always supervise siblings when feeding small babies.

* to satisfy increasing appetite
* to introduce new tastes and textures; this enables the baby to join in family meals, thus promoting cognitive and social development
* to develop new skills – use of feeding beaker, cup and cutlery.

For children from 6 to 8 months of age, you can gradually increase the amount of solid foods you give. By 12 months solid foods should form the main part of the diet, with breast or formula milk making up the balance (see Table 2.9).

Stage 1 Around 5–6 months	Stage 2 6–8 months	Stage 3 9–12 months
Mix a teaspoon of one of the following with the baby's usual milk (breast or formula): • vegetable purée – such as carrot, parsnip, potato or yam, or • fruit purée – such as banana, cooked apple, pear or mango, or • cereal (not wheat-based) – such as baby rice, sago, maize, cornmeal or millet Offer this before or after one of the usual milk feeds, or in the middle of a feed, if that works better. If the food is hot, make sure you stir and cool it and test it before giving it to the baby	Add to the vegetable, fruit and cereal purées other foods, such as: • purées of meat and poultry • purées of pulses such as lentils (dhal), hummus • full-fat milk products such as yoghurt or fromage frais – unless advised otherwise by the health visitor or general practitioner (full-fat cows' milk can also be used for cooking only, e.g. in cheese sauce, but avoid giving cows' milk as a drink) Try to give cereals just once a day; start to add different foods and different tastes. By using family foods – mashing, or puréeing a small amount – you help to get the baby used to eating with the family	Add a wider range of foods with a variety of textures and flavours: • finger foods such as toast, bread, breadsticks, pitta bread or chapatti, peeled apple, banana, carrot sticks, or cubes of cheese • pieces of meat from a casserole • 3–4 servings a day of starchy foods and fruit and vegetables – the vitamin C in fruit and vegetables helps our bodies absorb iron If the baby is following a vegetarian diet, give two servings a day of pulses (e.g. red lentils, beans or chickpeas), or tofu

Table 2.9: The three stages of weaning

Methods of weaning

Some babies take very quickly to solid food; others appear not to be interested at all. The baby's demands are a good guide for weaning; mealtimes should never become a battleground. Even babies as young as 4 months have definite food preferences and should never be forced to eat a particular food, however much thought and effort has gone into the preparation. The best foods to start with are puréed cooked vegetables, fruit and ground cereals such as rice. Chewing usually starts at around the age of 6 months, whether the baby has teeth or not, and coarser textures can then be offered. The baby should be in a bouncing cradle or high chair – not in the usual feeding position in the carer's arms.

Methods of **puréeing food**:

* rub through a sieve using a large spoon
* mash soft foods such as banana or cooked potato with a fork
* use a mouli-sieve or hand blender
* use an electric blender (useful for larger amounts).

Food allergies and special diets

* **Cows' milk protein intolerance or allergy:** babies who have an intolerance to cows' milk or an allergy to it should be referred to a dietician, who may recommend a soya-based formula or a cows' milk-based formula that has been specially modified for babies with an allergy or intolerance.
* **Lactose intolerance:** this is an intolerance to the sugar (lactose) found in milk. It is not an allergy, but babies will need to avoid milk; they may be given fermented milk products, such as yoghurt.
* **Gluten-free diet:** babies who have the rare condition coeliac disease must not be given any foods that contain gluten. This is found in cereals (wheat, rye, barley and oats) and all foods made with them, such as bread, pastries, biscuits and cakes. Gluten-free alternatives must be given. Dieticians will advise parents, and useful advice is provided by the Coeliac Society (www.coeliac.co.uk).
* **Dairy-free diet:** some babies with severe eczema may be advised to avoid dairy products such as milk, cheese and butter. Again, a dietician will give advice about a suitable diet.

Babies with special needs

* **Cleft lip and palate:** feeding can be difficult in babies with this condition, as the gap caused by the cleft palate can

---

GUIDELINES ON WEANING

* Try to encourage a liking for savoury foods.
* Introduce only one new food at a time.
* Be patient if the baby does not take the food – feed at the baby's pace, not yours.
* Do not add salt or sugar to feeds.
* Make sure that food is the right temperature.
* Avoid giving sweet foods or drinks between meals.

* Never leave a baby alone when she is eating.
* Limit the use of commercially prepared foods – they are of poorer quality and will not allow the baby to become used to home cooking.
* Select foods approved by the baby's parents.

ACTIVITY: WEANING A BABY ON TO SOLID FOOD

1. Prepare a booklet for parents on weaning. Include the following information:
   - when to start weaning a baby
   - what foods to start with
   - when and how to offer feeds
   - a weekly menu plan, which includes vegetarian options.
2. Visit a store that stocks a wide variety of commercial baby foods and note their nutritional content (e.g. protein, fat, energy, salt, sugar, gluten and additives). Make a chart that shows:

   - the type of food (e.g. rusks and cereals, savoury packet food, jars of sweet and savoury food)
   - the average cost in each category
   - the packaging – note particularly if manufacturers use pictures of babies from different ethnic backgrounds.
3. If possible, ask a parent who has recently used weaning foods what reasons they had for choosing one product over another.

cause milk to be regurgitated through the nose. Various specialist feeding bottles and teats can be used. A specially designed one-way valve and teat adjust milk flow to suit the baby's needs.

* **Down's syndrome:** some babies with Down's syndrome may have feeding problems in the first few weeks. They need to be able to sort out the complicated coordination necessary to suck, swallow and breathe at the same time and they may splutter and choke a bit. Try holding the baby fairly upright to feed and check first that the tongue is not sticking to the roof of the mouth. For a baby to suckle and obtain adequate milk the teat must be on the tongue (not under it). Specially adapted teats are available to help babies who have difficulty feeding. Do not hurry the feed. Babies with Down's syndrome often feed very slowly, so do not stop too quickly. If the baby falls asleep in the middle of a feed, try tickling her cheeks, chin and feet.

When caring for babies with special needs, try to find out as much as you can about the particular condition by consulting the relevant websites.

Consulting parents and other carers about feeding preferences

Parents usually have very definite ideas about what feed their baby should be given – and how often. You need to be aware of their preferences and to make sure that their instructions are followed. It is good practice to keep a record of when and how much food or milk is taken by babies in your care. You could record this information on a chart (see example on page 70).

The importance of rest and sleep

Rest and sleep are important for our health and well-being. By the end of the first year, most babies are having two short sleeps during the day – before or after lunch and in the afternoon – and sleeping through the night, although there is much variation between individual children. It is important to have 'quiet periods', even if the baby does not want to sleep.

When we sleep, we rest and gain energy for a new day. But sleep does more than that. When we dream, we process all the events of our daily life. After a night without enough sleep we often feel exhausted and irritable, but after

Feeding Chart		
Name: Molly Bates		
Date: 4/5/08		
Time	**Food/Drink**	**Comments**
8.40 am	Baby rice and 100 ml milk	Both enjoyed
10.30 am	200 ml milk	Taken well
12.45 pm	Puréed sweet potato, carrot and lentils Half a small mashed banana 150 ml boiled water	Only ate 4 teaspoons Really enjoyed banana!
4.15 pm	200 ml milk	Taken well
Key worker: H. Charles		

a good night's sleep we feel rested, refreshed and full of energy. It is important to parents that their child sleeps through the night, as it influences the entire family's life and well-being. Children need more sleep than adults because the brain is developing and maturing, and they are physically growing as well. Sleep is important to child health because:

* it rests and restores the body
* it enables the brain and the body's metabolic processes to recover (these processes are responsible for producing energy and growth)
* during sleep, growth hormone is released; this renews tissues and produces new bone and red blood cells
* dreaming is believed to help the brain sort out information stored in the memory during waking hours.

Children vary enormously in their need for sleep and rest. Some seem able to rush around all day with very little rest; others will need to 'recharge their batteries' by having frequent periods of rest. You need to be able to recognise the signs that a child is tired; these may include:

* looking tired – dark rings under the eyes and yawning
* asking for their comfort object
* constant rubbing of the eyes
* twiddling their hair and fidgeting with objects
* showing no interest in activities and in their surroundings
* being particularly emotional – crying or being stubborn
* withdrawing into themselves – sucking thumb and appearing listless.

Different views about sleep and rest

There are cultural differences in the how parents view bedtime and sleep routines. In some cultures it is normal for children to sleep with their parents and to have a much later bedtime in consequence. Some families who originate from hot countries where having a sleep in the afternoon is normal tend to let their children stay up in the evening. Such children are more likely to need a sleep while in day care; as long as the overall amount of sleep is sufficient for the child, it does not matter. It is always

GUIDELINES: ESTABLISHING A ROUTINE FOR REST AND SLEEP

Children will only sleep if they are actually tired, so it is important that enough activity and exercise is provided. Some children do not have a nap during the day but should be encouraged to rest in a quiet area.

When preparing children for a daytime nap, rest or bedtime sleep, you need to:

- treat each child uniquely; every child will have his or her own needs for sleep and rest
- find out all you can about the individual child's sleep habits; for example, some children like to be patted to sleep, while others need to have their favourite comfort object
- be guided by the wishes of the child's parents or carers; some parents, for example, prefer their child to have a morning nap but not an afternoon nap, as this fits in better with the family's routine
- reassure children that they will not be left alone, and that you or someone else will be there when they wake up
- keep noise to a minimum and darken the room; make sure that children have been to the lavatory beforehand – they need to understand the signals that mean it is time for everyone to have a rest or sleep
- provide quiet, relaxing activities for children who are unable, or who do not want to sleep; for example, jigsaw puzzles, a story tape or reading a book.

worth discussing bedtime routines with parents when toddlers are struggling to behave well. Some areas have sleep clinics, managed by the health visiting service, to help parents whose children have difficulty sleeping.

Even after they have established a good sleep routine, children's sleep patterns can become disrupted between the ages of 1 and 3 years. There are thought to be a number of reasons for this, including developmental changes and behavioural issues.

GUIDELINES: ESTABLISHING A BEDTIME ROUTINE FOR BABIES

Between 3 and 5 months, most babies are ready to settle into a bedtime routine.

- Give the baby a bath or wash, and put on a clean nappy and nightwear.
- Take her to say goodnight to other members of the household.
- Carry her into her room, telling her in a gentle voice that it is time for bed.
- Give the last breast- or bottle-feed in the room where the baby sleeps.
- Sing a song or lullaby to help settle her, while gently rocking her in your arms.
- Wrap her securely and settle her into the cot or cradle, saying goodnight.
- If she likes it, gently 'pat' her to sleep.

The routine can be adapted as the baby grows. Advice from the Foundation for the Study of Infant Deaths (FSID) is that the safest place for a baby to sleep is in a cot in the parents' room for the first six months. After this time, the baby can safely be left in her own room.

Preventing sudden infant death syndrome

Sudden infant death syndrome (SIDS) is often called 'cot death'. It is the term applied to the sudden unexplained and unexpected death of an infant. The reasons for cot deaths are complicated and the cause is still unknown. Although cot death is the commonest cause of death in babies up to 1 year old, it is still very rare, occurring in approximately 2 out of every 1000 babies.

'Side' sleeping is not as safe as sleeping on the back, but it *is* much safer than sleeping on the front. Healthy babies placed on their backs are *not* more likely to choke. To prevent a baby wriggling down under the covers, place the baby's feet at the foot of the cot and make the bed up so that the covers reach no higher than the shoulders. Covers should be securely tucked in so that they cannot slip over the baby's head. Duvets or quilts, baby nests and pillows have the potential to trap air and may increase the risk of overheating.

How to put babies down to sleep

*   Place babies on their back to sleep, with the feet near to the end of the cot to prevent the baby slipping under the covers ('feet to foot').
*   Make sure the room is not too hot or too cold (it should be about 18–20°C). If the room is warm enough for you to be comfortable wearing light clothing, then it is the right temperature for babies.
*   Do not overdress the baby – keep the head uncovered.
*   Do not place the baby's cot in direct sunlight or near a radiator.
*   Do not use duvets or quilts until the baby is over a year old.

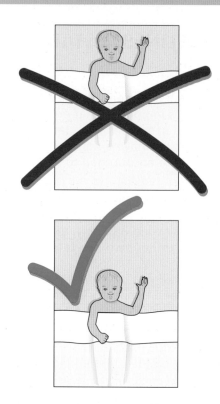

Fig 2.3. Feet-to-foot position

*   Do not smoke or let anyone else smoke near the baby.

How to help children to sleep

When preparing children for the night-time sleep, you need to follow the guidelines above and also warn the child that bedtime is approaching (e.g. after the bath and story) and then follow a set **routine** as outlined in the accompanying guidelines on page 71.

Promoting and maintaining good hygiene and care routines

(Unit 3 discusses hygiene routines in the child care setting.)

Caring for babies' skin and hair

A baby's skin is soft and delicate, yet also tough and pliant. Young babies do not have to be bathed every day because only their

GUIDELINES: A BEDTIME ROUTINE

- Take a family meal about 1½ hours before bedtime. This should be a relaxing, sociable occasion.
- After the meal, the child could play with other members of the family.
- Make bathtime a relaxing time to unwind and play with the child; this often helps the child to feel drowsy.
- Give a final bedtime drink followed by teeth cleaning. (Never withhold a drink at bedtime when potty-training – see below.)
- Read or tell a story; looking at books together develops a feeling of closeness between the child and their carer.
- Settle the child in bed, with curtains drawn and nightlight on if desired, and then say goodnight and leave.

bottom, face and neck, and skin creases get dirty and because the skin may tend to dryness. If a bath is not given daily, the baby should have the important body parts cleansed thoroughly – a process known as 'topping and tailing'; this limits the amount of undressing and helps to maintain good skin condition.

Whatever routine is followed, the newborn baby needs to be handled gently but firmly, and with confidence. Most babies learn to enjoy the sensation of water and are greatly affected by *your* attitude. The more relaxed and unhurried you are, the more enjoyable the whole experience will be.

GUIDELINES: TOPPING AND TAILING FOR BABIES

- Babies do not like having their skin exposed to the air, so should be undressed for the shortest time possible. Always ensure the room is warm – no less than 20°C (68°F) – and that there are no draughts.
- Warm a large, soft towel on a not-too-hot radiator and have it ready to wrap the baby in afterwards.
- Wash your hands. Remove the baby's outer clothes, leaving on her vest and nappy. Wrap the baby in the towel, keeping her arms inside.
- Using two separate pieces of cotton wool (one for each eye; this will prevent any infection passing from one eye to the other), squeezed in the boiled water, gently wipe the baby's eyes in one movement from the inner corner outwards.
- Gently wipe all around the face and behind the ears. Lift the chin and wipe gently under the folds of skin. Dry each area thoroughly by patting with a soft towel or dry cotton wool.
- Unwrap the towel and take the baby's vest off, raise each arm separately and wipe the armpit carefully. The folds of skin rub together here and can become quite sore. Again, dry thoroughly and dust with baby powder if used.
- Wipe and dry the baby's hands.
- Take the nappy off and place in a lidded bucket.
- Clean the baby's bottom with moist swabs, then wash with soap and water; rinse well with flannel or sponge, pat dry and apply protective cream.
- Put on clean nappy and clothes.

Caring for children's skin and hair

As children grow and become involved in more vigorous exercise, especially outside, a daily bath or shower becomes necessary. Most young children love bathtime and adding bubble bath to the water adds to the fun of getting clean.

Children should NEVER be left alone in the bath or shower, because of the risk of drowning and scalding.

Head lice

Head lice are a common affliction. Anybody can get them but they are particularly prevalent among children. Head lice:

* are tiny insects with six legs
* live only on human beings; they cannot be caught from animals
* have mouths like small needles, which they stick into the scalp and use to drink the blood
* are unable to fly, hop or jump
* are not the same as nits – nits are the egg cases laid by lice; nits may be found 'glued' on to the hair shafts; they are smaller than a pinhead and are pearly white
* are between 1 and 4 mm in size – slightly larger than a pin head

GUIDELINES: CARING FOR CHILDREN'S SKIN AND HAIR

* Wash face and hands in the morning. (Note: Muslims always wash under running water.)
* Always wash hands after using the toilet and before meals; dry hands thoroughly – young children will need supervision.
* After using the toilet, girls should be taught to wipe their bottom from front to back, to prevent germs from the anus entering the vagina and urethra.
* Wash hands after playing outside, or after handling animals.
* Nails should be scrubbed with a soft nailbrush and trimmed regularly by cutting straight across; never cut into the sides of the nails as this can cause sores and infections.
* Find out about any special skin conditions, such as eczema or dry skin, and be guided by parents' advice concerning the use of soap and creams.
* Children should have their own flannel, comb and brush, which should be cleaned regularly.
* Skin should always be dried thoroughly, taking special care of such areas as between the toes and the armpits; black skin tends to dryness and may need massaging with special oils or moisturisers.
* Babies' and young children's hair should ideally be washed during bathtime using a specially formulated mild baby soap or shampoo. (Adult shampoos contain many extra ingredients, such as perfumes and chemicals, all of which can lead to irritation of children's delicate skin.)
* Hair usually only needs washing twice a week; children with long or curly hair benefit from the use of a conditioning shampoo, which helps to reduce tangles. Hair should always be rinsed thoroughly in clean water and not brushed until it is dry – brushing wet hair damages the hair shafts. A wide-toothed comb is useful for combing wet hair.
* African-Caribbean hair tends to dryness and may need special oil or moisturisers; if the hair is braided (with or without beads), it may be washed with the braids left intact, unless advised otherwise.
* Rastafarian children with hair styled in dreadlocks may not use either combs or shampoo, preferring to brush the dreadlocks gently and secure them with braid.
* Regular combing and brushing will also help to prevent the occurrence of head lice.

ACTIVITY: PREVENTION AND TREATMENT OF HEAD LICE

1. Find out how to prevent head lice.
2. Find out how to treat an individual child with head lice.
3. Prepare a fact sheet to give to parents that explains:

(a) what head lice are and why children are particularly susceptible to them

(b) how head lice can be prevented

(c) the different methods of treatment and where to obtain them.

---

* live on, or very close to, the scalp, and don't wander down the hair shafts for very long
* are caught just by coming into contact with someone who is infested; when heads touch, the lice simply walk from one head to the other.
* do not discriminate between clean and dirty hair, but tend to live more on smooth, straight hair.

Care of children's teeth

Care of the first, 'milk', teeth is as important as for permanent teeth, since it promotes good habits and encourages permanent teeth to appear in the proper place. Every time the child eats sweet things, acid is produced which attacks the enamel of the tooth. Saliva protects the teeth from this and more saliva is produced during meals. The protective effect lasts for about half an hour so the more frequently the child eats sweets or sugary drinks, the more exposure to acid the teeth have. After the child's first birthday, they can be taught to brush their own teeth, but they will need careful supervision. You can help by following the guidelines presented here.

The use of dummies

Parents often have strong views about the use of soothers and dummies. These are only likely to be harmful to tooth development if they are used constantly and habitually, or if they are sweetened, which is likely to cause

---

GUIDELINES: CARING FOR CHILDREN'S TEETH

* Babies under 1 year should have their teeth brushed with a soft brush once or twice a day using gentle toothpaste.
* Drinks should be given after meals, with water between meals. Bottles and cups should not contain fizzy or sweetened drinks, and fruit juice should be limited to mealtimes.
* Babies should not be allowed to have constant access to a bottle or cup
* Babies should be encouraged to drink from a cup between 12 and 15 months
* Teach children to brush their teeth after meals: show them how to brush up and away from the gum when cleaning the lower teeth and down and away from the gum when cleaning the upper teeth. (Younger children will need help in brushing the back teeth.)
* Crusty bread, crunchy fruit and raw vegetables, such as carrot or celery, help to keep teeth healthy and free of **plaque** – a substance that builds up on the teeth, attracting bacteria and causing tooth decay.
* Sweets may be given after meals, if at all.
* Take children to the dentist regularly so that they get used to the idea of having their mouth looked at.

decay. Dummies should be sterilised regularly and changed if they have been dropped on the floor. Dummies should *never* be sucked by adults before giving to babies as this merely transfers bacteria from adult to child and can cause stomach upsets.

Equipment for physical care

There is a wide variety of equipment that may be used when physically caring for children. Children will find it easier to be independent in their hygiene routines if they are provided with suitable equipment (e.g. a stool that enables them to reach the washbasin, or a child-sized toothbrush).

The development of bowel and bladder control

Children will not achieve control over their bowel or bladder function until the nerve pathways that send signals to the brain are mature enough to indicate fullness. This usually happens between 2 and 3 years of age, with most children achieving control by 4 years. Gaining control over these basic functions is a major milestone that relies on both psychological and physical readiness.

* Toilet training should be approached in a relaxed, unhurried manner. If the potty is introduced too early, or if a child is forced to sit on it for long periods of time, they may rebel and the whole issue of toilet training becomes a battleground.
* Toilet training can be over in a few days or may take some months. Becoming dry at night takes longer, but most children manage this before the age of 5.
* There is no point in attempting to start toilet training until the child shows that he or she is ready, and this rarely occurs before the age of 18 months.

There are different opinions on using a potty or placing the child straight on the toilet. Privacy must be considered within the nursery setting and the potty placed in a cubicle if the child is used to a potty;

GUIDELINES: TOILET TRAINING

- Toilet training must be discussed with the parents and the decision on when to start agreed.
- Parents must not feel pressured into toilet training their child; however, children do exhibit certain signs and behaviours that will indicate that they are developmentally ready to consider training – that is, they are likely to achieve control successfully and without too much difficulty – and parents may find this information helpful.
- You should understand how to recognise the signs that children are ready to be toilet trained; these include:
  - ability to pull down pants
  - has bowel movements at regular times (e.g. after breakfast)
  - is willing to sit on the toilet or potty without crying or fuss
  - shows an interest in using it and will usually pass urine if placed on toilet/potty
  - has a word or gesture to indicate a wet or soiled nappy.
- Anticipate when the child is likely to need the toilet – such as after meals, before sleep and on wakening – and sit the child on the potty or toilet.
- Give children praise on 'going' and have a practical and sympathetic attitude to 'accidents'.
- Demonstrate that using the toilet is a normal activity that everyone does when they are old enough to manage it.

however, if the toilet is 'child sized' then they can be encouraged to use it. Aids such as clip-on seats and steps are available to enable children to use an adult-sized toilet and still feel safe – some children are anxious about falling down the toilet.

Dealing with accidents

Even once a child has become used to using the potty or toilet, there will inevitably be occasions when they have an 'accident' – that is, they wet or soil themselves. This happens more often during the early stages of toilet training, as the child may still lack the awareness or the control to allow enough time to get to the potty. Older children may become so absorbed in their play that they simply forget to go to the toilet.

You can help children when they have an accident by:

* not appearing bothered; let the child know that it is not a big problem, just something that happens from time to time
* reassuring the child by using a friendly tone of voice and offering a cuddle if they seem distressed
* being discreet; deal with the matter swiftly – wash and change them out of view of others and with the minimum of fuss
* if older children want to manage the incident themselves, encouraging them to do so, but always checking tactfully afterwards that they have managed
* always following safety procedures in the setting (e.g. wearing disposable gloves and dealing appropriately with soiled clothing and waste).

Other developmental areas and gaining control

As we have seen before, all the areas of development are closely linked with each other and the stages of development reached in one area will have an effect on the way in which independence in toilet needs is reached.

* **Physical development**: a child with a spinal injury or other physical disability may not receive the messages to the brain that tell them that their bladder is full; independence is therefore restricted.
* **Cognitive and language development:** children who have communication difficulties may need the support of a signed language such as Makaton or Signalong in order to signal their toilet needs.
* **Emotional and social development:** if a child is feeling insecure or under stress, this may affect the rate at which they gain control over their bladder and bowel function. Sometimes, children who have previously been both dry and clean may begin to have more 'accidents'. This is known as regression and is usually a temporary response to an emotional upset (e.g. the birth of a sibling in the family).

Signs of illness or abnormality

When you help children to use the potty or the toilet you should always be alert to any problems they may have. All observations should be reported to the child's parents, or, if this is not appropriate, to your immediate supervisor. Some of the signs to look for are:

* **diarrhoea** – some nursery-age children are prone to bouts of diarrhoea, which is not usually a sign of infection but a result of the immaturity of the nervous system affecting the speed of digestion
* **constipation** – a child may have difficulty and feel pain when passing a motion
* **pain when passing urine** – this may be caused by a bladder infection (cystitis) and will require treatment

* **rashes around the nappy and genital area** – nappy rash or thrush may cause red spots around the nappy area
* **bruising or other marks** – these could indicate abuse (see Unit 3 for further information).

Care of children's feet

Babies do not need shoes: the bones of the feet are not fully developed during the first year and can easily be damaged by shoes – and even socks – as these restrict the natural movement of the toes and feet, especially if they are too small. The feet of babies and young children grow very quickly, so that both socks and shoes can become too small in a matter of weeks. Although miniature versions of adult shoes are available in sizes to fit babies they should be discouraged; unfortunately, because of the availability of such products, there is a tendency to believe they are not harmful. Babies should be left barefoot as much as possible, especially once they become mobile, because their attempts to balance and efforts at walking strengthen and develop the supporting muscles of the foot, including the arch.

Children's footwear: parents and carers should always go to a shoe shop where trained children's shoe fitters can help them choose from a wide selection of shoes. Second-hand shoes should never be worn as all shoes take on the shape of the wearer's foot.

CLOTHING FOR CHILDREN

Parents and carers should expect children to become dirty as they explore their surroundings and should not show disapproval when clothes become soiled. Clothes for children need to be:

* hard-wearing
* comfortable

GUIDELINES: CHANGING NAPPIES IN A GROUP SETTING

Nappy changing is an important time and you should ensure that the baby feels secure and happy. Chatting and singing should be built in to the procedure to make it an enjoyable experience. Each setting will have its own procedure for changing nappies. The following is an example.

* Nappies should be checked and changed at regular periods throughout the day.
* A baby should never knowingly be left in a soiled nappy.
* Collect the nappy and the cream needed. Put on apron and gloves. Ensure you have warm water and wipes.
* Carefully put the baby on the changing mat, talking to and reassuring him or her.
* Afterwards, dispose of the nappy and discard the gloves.
* Thoroughly clean the nappy mat and the apron with an anti-bacterial spray.
* Wash your hands to avoid cross-contamination.
* Record the nappy change on the baby's nappy chart, noting the time, whether it was wet or dry, whether there had been a bowel movement. Note any change you have observed – for example, in the colour or consistency of the stools – or if the baby had difficulty in passing the stool. Also note whether there is any skin irritation or rash present.
* Check nappy mats for any tears or breaks in the fabric and replace if necessary.
* **Never** leave a baby or toddler unsupervised on the changing mat.

* easy to put on and take off, especially when going to the toilet
* washable.

Underwear should be made of cotton, which is comfortable and sweat-absorbent.

Sleep suits – all-in-one pyjamas with hard-wearing socks – are useful for children who kick the bedcovers off at night. (Note: these must be the correct size to prevent damage to growing feet.)

Daytime clothes should be adapted to the stage of mobility and independence of the child; for example, a dress will hinder a young girl trying to crawl; dungarees may prove difficult for a toddler to manage when being toilet trained. Suitable daytime wear includes: cotton jersey tracksuits, T-shirts and cotton jumpers.

Outdoor clothes must be warm and loose enough to fit over clothing and still allow freedom of movement; a shower-proof anorak with a hood is ideal as it can be washed and dried easily.

Choose clothes that are appropriate for the weather: for example, children need to be protected from the sun with wide-brimmed hats with neck shields; they need warm gloves, scarves and woolly or fleece hats in cold, windy weather, and waterproof coats and footwear when out in the rain.

Caring for children's clothes

Many nannies have total responsibility for the care of children's clothes and bed linen. When caring for clothes, you should:

* look at the laundry care labels on each garment and make sure that you are familiar with the different symbols
* check and empty all pockets before laundering
* be guided by the parents regarding choice of washing powder – some detergents can cause an adverse skin reaction in some children
* dry clothes thoroughly before putting them away
* label children's clothes with name tapes before they go into group settings.

THE IMPORTANCE OF ROUTINES

(**Routine** = the usual way tasks or activities are arranged.)

One aspect of children's need for love and security is the need for **routine** and predictability. This is why having daily routines is so important in all aspects of child care. By meeting children's need for routine, parents and carers are helping the child:

* to feel acknowledged
* to feel independent
* to increase self-esteem.

Routines – for example, around mealtimes and bedtimes – can be very useful in helping babies and toddlers to adapt both physically and emotionally to a daily pattern; this will suit both them and those caring for them. It will prove especially helpful during times of **transition** and change in their lives, such as starting nursery or moving house. If certain parts of the day remain familiar, they can

---

The **health and safety** requirements when working with children from birth to age 5 years are covered in Unit 3.
The principles of **effective communication** when working with families and their children are discussed in Unit 5.

cope better with new experiences. Having routines for everyday activities also ensures that care is consistent and of a high quality.

All settings that provide care and education for children have **routines** for daily activities. This does not mean that every day is the same; rather, it means that there is a recognised structure to the child's day – one that will help children to feel secure and safe. Such routines include:

* hygiene – changing nappies and toileting older children; ensuring there is a hand-washing routine after messy activities, and before eating and drinking
* health and safety – tidying away toys and activity equipment; making regular checks on equipment for hazards
* safety at home times and trips away from the setting – ensuring there is a correct ratio of adults to children, permission from parents and contact numbers, etc.
* meal and snack times – serving of meals and drinks under close supervision (see Unit 7)
* sleep and rest
* outdoor play.

Supporting hygiene routines

All children benefit from regular routines in daily care. You need to encourage them to become independent by helping them to learn how to take care of themselves. Ways of helping children to become independent include:

* teaching them how to wash and dry their hands before eating or drinking
* making sure that they always wash and dry their hands after going to the toilet and after playing outdoors
* providing children with their own combs and brushes, and encouraging them to use them every day

Fig 2.4. Child washing hands

* providing a soft toothbrush, and teaching children how and when to brush their teeth
* ensuring that you are a good role model for children – for example, when you cough or sneeze, always cover your mouth
* devise activities that develop an awareness in children of the importance of hygiene routines – for example, you could invite a dental hygienist or dental nurse to the setting to talk to children about daily tooth care
* make sure that children are provided with a healthy diet and that there are opportunities for activity, rest and sleep throughout the nursery or school day.

Planning routines to meet individual needs

Anyone looking after children should be able to adapt to their individual needs, which will change from day to day. You therefore need to be flexible in your approach and allow, whenever feasible, the individual child to set the pattern for the day – as long as all the child's needs are met. Obviously, parents and carers have their own routines and hygiene

GUIDELINES: EVERYDAY ROUTINES FOR BABIES AND YOUNG CHILDREN

- Be patient – even when pressed for time, try to show children that you are relaxed and unhurried.
- Allow time for children to experiment with different ways of doing things.
- If you work directly with parents, encourage them to make a little extra time in the morning and evening for children to dress and undress themselves. Children could be encouraged to choose their clothes the night before from a limited choice (the choosing of clothes to wear is often fertile ground for disagreements and battles of will).

- Resist the urge to take over if children are struggling, since this deprives them of the sense of achievement and satisfaction of success.
- Show children how to do something and then let them get on with it. If they ask for help, they should be shown again. If adults keep doing things for children that they could do for themselves they are in danger of creating 'learned helplessness'.
- Offer praise and encouragement when children are trying hard, not just when they succeed in a task.

practices, and these should always be respected. (For example, Muslims prefer to wash under running water and Rastafarians wear their hair braided so may not use a comb or brush.)

Whenever you are caring for children, you should always treat each child as an individual. This means that you should be aware of their individual needs at all times.

* Sometimes a child may have special or additional needs.
* Children may need specialist equipment or extra help with play activities.
* Routines may need to be adapted to take into account individual needs and preferences.

Section 5

Supporting children through transitions

A transition is a change of passage from one stage or state to another. Children and young people naturally pass through a number of stages as they grow and develop. Often, they will also be expected to cope with changes such as movement from nursery education to primary school, and from primary to secondary school.

You may have just made the transition from secondary school to a tertiary college or sixth form. Along with the excitement of a new course and possibly making new friends, you are likely to have felt some apprehension about the change to your life. This is likely to affect you more if you have experienced many changes in your life.

These changes are commonly referred to as **transitions**. Some children may have to cope with personal transitions that – unlike the transition to school at a certain age – are not necessarily shared or understood by all their peers.

You need to be able to identify transitions and understand what you can do to support children through them. Before we can fully understand the importance of transitions in children's lives, we need to explore the concepts of attachment, separation and loss.

ATTACHMENT

Attachment means a warm, affectionate and supportive bond between a child and his or her carer, which enables the child to develop **secure relationships**. When children receive warm, responsive care, they feel safe and secure.

* Secure attachments are the basis of all the child's future relationships. Because babies experience relationships through their senses, it is the expression of love that affects how they develop and that helps to shape later learning and behaviour.

* Children who are securely attached will grow to be more curious, get along better with other children and perform better in school than children who are less securely attached.

* With children who have a strong attachment to their parent or primary carer, the process of becoming attached to the worker is easier, not harder, than it is for children with a weaker attachment. Remember, though, that all parents find separation difficult, whether they have formed a strong attachment with their child or not.

SEPARATION

Many of the times which are difficult for children have to do with separation. Going to bed is separation from the main carer and is often a source of anxiety in children. Some young children can be terrified as a parent walks out of the room. How children react to separation is as varied as children are themselves. For some children each new situation will bring questions and new feelings of anxiety. Other children love the challenge of meeting new friends and seeing new things.

THE EFFECTS OF MULTIPLE TRANSITIONS

Children who have had to make many moves or changes may feel a sense of loss and grief. These changes may have a profound effect on their emotional and social development. Reasons for transitions include the following.

* **Divorce or separation:** children whose parents have separated or divorced may have to live and get along with several 'new' people (e.g. stepfathers, stepmothers, half-brothers and sisters).

* **Changes in child care arrangements:** children may experience many different child care arrangements (e.g. frequent changes from one nanny or childminder to another).

* **Children who are in local authority care** – either in residential children's homes or in foster care.

* **Children whose families have moved house several times** – for example, for employment reasons, or as travellers.

Children who have experienced multiple transitions need to feel supported each time they enter a new setting. They may feel:

* **disorientated** – no sooner have they settled in one place and got to know a carer, they may be uprooted and have to face the same process again

* **a sense of loss** – each time they make a move they lose the friends they have made and also the attachments they have formed with their carers

* **withdrawn** – children may withdraw from new relationships with other children and with carers, because they do not trust that the separation will not happen again.

BOWLBY'S THEORY OF ATTACHMENT

John Bowlby (1907–90) used many of the ideas from psychodynamics (e.g. Freud's theory) to form his basic theory. However, he also believed that the psychodynamic approach put too much emphasis on the child's fantasy world and not nearly enough on actual events.

The main principles of Bowlby's theory are that:

- children need a **close continuous relationship** with their mothers for successful personality development
- the child must **form an attachment** by about 6 months of age; after that and until the age of 3 children strongly need to be close by their mothers
- any obstacle to forming an attachment, and any disruption of the relationship, constitutes **maternal deprivation**.

Secure attachment and continuous relationships are far more likely to be provided within the child's natural family than anywhere else. Bowlby did not say that the most important attachment figure *must* be the natural mother. He did stress, however, that babies need one central person who is the 'mother figure'.

Bowlby's theory has been criticised for placing too much emphasis on the mother's role as primary caregiver; what is important for children is that there is familiarity, trust and continuity in their first relationships. It is now accepted that babies and young children can form **several close attachments**, and that it is only when such close relationships are broken that emotional damage results.

Bowlby's research had an enormous impact on the delivery of care both to mothers in post-natal wards and to children in institutions. Above all, his theory led to further research and highlighted the importance of meeting children's emotional needs as well as their physical and intellectual needs. Some of the changes made in response to his theory of attachment are as follows:

- babies are kept with their mothers after birth when at all possible
- parents are helped to look after their newborn babies in special care baby units
- children are allowed to visit their parents in hospital
- parents are encouraged to stay overnight when their children are in hospital, and to participate in their care
- parents are encouraged to stay and help to settle their children in nurseries and playgroups before leaving them
- children in many day nurseries and in residential care have a key worker assigned to them; this means that one person is responsible for their care when at the nursery and so becomes another attachment figure.

As children become older, they start to cope better with being separated from their parents or main carers; however, the way they cope will still depend on their early experiences of separation and how earlier transitions were managed. Children who have had to change schools many times – maybe because of a parent's job being changed – often find it harder to settle in and make new friends and relationships.

HOW TO SUPPORT CHILDREN THROUGH TRANSITIONS

The first few days at a nursery or playgroup can be very daunting for some children. They may not have been left by their parents or primary carers ever before and some children will show real distress. You need to be able to recognise their distress and to find ways of dealing with it. Children show their distress at being separated from their carer by crying and refusing to join in with activities. Parents too can feel distressed when leaving their children in the care of others; they may feel guilty because they have to return to work, or they may be upset because they have never before been separated from their child.

You can help a child to settle in by following the suggestions given below.

* **Trying to plan for the separation:** nursery staff can help by visiting the child and their parents at home. This gives both parents and children the opportunity to talk about their fears and helps them to cope with them. When children know in advance what's going to happen and not happen they can think about and get used to their feelings about it. Parents can be encouraged to prepare their child for the change by:
  - visiting the nursery with their child so that they can meet the staff
  - reading books about starting at a nursery or going to hospital, and
  - involving their child in any preparation, such as buying clothing or packing a 'nursery bag'.
* **Encouraging parents to stay with their child until the child asks them to leave:** this does not mean that the parents should cling to their child. Children can always sense a parent's uncertainty. Although young children do not have a very good sense of time, parents and carers should make it very clear when they will be back (e.g. saying 'I'll be back in one hour').
* **Allowing the child to bring a comforter** – for example, a blanket or a teddy bear – to the nursery. If it is a blanket, sometimes the parent can cut a little piece and put it in the child's pocket if they think there will be any

embarrassment. Then the child can handle the blanket and feel comforted when feeling lonely.

* **Having just one person to settle the child:** hold and cuddle the child and try to involve him or her in a quiet activity with you (e.g. reading a story). Most child care settings now employ a **key person** who will be responsible for one or two children during the settling-in period.
* **Contacting the parent or primary carer** if the child does not settle within 20 minutes or so. Sometimes it is not possible to do this, and you will need to devise strategies for comforting and reassuring the child. Always be honest with parents regarding the time it took to settle their child.

OTHER TRANSITIONS

Where children are facing other transitions or changes in their lives – such as bereavement or loss, or the arrival of a new sibling – their key worker will need to be especially sensitive to their feelings and always take time to talk with them about how they are feeling. Opportunities should be provided for children to express their feelings in a safe and unthreatening environment. For example, some children may be encouraged to use play dough to release pent-up feelings of frustration; others may choose to use role play.

THE ROLE OF THE KEY PERSON OR KEY WORKER

Each family is given a key person at nursery who gets to know them well, and this helps everyone to feel safe. A baby or young child knows that this special person and the important people at home often do the same things for them:

*   they help you manage through the day
*   they think about you
*   they get to know you well
*   they sometimes worry about you
*   they get to know each other
*   they talk about you.

The Sure Start programme makes a distinction between the **key worker** role and the **key person** role. The term 'key worker' is often used in nurseries to describe how staff work, to ensure liaison between different professionals, and to enhance smooth organisation and record keeping. The key person role is defined as a special emotional relationship with the child and the family. For more information on the key worker or person role, see Unit 7, pages 193–194.

Activities relating to Unit 2

ACTIVITY: HELPING CHILDREN TO SETTLE IN

This activity will help a child who is new to the setting to realise that he or she is not alone, and that other children also feel shy and alone at times.

*   **Introduction:** choose a teddy and introduce him to the group, saying something like 'Teddy is rather shy and a little bit lonely. How can we help him to feel better?'
*   **Discussion and display:** take photos of teddy – using a digital camera if possible – with different groups of children, and in different places in the nursery (e.g. playing in the sand, reading a book, doing a puzzle), and use them later for discussion and display.
*   **Circle time:** in circle time, pass teddy round and encourage each child to say something to him – for example, 'Hello Teddy, my name is Lara' or 'Hello Teddy, I like chocolate . . .

*   **Taking teddy home:** each child takes it in turns to take teddy home. Include a notebook and encourage parents to write a few sentences about what teddy did at their house that evening. The children can draw a picture.
*   **Story time:** read and act out the story of 'Goldilocks and the Three Bears', with the different-sized bowls, beds and chairs.
*   **Cooking:** use a shaped cutter to make teddy-shaped biscuits or dough teddies.
*   **Teddy bears picnic:** arrange a teddy bears picnic where each child brings in a favourite bear – 'What does your teddy like to eat?', 'Are there enough plates, biscuits and cups for all the bears?'

You can probably think of many more teddy-related ideas that will help children gain a sense of belonging.

ACTIVITY: OBSERVING SOCIAL NEEDS

1. In your work placement, plan to observe an individual child's social needs during a whole session. Make a checklist that includes the following needs.
   - Interaction with other children: observe how the child plays – for example, does he or she play alone (**solitary play**), alongside others but not with them (**parallel play**), or actively with other children.
   - **Attention from adults:** does the child seek attention from one particular adult, or from any adult? Note the number of occasions a child seeks adult attention and describe the interaction.
   - **Self-help skills and independence:** observe the child using self-help skills (e.g. putting on coat to go outside, washing hands and going to the lavatory).

2. Identify the stage of social development the child is passing through and list the ways in which you can ensure that their social needs are met within the setting.

MULTIPLE-CHOICE QUESTIONS

Unit 2 is assessed through multiple-choice questions (MCQs). You will find some that you can use for practice – along with the correct answers – in the Appendix at the back of the book. Good luck!

Unit 3

Safe, Healthy and Nurturing Environments for Children

Contents

Unit 3 is divided into three sections:

Section 1

Supporting and maintaining a safe environment for children

A safe environment is one in which the child or adult has a low risk of becoming ill or injured. Safety is a basic human need.

* Children should be supervised at all times.
* The early years environment and all materials and equipment should be in a safe condition.
* There must be adequate first aid facilities and staff should be trained in basic first aid.
* Routine safety checks should be made daily on premises, both indoors and outdoors.
* Fire drills should be held twice a term in schools and nurseries, and every six weeks in day nurseries.
* Children should only be allowed home with a parent or authorised adult.

A HEALTHY ENVIRONMENT

Children need a clean, warm and hygienic environment in order to stay healthy. Although most large early years settings employ a cleaner, there will be many occasions when you have to take responsibility for ensuring that the environment is kept clean and safe – for example, if a child has been sick or has had a toileting accident. You can help in the following ways.

* Be a good role model by, for example, always looking neat and tidy, washing your hands, wearing an apron during messy activities, etc.
* Encourage children to cover their mouths when coughing.

* Make sure that food is stored at the correct temperature and that snacks are prepared hygienically.
* Find out about the more common childhood illnesses (such as infectious diseases and asthma) and how to deal with a child who is ill.
* Prevent accidents by keeping the environment clean, tidy and uncluttered.

UNDERSTANDING SAFETY ISSUES RELEVANT TO CHILD CARE

The likelihood of different types of accidents occurring depends on:

* **the age and developmental capabilities** of the child; for example, bicycle accidents are more likely in older children, accidents involving poisoning are commoner in younger children
* **the environment** – indoor or outdoor, child-aware or not; for example, toddlers visiting childless relatives are more likely to find hazards – such as trailing electrical flexes, loose rugs or unsecured cupboards containing potentially dangerous cleaning products – than in a household with children
* **the degree of supervision** available; for example, inquisitive toddlers with little appreciation of danger need more supervision in an environment that is not child-aware; at the same time, the adult may be less aware of potential dangers due to the distractions – for example, holding an adult conversation with a friend, talking on the phone (especially mobile phones) or in a busy shopping centre where there is a lot of visual stimulation

* **policies** relating to risk and **risk assessment** must be made clear to parents before the child is accepted.

Preventing accidents

Accidents are the most common cause of death in children between the ages of 1 and 14 years old. The pattern of accidents varies with the child's age, in keeping with:

* the child's stage of development, and
* their exposure to new hazards.

Table 3.1 shows the most common injuries to children and the age group that is most vulnerable to them.

HEALTH AND SAFETY LEGISLATION

The most relevant laws relating to health and safety in child care settings in the UK are:

* the Health and Safety at Work Act 1974
* the Management of Health and Safety at Work Regulations 1999
* COSSH (Control of Substances Hazardous to Health) 2002
* RIDDOR (Reporting of Injuries, Diseases and Dangerous Occurrences Regulations) 1995
* the Electricity at Work Regulations 1989

Choking and suffocation	High-risk age	Burns and scalds	High-risk age
Use of pillows Unsupervised feeding Play with small parts of toys Plastic bags Peanuts Cords and ribbons on clothes	Under 1 year	Matches, lighters, cigarettes Open fires and gas fires Baths Kettles and irons Cookers Bonfires and fireworks	From 9 months on, when children are newly mobile
Falls	High-risk age	**Poisoning**	High-risk age
Stairs Unlocked windows Bouncing cradles left on worktops, etc. Push chairs and high chairs Climbing frames	Under 3 years	Household chemicals, e.g. bleach and disinfectant Medicines Berries and fungi Waste bins Vitamins	1 to 3 years
Electric shocks	High-risk age	**Road accidents**	High-risk age
Uncovered electric sockets Faulty wiring	Under 5 years	Running into the road Not wearing child restraints in cars Playing in the road	All ages up to 14 years
Drowning	High-risk age	**Cuts**	High-risk age
Unsupervised in the bath Ponds and water butts Swimming pools, rivers and ditches	Under 4 years	Glass doors Knives, scissors and razor blades Sharp edges on doors and furniture	1 to 8 years

Table 3.1: Risks of injury to children

* the Manual Handling Operations Regulations 1992
* the Fire Precautions at Work Regulations 1997
* the Children Acts 1989 and 2004.

Regulation and inspection

In order to ensure the safety of babies and children when they are cared for by people other than family members, both the providers of child care and the premises in which children are cared for are regulated and inspected. Within the scope of the Children Acts 1989 and 2004, which are concerned with safeguarding the welfare of children, all child care providers are expected to meet minimum standards of care as detailed in the **National Standards**, which cover all the different types of provision available for babies and children: full day care, sessional day care, crèches, out of school care, and childminding. The National Standards apply across the four countries of the United Kingdom, although there are some minor differences in application. Providers of child care are inspected by the relevant regulatory bodies on their compliance with the National Standards (in England with Ofsted, in Wales with the Care Standards Inspectorate for Wales, in Scotland with the Care Commission and in Northern Ireland with the local health and social services trust). In addition to the National Standards, there are many regulations, laws and guidelines that deal specifically with health and safety in early years settings. You do not need to know the detail, but you must know where your responsibilities begin and end.

Policies and procedures

Each early years setting will have **policy documents** covering such areas as:

* safety

* health and hygiene
* safety at arrival and departure times, and on outings
* first aid and prevention of illness
* fire prevention
* staffing ratios and supervision.

In group care and education settings, a member of staff is usually nominated as being responsible for health and safety; in a childminder's home or if you are working as a nanny, you can contact the local Childminding Association or nanny agency for information on health and safety.

YOUR ROLES AND RESPONSIBILITIES

Your responsibilities include:

* taking reasonable care for **your own safety** and that of others
* working with your employer in respect of **health and safety** matters
* knowing about the **policies and procedures** in your particular place of work – these can all be found in the setting's **health and safety policy** documents
* not intentionally damaging any health and safety equipment or materials provided by the employer
* **reporting all accidents**, incidents and even 'near misses' to your manager; as you may be handling food, you should also report any **incidences of sickness** or diarrhoea; if you are unable to contact the sick child's parents (or other emergency contact person), then you will need to seek medical advice; always ask your supervisor or manager if in doubt
* **reporting any hazards** immediately you come across them.

Apart from your legal responsibilities, knowing how to act and being alert and vigilant at all times can prevent accidents, injury, infections and even death – this could be in relation to you, your fellow workers or the children in your care.

THE EMERGENCY PROCEDURES FOLLOWED IN A RANGE OF SETTINGS

Everyone who works with children should attend a first aid course. There are now specialist courses, such as St John Ambulance's **Early Years First Aid** and the British Red Cross's **First Aid for Child Carers**. The Sure Start Childcare Approval Scheme for nannies requires candidates to hold a relevant paediatric First Aid Certificate.

Once you have learnt how to respond to an emergency you never lose that knowledge, and knowing how means that you could save a life one day.

The following sections explain the major first aid techniques, but should not be used as a substitute for attending a first aid course with a trained instructor.

The ABC of resuscitation

A is for Airway, B is for Breathing, C is for Circulation
The ABC of assessing a casualty in a medical emergency

ABC of resuscitation: babies up to 1 year old

If a baby appears unconscious and gives no response

A   Airway – open the airway

* Place the baby on a firm surface.
* Remove any obstruction from the mouth.
* Put one hand on the forehead and one finger under the chin, and gently tilt the head backwards *very slightly*. (If you tilt the head too far back, it will close the airway again.)

If there is no pulse, or the pulse is slower than 60 beats per minute, and the baby is not breathing, start chest compressions.

* Place two fingers in the centre of the chest.
* Compress the chest by approximately one-third of its depth.

B   Breathing – check for breathing

* Put your ear close to the baby's mouth.
* Look to see if the chest is rising and falling.
* Listen and feel for the baby's breath on your cheek.
* Do this for five seconds.

If the baby is not breathing

1. Start **mouth to mouth-and-nose resuscitation**:
    * seal your lips around the baby's mouth and nose
    * blow GENTLY into the lungs until the chest rises
    * remove your mouth and allow the chest to fall.
2. Give **FIVE** of these initial rescue breaths.
3. Check the pulse.
4. After 30 compressions, blow gently into the lungs **TWICE**.
5. Continue the cycle for one minute.
6. Carry the baby to a phone and dial 999 for an ambulance.

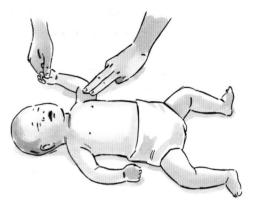

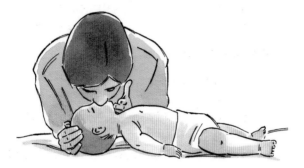

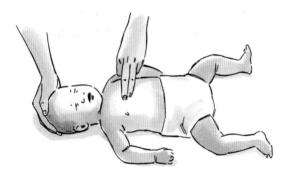

7. Continue resuscitation, checking the pulse every minute until help arrives.

If the baby is not breathing but does have a pulse

1. Start **mouth to mouth-and-nose resuscitation**, at the rate of one breath every three seconds.
2. Continue for one minute, then carry the baby to a phone and **dial 999** for an ambulance.

C   Circulation – check the pulse

Lightly press your fingers towards the bone on the inside of the upper arm and hold them there for five seconds.

If the baby does have a pulse and is breathing

1. Lay the baby on its side, supported by a cushion, pillow, rolled-up blanket or something similar.
2. Dial 999 for an ambulance.
3. Check breathing and pulse every minute, and be prepared to carry out resuscitation.

ABC of resuscitation: children aged 1 to 10

A   Airway – open the airway

* Lay the child flat on their back.

* Remove clothing from around the neck.
* Remove any obstruction from the mouth.
* Lift the chin and tilt the head back slightly to open the airway.

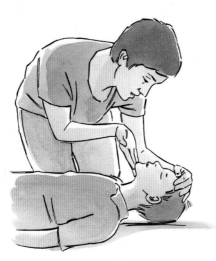

If the child is unresponsive and not breathing normally

1. Give **FIVE initial rescue breaths**.
2. Begin a cycle of **30 chest compressions** and **TWO breaths** (see 'mouth-to-mouth resuscitation'). Continue for one minute.
3. Dial 999 for an ambulance.
4. Continue at the rate of **TWO breaths** to **30 compressions** until help arrives.

If the child is not breathing but does have a pulse

1. Give 20 breaths (see 'mouth-to-mouth resuscitation') in one minute.
2. Dial 999 for an ambulance.
3. Continue mouth-to-mouth resuscitation, rechecking the pulse and breathing after each set of 20 breaths, until help arrives or until the child starts breathing again. When breathing returns, place the child in the recovery position.

B   Breathing – check for breathing

* Keep the airway open and place your cheek close to the child's mouth.
* Look to see if their chest is rising and falling.
* Listen and feel for their breath against your cheek.
* Do this for five seconds.
* If the child is not breathing, give five rescue breaths (see 'mouth-to-mouth resuscitation'), then check the pulse.

Mouth-to-mouth resuscitation

1. Open the airway by lifting the chin and tilting back the head.
2. Close the child's nose by pinching the nostrils.
3. Take a deep breath and seal your mouth over the child's.
4. Blow firmly into the mouth for about two seconds, watching the chest rise.
5. Remove your mouth and allow the child's chest to fall.
6. Repeat until help arrives.

C Circulation – check the pulse

✳ Find the carotid pulse by placing your fingers in the groove between the Adam's apple and the large muscle running down the side of the neck.

✳ Do this for five seconds.

Chest compression

1. Make sure the child is lying on their back on a firm surface (preferably the ground).
2. Use one or two hands in the centre of the chest to achieve an adequate depth of compression.
3. Continue until help arrives.

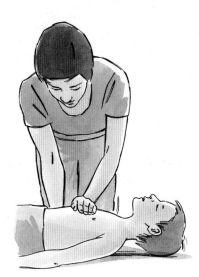

The recovery position

Any child who is breathing and who has a pulse should be placed in the recovery position while you wait for an ambulance or other medical assistance. This safe position allows fluids to drain out of the child's mouth so that they are not inhaled into the lung. (An unconscious baby should be held securely, with the head tilted back slightly to keep the airway open.)

For an unconscious child

1. Roll the child onto his or her side. Grasp the thigh furthest away from you and roll the child over by pulling the bent leg towards you. As you roll, put the child's hand against his or her cheek.
2. Bend the top leg at a right angle and adjust the position of the bottom arm to prevent the child from rolling forwards. Tilt the head back to keep the airways open. Make sure that someone stays with the child until the ambulance arrives, and check both breathing and pulse frequently.

Note: If the child has a suspected spinal (back or neck) injury, put them in the recovery position only if their breathing is obstructed. You should aim to keep the child's head, neck and spine aligned at all times.

Choking

Choking is when a child struggles to breathe because of a blockage in the airway. Children under 3 years are particularly vulnerable to choking because their airways are small and they've not yet developed full control of the muscles of their mouth and throat.

What causes it?

Usually, choking in small children is caused by a small foreign object blocking one of the major airways. This may be a small toy they've put in their mouth and inadvertently 'swallowed', or a small piece of food they haven't chewed properly.

Symptoms

Choking often begins with small coughs or gasps as the child tries to draw in breath around the obstruction or clear it out. This may be followed by a struggling sound or squeaking whispers as the child tries to communicate their distress. The child may thrash around and drool, and their eyes may water. They may flush red and then turn blue. However, if a small item gets stuck in a baby or toddler's throat, you may not even *hear* them choking – they could be silently suffocating as the object fills their airway and prevents them from coughing or breathing.

If a child is choking, **ACT QUICKLY!**

* **First check inside the child's mouth:** if the obstruction is visible, try to hook it out with your finger, but don't risk pushing it further down. *If this doesn't work . . .*
* *For a baby:* lay the baby down along your forearm, supporting her head and neck with your hand. The baby's head should be lower than her bottom.
* *For an older baby or toddler:* sit down and put the child face down across your

knees with head and arms hanging down. Keep the child's head lower than the chest.
* **Give five brisk slaps** between the shoulder blades.
* **Turn the child over**, check the mouth again and remove any visible obstruction.
* **Check for breathing**.
* If the child is not breathing, give **five 'rescue breaths'** (see ABC of resuscitation).
* If the airway is still obstructed, give **five chest compressions**.
* If the child is still not breathing, **repeat the cycle** of back slaps, mouth-to-mouth breathing and chest compressions.
* After two cycles, if the child is not breathing, **dial 999 for an ambulance**.

(*Never* hold a baby upside down by the ankles and slap its back – you could break its neck.)

Bleeding, cuts, grazes and nosebleeds

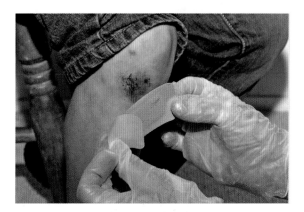

Minor cuts and grazes

1. Sit or lie the child down and reassure them.
2. Clean the injured area with cold water, using cotton wool or gauze.
3. Apply a dressing if necessary.
4. Do not attempt to pick out pieces of gravel or grit from a graze; just clean gently and cover with a light dressing.

5. Record the injury and treatment in the **Accident Report Book** and make sure the parents/carers of the child are informed.

Severe bleeding

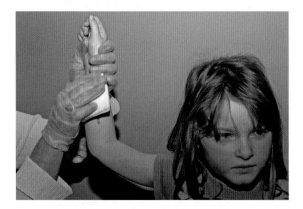

1. Summon medical help: dial 999 or call a doctor.
2. Try to stop the bleeding:
   * apply direct pressure to the wound; wear gloves and use a dressing or a non-fluffy material, such as a clean tea towel
   * elevate the affected part if possible.
3. Apply a dressing. If the blood soaks through, *do not* remove the dressing, apply another on top, and so on.
   * Keep the child warm and reassure them.
   * *Do not* give anything to eat or drink.
   * Contact the child's parents or carers.
   * If the child loses consciousness, follow the ABC procedure for resuscitation.

Note: always record the incident, and the treatment given, in the Accident Report Book. Always wear disposable gloves if in an early years setting, to prevent cross-infection.

Nosebleeds

1. Sit the child down with her head well forward.

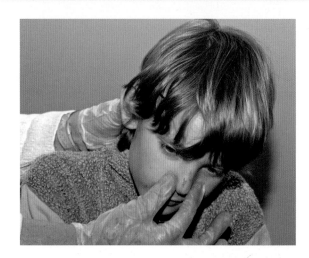

2. Ask her to breathe through her mouth.
3. Pinch the fleshy part of her nose, just below the bridge.
4. Reassure her, and tell her not to try to speak, cough or sniff as this may disturb blood clots.
5. After 10 minutes, release the pressure. If the nose is still bleeding, reapply the pressure for further periods of 10 minutes.
6. If the nosebleed persists beyond 30 minutes, seek medical aid.

Minor burns and scalds

1. Place the injured part under slowly running cold water, or soak in cold water for 10 minutes.
2. Gently remove any constricting articles from the injured area before it begins to swell.

3. Dress with clean, sterile non-fluffy material:
   * DO NOT use adhesive dressings
   * DO NOT apply lotions, ointments or grease to burn or scald
   * DO NOT break blisters or otherwise interfere.

Sprains and strains

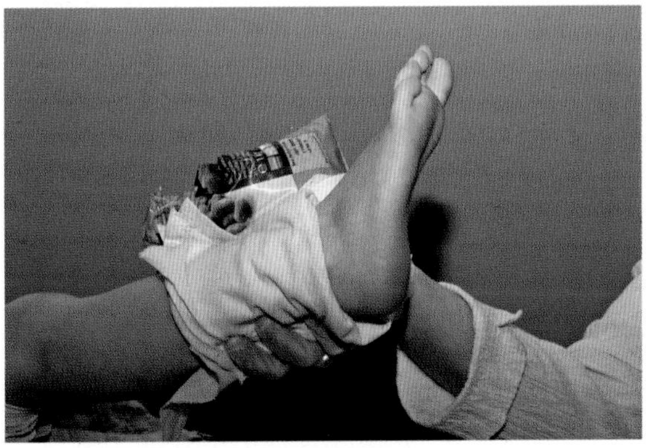

Follow the **RICE** procedure:

* **R** – **rest** the injured part
* **I** – apply **ice** or a cold compress
* **C** – **compress** the injury
* **E** – **elevate** the injured part.

1. Rest, steady and support the injured part in the most comfortable position for the child.
2. Cool the area by applying an ice pack or a cold compress. (This could be a pack of frozen peas wrapped in cloth.)
3. Apply gentle, even pressure by surrounding the area with a thick layer of foam or cotton wool, secured with a bandage.
4. Raise and support the injured limb, to reduce blood flow to the injury and to minimise bruising.

HOW TO GET EMERGENCY HELP

1. **Assess the situation:** stay calm and don't panic.
2. **Minimise any danger to yourself and to others** – for example, make sure someone takes charge of other children at the scene.
3. **Send for help:** notify a doctor, hospital, parents etc. as appropriate. If in any doubt, call an ambulance: **dial 999**.

Be ready to assist the emergency services by answering some simple questions:

* your name and the telephone number you are calling from
* the location of the accident – try to give as much information as possible (e.g. familiar landmarks such as churches or pubs nearby)
* explain briefly what has happened – this helps the paramedics to act speedily when they arrive
* tell them what you have done so far to treat the casualty.

UNDERSTAND YOUR ROLE AND RESPONSIBILITY IN REPORTING AND RECORDING ACCIDENTS

Reporting to parents

All accidents, injuries or illnesses that occur to children in a group setting must be reported to the child's parents or primary carers. If the injury is minor (e.g. a bruise or a small graze to the knee) the nursery or school staff will inform parents when the child is collected at the end of the session; or they may send a notification slip home if the child is collected by someone else. The parents are notified about:

* the nature of the injury or illness
* any treatment or action taken
* the name of the person who carried out the treatment.

In the case of a major accident, illness or injury, the child's parents or primary carers must be notified as soon as possible. Parents need to know that the staff are dealing with the incident in a caring and professional manner, and to be involved in any decisions regarding treatment.

THE ACCIDENT REPORT BOOK

Every workplace is, by law, required to have an Accident Report Book and to maintain a record of accidents. Information recorded includes:

* name of person injured
* date and time of injury
* where the accident happened (e.g. in the garden)
* what exactly happened (e.g. Kara fell on the path and grazed her left knee)
* what injuries occurred (e.g. a graze)
* what treatment was given (e.g. graze was bathed and an adhesive dressing applied)
* name and signature of person dealing with the accident
* signature of witness to the report
* signature of parent or guardian.

One copy of the duplicated report form is given to the child's parent or carer; the other copy is kept in the Accident Report book at the early years setting.

If you are working in the family home as a nanny, you should follow the same reporting procedure, even though you do not have an official Accident Report Book.

THE FIRST AID BOX

Every place of work must, by law, have an accessible first aid box with the following recommended basic contents:

* 20 individually wrapped sterile adhesive dressings – in assorted sizes
* 2 sterile eye pads
* 6 individually wrapped triangular bandages

* 6 safety pins
* 6 medium-sized individually wrapped sterile wound dressings
* 2 large individually wrapped sterile wound dressings
* 3 extra-large individually wrapped sterile wound dressings
* 2 pairs of disposable gloves
* 1 pair of blunt-ended scissors.

Large nurseries and schools may have more than one first aid box and the contents will vary according to individual needs; for example, a nursery setting will have a larger number of small adhesive dressings or plasters.

* The first aid box must be a strong container that keeps out both dirt and damp.
* It should be kept in an accessible place, but one that is out of reach of children.
* All employees should be informed where the first aid box is kept and it should be moved from this safe place only when in use.
* Supplies must be replaced as soon as possible after use.

Some first aid boxes also contain a small first aid manual or booklet.

HOW TO IDENTIFY RISKS IN THE SETTING

Babies and young children are at particular risk of harm because they:

* lack any appreciation of danger
* are naturally inquisitive
* love to explore and test the boundaries of their world.

You need to help young children to explore within safe boundaries, but to adjust those boundaries according to their capabilities and increasing skill. Useful skills to employ when dealing with inquisitive toddlers include: recognising the value of **distraction** – guiding attention away from something dangerous and towards something potentially more interesting; physically removing the child (e.g. 'Harry, come with me – I want to show you something . . .').

Even so, no environment – however carefully planned and designed – can ever be totally without risk to developing children.

THE RISK ASSESSMENT PROCESS

Risk assessment is a method of preventing accidents and ill health by helping people to think about what could go wrong and devising ways to prevent problems. Figure 3.1 shows how you carry out a risk assessment.

If you work in a setting with others, there is likely to be a designated person who is a

The most important factor in preventing accidents is *you*!

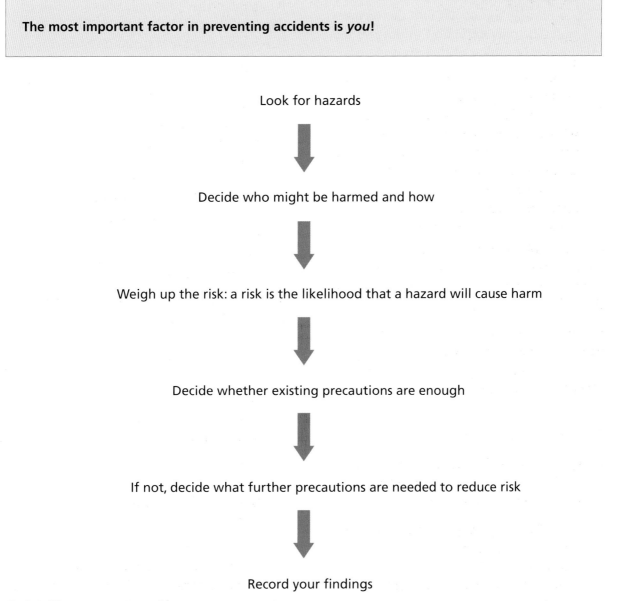

Look for hazards

Decide who might be harmed and how

Weigh up the risk: a risk is the likelihood that a hazard will cause harm

Decide whether existing precautions are enough

If not, decide what further precautions are needed to reduce risk

Record your findings

Fig 3.1. How to carry out a risk assessment

KEY TERMS

Hazard A source of potential harm or damage, or a situation with potential for harm or damage.

Risk assessment The assessments that must be carried out in order to identify hazards and find out the safest way to carry out certain tasks and procedures.

qualified in **first aid**, and he or she should be called to deal with the situation. Remember, it is essential that you do not make the situation worse and it is better to do the minimum to ensure the child's safety, such as putting him or her into the recovery position. The only exception to this is if the child is not breathing or there is no heartbeat.

SAFE WORKING PRACTICES

All areas where children play and learn should be checked for hygiene and safety at the start of every session and again at the end of each session – but do be alert at all times. Look at your setting's written **policy** for health and hygiene issues. Find out from your manager how to clean toys and other equipment, and remember that many objects (plastic toys and soft toys) end up in children's mouths, which is a good way of passing on and picking up an infection.

Remember that *you* could also be a risk to children's health. For example, if you have a heavy cold or have suffered from diarrhoea or vomiting within the previous 24 hours, you must not attend work as you could pass on a serious infection to the children.

The home, garden and nursery setting should be made as accident-proof as possible. Remember that playing should be fun and is an important part of growing up. Your role is to make sure that it stays fun and does not lead to a serious accident.

The following guidelines apply both to the home setting and to nursery and other group settings.

SAFETY AND HYGIENE GUIDELINES

Safety guidelines for playing indoors
- Try to keep very young children out of the kitchen, even when an adult is there.
- Put them in a playpen or high chair if there is no alternative; or you could try putting a stair gate in the doorway.
- Put safety film over glass doors and beware of children playing rough-and-tumble games near glass doors or low windows.
- Encourage children not to play on the stairs or in the main walkways in group settings

In a flat or maisonette
- Always supervise children on balconies – they may be tempted to climb up or over the railings.

Playing with toys
- Keep toys and other clutter off the floor so that no one trips up – use a toy box (e.g. a large, strong cardboard box).
- Choose toys suitable for the child's age and stage of development. Keep toys for older children away from younger brothers or sisters to prevent them from choking on small parts.

- Check the toys in family homes and group settings. Go through the toy box regularly and clear out any broken and damaged toys. Don't hand them on to jumble sales or charity shops, where they could cause injury to another child.

Safety guidelines for playing outdoors

If there is a garden or outdoor play area

- Make sure the children can't get out on their own: block up gaps in the fence and keep the gates locked.
- Set up garden toys properly, and check they are stable and with no loose nuts and bolts.
- Have something soft under climbing frames – regularly watered grass is fine, but dried earth can be as hard as concrete.
- Watch children at all times in the paddling pool and empty it straight away after use. Remember: *small children can drown in just a few inches of water.*
- Cover, fence off or fill in the garden pond to keep small children away.

Playgrounds are good places for children to run around and play, but some are safer than others. You should always:

- teach children to use the equipment properly – make sure they understand your instructions (e.g. teach children never to run in front or behind children using swings)
- keep a close eye on very young children at all times
- avoid old, damaged or vandalised equipment, which could hurt a child
- try to keep to playgrounds with safety surfaces like bark chippings (they are not completely safe but may mean a less serious injury)
- check for rubbish such as broken glass or even syringes, particularly if you are somewhere where older children or adults meet (if these problems persist, report them to the playground owners)
- watch out for nearby hazards such as roads and streams.

Note: Always be aware of children with special needs – for example, those with mobility problems or a visual impairment. Whenever children are playing with or near water – even indoors at the water play area – they must be constantly supervised.

Safety and hygiene guidelines: checking equipment regularly

- *Floors and surfaces:* floors and surfaces must be checked for cleanliness.
- *Plastic toys:* throw out any plastic toys that have cracks or splits in them, as these cracks can harbour germs; also check for splits and cracks when you clean them; plastic toys such as Duplo bricks should be washed weekly.
- *Metal equipment:* check tricycles, pushchairs and prams for rust and/or broken hinges or sticking-out screws, etc.
- *Wooden equipment:* check wooden blocks or wheeled carts for splinters and rough edges; remove any that are damaged, and report this to your supervisor.
- *Dressing-up clothes and soft toys:* all toys and play equipment should be cleaned at least once a week. This includes dressing-up clothes and soft toys – and you should always remove from the nursery any toy that has been in contact with a child who has an infectious illness. Particular care should be taken to keep hats, head coverings and hairbrushes clean, in order to help prevent the spread of head lice.
- *Water tray:* water trays should be emptied daily, as germs can multiply quickly in pools of water.
- *Sandpit:* check that sandpits or trays are clean, and that toys are removed and cleaned at the end of a play session; if the sandpit is kept outside make sure it is kept covered when not in use.
- *Home area:* the home area often contains dolls, saucepans and plastic food; these need to be included in the checking and in the regular wash.

- *Ventilation:* adequate ventilation is important to disperse bacteria or viruses transmitted through sneezing or coughing. Make sure that windows are opened to let fresh air in to the nursery – but also make sure there are no draughts.

- *Outdoor play areas:* these should be checked before any play session for litter, dog or cat faeces, or any other object that could cause children harm.

YOUR ROLE IN PREVENTING ACCIDENTS

There are different views on whether the environment should be made 'toddler-proof' by removing all potentially dangerous items and ensuring adult supervision at all times, or whether by helping children to develop skills, including self-control, they can be encouraged to recognise and manage a degree of risk appropriate to their capabilities. The guidelines shown in Table 3.2 will help you to ensure that children in your care are protected from some common hazards.

MAINTAINING AND PROMOTING THE PERSONAL HEALTH AND SAFETY OF THE CHILD

Children who play closely together for long periods are more likely than others to develop an infection – and any infection can spread quickly from one child to another and to the adults who care for them.

Good hygiene will help to prevent infection and the spread of disease. Being clean also increases self-esteem and social acceptance, and helps to prepare children in skills of independence and self-caring.

Here, as elsewhere, you should be a good role model with your personal hygiene and by wearing the right clothes. You should help children to develop good **personal hygiene routines** – for example, by encouraging children to keep their face clean by using a clean flannel.

Teach children how and when to wash their hands

The chief way of preventing the spread of infection is through the washing of hands. Regular hand washing should be practised and promoted within all early years settings.

* Teach children **how** to wash and dry their hands.
* Make sure they always wash their hands **before eating and drinking**.
* Make sure they always wash their hands **after going to the toilet**.
* Make sure they always wash their hands **after playing outdoors**.
* Make sure they always wash their hands **after handling pets or other animals**.
* Make sure they always wash their hands **after blowing their nose**.

Teach children how to play safely

Children need a safe environment, so that they can explore, and thus learn and grow. As

Preventing burns and scalds	Preventing poisoning
• Never carry a hot drink through a play area or place a hot drink within reach of children.	• Make sure that all household chemicals are out of children's reach.
• Make sure the kitchen is safe for children – kettle flexes coiled neatly, cooker guards used and saucepan handles turned inwards.	• Never pour chemicals or detergents into empty soft drink or water bottles.
• Make sure the kitchen is inaccessible to children when no one is in it.	• Keep all medicines and tablets in a locked cupboard.
• Never smoke in child care settings, and keep matches and lighters out of children's reach.	• Use child-proof containers.
	• Teach children not to eat berries or fungi in the garden or park.
Fire safety	**Preventing falls**
In the case of fire or other emergency you need to know what to do to evacuate the children and yourselves. You should also always practise fire safety.	Babies need to be protected from falls – close supervision is needed. All children will trip and fall at some time, but children should not be put at risk of *serious* injury.
• Remember that no smoking is allowed in any child care setting.	• Never leave a baby unattended on a table, work surface, bed or sofa.
• Keep handbags containing matches or lighters securely away, out of children's reach.	• Make sure young children cannot climb up near windows – and ensure window catches are used.
• The nursery cooker should not be left unattended when turned on.	• Always clean and dry a floor where children are playing.
• Fire exits and other doors should be free of obstructions on both sides.	• Make sure that clutter is removed from floors.
• Ensure you know where the fire extinguishers are kept and how to use them.	• Make sure you know how to use safety equipment, such as stair gates, reins and harnesses, adjustable changing tables and car seats.
• Regularly check electrical equipment for any faults.	• Use safety gates when working in home settings.

Table 3.2: Protecting children in your care from common hazards

they develop children need to learn how to tackle everyday dangers so that they can become safe adults. You have an important role – not only in ensuring that children are kept as safe and secure as possible – but also in teaching them to be aware of safety issues. Every opportunity should be made to teach children about different aspects of keeping themselves – and others – safe. Above all, children should be taught the following.

* **Road safety:** how and when to cross roads safely (even *with* adults holding on to them).
* **Fire safety:** never to play with matches, lighters, cigarettes, sparklers, etc.
* **Water safety**: not to play near ponds and rivers (ideally teach young children how to swim).

* **Food safety:** how germs spread, and the importance of hand washing
* **Play safety:** for example:
  - to carry things carefully
  - never to run with anything in their mouths – this includes sweets and other food
  - never to run while carrying a glass, scissors or other pointed objects; if a child falls he can stab himself with something as simple as a pencil
  - never to throw sand
  - to take turns when using bikes, slides and climbing frames.

Always give reasons for the safety message:

* 'You mustn't throw sand because you'll hurt your friend.'

* 'Never run into the road, because you could be hit by a car.'
* 'Don't run with a stick in your hand as it would hurt you if you fall.'

When teaching young children about safety, you will need to find ways to communicate with each child according to their needs – for example, by the following means.

* **Repetition:** children learn best by doing or practising things – over and over again – but first you have to make the activity enjoyable.
* **Adapting** your approach, according to the message you're trying to convey – for example, making sure that *all* children in the group can join in and benefit from the activity.
* **Modifying the message:** children with hearing difficulties, for example, will need both children and adults to face them so that they can see any signs, and lip-read if the hearing loss is severe.
* **Using real-life examples:** children remember what they have seen and/or experienced themselves – so, if a child has had sand thrown in his eyes, this would be a good moment to teach other children about the dangers of throwing sand.

Practise sun safety

Strong sun can easily burn the skin. For people with fair skin, the more sun that you get, the more likely you are to get skin cancer later on. Sunburn is especially bad; it hurts a lot at the time, and sunburnt children may be especially prone to skin cancer later in life. Follow these guidelines.

* Keep children out of the sun between 11 a.m. and 2 p.m. This is the time to let them read, do some drawing, watch a video or play with toys and games.
* Cover the children up. It's better to wear some clothes than nothing at all. The

most protection comes from clothes that are loose, long-sleeved and made of tightly woven materials (like T-shirts).

* Provide floppy sun hats. Try to shade the head, face, neck and ears.
* Coat children with sun cream. Choose a high sun protection factor (SPF), anything less than factor 8 is no help at all. It won't last all day, so put more on from time to time, especially if the children are in and out of water.

Note: Babies under 6 months old should be kept out of direct sunlight altogether.

Fig 3.2. The Sun Safety Code

Keep children safe during meal and snack times

One of the most common accidents in babies and children under 5 is choking. Babies are most at risk from choking when left unsupervised either eating or playing. Young children are most at risk of choking when they are tired or crying, or when they are running around. Half of all cases of choking in children under 4 years involve **food**. (Only 6 per cent of cases are due to toys.)

* *Never* leave a child propped up with a bottle or feeding beaker.
* *Always* supervise babies and young children when eating and drinking. If a toddler goes to the toilet – or leaves the table for any reason – during meal or snack time, make sure an adult accompanies him or her. (Accidents in nursery settings have occurred when a child chokes silently on food when no adult is present.)
* *Never* give peanuts to children under 4 years old as they can easily choke on them or inhale them into their lungs, causing infection and lung damage.
* Make sure you know what to do if a child is choking (see the first aid section on page 95).

Food hygiene

In promoting the health of young children it is important that you understand the basics of food hygiene as they generally apply to you in the early years setting. Your role may involve serving children's food and drinks, and supervising them when they are eating and drinking. Often you will have to prepare simple snacks for the children. You need to be confident that you are doing everything in your power to provide children with food and drink that is safe to eat and free from illness-causing bacteria. As you progress in your career, you may become more involved in food preparation and will then be required to attend an accredited food hygiene course.

Young children are particularly vulnerable to the bacteria that can cause food poisoning or gastroenteritis. Bacteria multiply rapidly in warm, moist foods, and can enter food without causing it to look, smell or even taste bad. So it is very important to store, prepare and cook food safely, and to keep the kitchen clean.

The prevention of food poisoning

Storing food safely

* Keep food cold. The fridge should be kept as cold as it will go without actually freezing the food (1–5°C, or 34–41°F).
* Cover or wrap food with food wrap or microwave cling film.
* Never refreeze food that has begun to thaw.
* Do not use foods that are past their sell-by or best-before date.
* Always read instructions on the label when storing food.
* Once a tin is opened, store the contents in a covered dish in the fridge.
* Store raw foods at the bottom of the fridge so that juices cannot drip onto cooked food.
* Thaw frozen meat completely before cooking.

Preparing and cooking food safely

* Always wash hands in warm water and soap, and dry on a clean towel, before handling food and after handling raw foods, especially meat.
* Wear clean protective clothing that is solely for use in the kitchen.
* Keep food covered at all times.
* Wash all fruits and vegetables before eating. Peel and top carrots, and peel fruits such as apples.
* Never cough or sneeze over food.
* Always cover any septic cuts or boils with a waterproof dressing.
* Never smoke in any room that is used for food.
* Keep work surfaces and chopping boards clean and disinfected; use separate boards for raw meat, fish, vegetables, etc.
* Make sure that meat dishes are cooked thoroughly.
* Avoid raw eggs; they sometimes contain *Salmonella* bacteria, which may cause

food poisoning. (Also avoid giving children *uncooked* cake mixture, home-made ice creams, mayonnaise or desserts that contain uncooked raw egg.) When cooking eggs, the egg yolk and white should be firm.

* When re-heating food, make sure that it is piping hot all the way through, and allow to cool slightly before giving it to children. When using a microwave, always stir and check the temperature of the food before feeding children, to avoid burning from hot spots.

* Avoid having leftovers – they are a common cause of food poisoning.

Keeping the kitchen safe

* Teach children to wash their hands after touching pets and going to the toilet, and before eating.

* Clean tin openers, graters and mixers thoroughly after use.

* Keep flies and other insects away – use a fine mesh over open windows.

* Stay away from the kitchen if you are suffering from diarrhoea or sickness.

* Keep the kitchen clean – the floor, work surfaces, sink, utensils, cloths and waste bins should be cleaned regularly.

* Tea towels should be boiled every day and dishcloths boiled or disinfected.

* Keep pets away from the kitchen.

* Keep all waste bins covered, and empty them regularly.

* Keep sharp knives stored safely where children cannot reach them.

How to keep children safe on outings

Any outing away from the children's usual setting – for instance, trips to farms, parks and theatres – must be planned with safety and security issues as a top priority. Many schools now employ an Educational Visit Coordinator to oversee the safety of school trips. Each setting must consider the following points.

* **Planning:** you may need to visit the place beforehand and discuss any particular requirements – for example, what to do if it rains, or specific lunch arrangements.

* **Contact numbers:** you need to have a copy of the children's contact information with you on the outing and you should regularly check the names of the children against the day's attendance list.

* **Permission:** the manager or head teacher must give permission for the outing, and a letter should be sent to all parents and guardians of the children.

* **Help:** usually, help is requested from parents so that adequate supervision is ensured.

* **Informing parents:** about what is involved on the outing; what the child needs to bring (e.g. packed meal,

---

GUIDELINES: FOOD HYGIENE

When serving food and clearing away after meals and snacks, you should observe the rules of food hygiene.

* Wash your hands using soap and warm water, and dry them on a clean towel.
* Wear clean protective clothing.
* Ensure any washing-up by hand is done

thoroughly in hot water, with detergent (and use rubber gloves).

* Cover cups/beakers with a clean cloth and air-dry where possible.
* Drying-up cloths should be replaced every day with clean ones.
* Never cough or sneeze over food.

waterproof coat) – emphasise *no* glass bottles and *no* sweets, spending money if necessary (state the advised maximum amount).

*   **Supervision:** arrange adequate adult supervision. There should always be trained staff on any outing, however local and low-key. The adult:child ratio should never exceed 1:4. If the children are under 2 years old or have special needs, then you would expect to have fewer children per adult. Swimming trips should be attempted only if the ratio is 1 adult to 1 child for children under 5 years. The younger the children, the more adults are required, particularly if the trip involves crossing roads, when an adult must be available to hold the children's hands.
*   **Transport:** if a coach is being hired, check whether it has seat belts for children. New laws require all new minibuses and coaches to have seat belts fitted, and minibus drivers have to have passed a special driving test.

Safety at arrival and departure times

Any early childhood setting or school should be secure so that children cannot wander off without anyone realising. There should also be a policy that guards against strangers being able to wander in without reason. Many child care settings now have door entry phones, and staff wear name badges. It is a matter of courtesy and security for all visitors for them to give advance notice of their visit.

At home time, staff *must* ensure that the child is collected by the appropriate person. If parents know that they will not be able to collect their child on a particular occasion, they should notify the setting, giving permission for another **named person** to collect their child. The child's **key person**

should, where possible, be responsible for handover when the child arrives and when he or she leaves the setting.

Child protection

Child protection means protecting children from physical, emotional or sexual abuse or neglect. It also means helping children to grow up into confident, healthy and happy adults. Although child abuse is not common, it is important to recognise that there are, and will always be, children who are victims of abuse in one way or another.

TYPES OF CHILD ABUSE

The categories of child abuse are:

*   physical abuse
*   emotional abuse
*   neglect
*   sexual abuse.

Physical abuse

Physical abuse, or non-accidental injury (NAI), involves someone deliberately harming a child. This may take the form of:

*   bruising – from being slapped, punched, shaken or squeezed
*   cuts – scratches, bite marks, a torn frenulum (the web of skin inside the upper lip)
*   fractures – skull and limb fractures from being thrown against hard objects
*   burns and scalds – from cigarettes, irons, baths and kettles.

Often the particular injuries can be explained easily, but you should always be suspicious if a child has any bruise or mark that shows the particular pattern of an object (e.g. a belt strap mark, teeth marks or the imprint of an iron). Also look out for behavioural disturbances in the child, such as aggressiveness towards others or a withdrawn attitude.

Emotional abuse

Emotional abuse occurs when a child consistently faces threatening ill-treatment from an adult. This can take the form of verbal abuse, ridiculing, mocking and insulting the child. It is difficult to find out how common this form of abuse is, because it is hard to detect. However, signs of emotional abuse include:

* withdrawn behaviour – child may not join in with others or appear to be having fun
* attention-seeking behaviour
* self-esteem and confidence are low
* stammering and stuttering
* tantrums beyond the expected age
* telling lies, and even stealing
* tearfulness.

Emotional neglect means that children do not receive love and affection from the adult. They may often be left alone without the company and support of someone who loves them.

Neglect

Physical neglect occurs when the adult fails to give their child what they need to develop physically. They often leave children alone and unattended. Signs of physical neglect include:

* being underweight for their age and not thriving
* unwashed clothes, which are often dirty and smelly
* child may have poor skin tone, dull, matted hair and bad breath; a baby may have a persistent rash from infrequent nappy changing

* being constantly tired, hungry and listless or lacking in energy
* frequent health problems, and prone to accidents
* low self-esteem and poor social relationships – delay in all areas of development is likely because of lack of stimulation.

Sexual abuse

There is much more awareness today about the existence of sexual abuse. Sexual abuse means that the adult uses the child to gratify their sexual needs. This could involve sexual intercourse or anal intercourse. It may involve watching pornographic material with the child. Sexual abuse might also mean children being encouraged in sexually explicit behaviour or oral sex, masturbation or the fondling of sexual parts. Signs of sexual abuse include the following:

* bruises or scratches as in a non-accidental injury or physical injury
* itching or pain in the genital area
* wetting or soiling themselves
* discharge from the penis or vagina
* poor self-esteem and lack of confidence
* may regress and want to be treated like a baby
* poor sleeping and eating patterns
* withdrawn and solitary behaviour.

YOUR ROLE IN REPORTING SUSPECTED ABUSE

You need to be aware of the indicators of child abuse as outlined above. However, it is important not to jump to conclusions. If you have any cause for concern, you should always talk to your immediate superior or to the head of the nursery or school. Every child care setting has a **policy** for dealing with suspected child abuse.

If you suspect child abuse in the **home setting**, then you should contact your local Social Services or the National Society for the Prevention of Cruelty to Children (NSPCC).

If a child tells you he or she has been abused

You should:

* reassure the child, saying that you are glad that they have told you about this
* believe the child; tell the child that you will do your best to protect them, but don't *promise* that you can do that
* remember that the child is not to blame, and that it is important that you make the child understand this
* do a lot of listening; don't ask questions
* report your conversation with the child to your immediate superior
* write down what was said by the child as soon as possible after the conversation.

Children at risk of abuse

Child abuse occurs in all different social groups of people from all walks of life. It is often believed that only parents are to blame or, in the case of sexual abuse, that strangers are to blame. However, children can become victims of abuse by anyone, whether parents, relatives, neighbours, family friends, acquaintances or strangers. Even those people who are entrusted to care for children – such as teachers, child care providers, church workers or foster parents – may abuse children. Abusers may be male or female. Their age may vary and could even include children and adolescents. There is no one profile of someone who abuses and there are many reasons why adults abuse children.

Certain factors within the family home can mean that children are at a higher risk of being abused.

* **Drug or alcohol abuse** by parents can lead to children being put at risk, even if the parents are not actually mistreating them; such abuse is a familiar trigger for **violence** in the home and can also lead to parents having a disordered lifestyle, which can leave children in danger.
* **Mental illness:** although this does not prevent individuals from being good parents, it can sometimes move a child up the scale from being one in need to one at significant risk of harm.

SOME FACTS ABOUT CHILD ABUSE

* All sections of society produce adults who abuse or neglect children. It is very dangerous to form stereotypes about the kind of people who might violate a child's rights or about the situations that could lead to child abuse or neglect.
* As evidence gathers on the subject of child protection, it is becoming apparent that the abusive or neglectful person is almost always known to the child (e.g. a parent, a family member, a friend of the family, a carer or co-habitee).
* Premature babies and children of 0–4 years of age are most likely to be abused or neglected.

* Separation of the mother and the baby for a period of time after birth can be associated with child abuse or neglect.
* Children who cry a great deal are much more likely to be abused or neglected.
* Children who do not enjoy eating are more likely to be abused or neglected.
* Stepchildren are vulnerable.
* Children with disabilities are more likely to be abused or neglected.
* Children who are boys when parents wanted girls, or girls when parents wanted boys, are more likely to be neglected.

Section 3

Understanding children's behaviour

Behaviour is observable (can be seen and/or heard). It is the way we act, speak and treat other people and our environment. It does not include our thoughts, although these usually prompt what we do.

Behaviour is influenced in the following ways:

* by the customs and practices of the society or culture
* by the rules, standards and expectations of the family
* by copying others – with children, particularly through play
* by receiving rewards or treats, or respect from others
* by being punished or penalised, or feeling humiliated
* by the actions and attitudes of a peer group
* by the desire to be useful to others and achieve satisfaction for doing something worthwhile.

The following stages are, of course, linked only loosely to the ages shown. As with any normative measurements, they serve only as a rough guide to help understand children's behaviour and how best to respond to it. Much will depend upon children's experiences and the way they have been helped to develop good relationships.

At age 1–2 years, children:

* have developed their own personalities and are sociable with close family and friends
* still become shy and anxious when parents or carers are out of sight
* are developing their speech, and can attract attention by calling out or crying

* can become possessive over toys, but can often be distracted to something else
* are discovering that they are separate individuals
* are self-centred (see things from their own point of view)
* are gaining mobility, improving their ability to explore their surroundings – this results in conflicts, often regarding safety
* begin to understand the meaning of 'No', and firm boundaries can be set
* can be frustrated by their own limitations, but resist adult help (perhaps saying 'me do it').

At age 2–3 years, children:

* are not yet able to share easily
* are developing greater awareness of their separate identities
* are developing their language abilities, which help them to communicate their needs and wishes more clearly and to understand 'in a minute'
* can still be distracted from the cause of their anger
* have tantrums (usually when parents or main carers are present) when frustrated – possibly caused by their efforts to become self-reliant (e.g. feeding or dressing themselves) or having ideas that the adult does not want them to carry out
* experience a range of feelings – being very affectionate and cooperative one minute and resistant the next
* are aware of the feelings of others and can respond to them.

At age 3–4 years, children:

* are very aware of others and imitate them – especially in their play; with developing speaking and listening skills they are liable to repeat swear words they hear
* are more able to express themselves through speech and, therefore, there is often a reduction in physical outbursts;

however, they are still likely to hit back if provoked

* can be impulsive and will be less easily distracted
* become more sociable in their play and may have favourite friends
* can, sometimes, be reasoned with and are just becoming aware of the behaviour codes in different places or situations
* like, and seek, adult approval and appreciation of their efforts

At age 4–5 years, children:

* can behave appropriately at mealtimes and during other 'routine' activities and may begin to understand why 'Please' and 'Thank you' (or their equivalent) are important
* are able to share and take turns, but often need help
* are more aware of others' feelings and will be concerned if someone is hurt
* are becoming more independent and self-assured, but still need adult comfort when ill or tired
* will respond to reason, can negotiate and be adaptable, but can still be distracted
* are sociable and becoming confident communicators able to make more sense of their environment; there will continue to be conflicts that they cannot resolve on their own and with which they will need adult help
* can sometimes be determined, may argue and show aggression.

At age 5–6 years, children:

* understand that different rules apply in different places (e.g. home, school, grandparents' house) and can adapt their behaviour accordingly
* are developing control over their feelings – they argue with adults when they feel secure and need to feel there are firm boundaries in place
* will respond to reason and can negotiate,

but are less easily distracted – anger can last longer and they need time to calm down

* are able to hide their feelings in some situations
* can cooperate in group play, but are not yet ready for team games
* may show off and boast (e.g. when they celebrate an achievement)
* will continue to need adult support to resolve conflicts
* will share and take turns, and begin to have an understanding of what is 'fair' if given an explanation.

At age 6–8 years, children:

* can quickly adapt behaviour to suit the situation
* can play games with rules
* can argue their viewpoints
* are growing in confidence and becoming independent
* are developing some moral values and understanding of 'right' and 'wrong'
* can be friendly and cooperative
* can control how they feel much of the time but there are still times when they want to do things their way and quarrels develop.

From ages 8–12 years, children:

* enjoy playing and inventing games with rules
* tend to be cooperative and enjoy being given responsibility
* tend to be closely attached to parental figures; make friends often with same-gender peers, usually based on proximity, common interest/hobbies or other perceived commonalities; girls tend to have fewer, but emotionally closer, friends than boys.

From ages 12–16 years, children and young people:

* often question rules at home and try to push the boundaries

* may show *avoidance* behaviours (e.g. truanting, bullying and behaving disruptively in class), often caused by low self-esteem and some may experience bullying themselves.

LINKING BEHAVIOUR TO CHILD DEVELOPMENT

When assessing children's behaviour it is important to bear these developmental stages in mind and to view the behaviour in the context of overall development.

Here are two examples.

1. It is well known that **tantrums** are a common, even expected, feature of a 2-year-old's behaviour. There is bound to be some cause for concern, however, if they are a regular feature of a 6-year-old's behaviour. However, some adults have unrealistic expectations of children and express surprise when unwanted behaviour occurs.
2. A 5-year-old becomes fidgety and whines during a Christmas pantomime. The adults will view the occasion as a treat and may feel resentment that their child is complaining, but it is reasonable that a 5-year-old should lose concentration, be unable to sit still for a lengthy period or understand all of what is going on.

In trying to understand behaviour it is helpful to note whether there are particular incidents or situations that seem to trigger unwanted behaviour. Some of these can be avoided altogether by minor changes in routine or approach, but others, such as siblings teasing each other, will occur frequently and so children need to be given some strategies and support to be able to cope with them effectively. It is important never to reject the child but only what the child has done (e.g. 'That was an unkind thing to say' rather than 'You are unkind').

The A-B-C of behaviour

* **Antecedent:** what happens before, or leads up to, the observed behaviour.
* **Behaviour:** the observed behaviour – what the child says and how s/he acts (this is any behaviour, both positive and negative).
* **Consequence:** what happens following the observed behaviour.

Part of your role is to observe children's behaviour, whether or not you make a written record, so that you can contribute to discussions about a child's behaviour and develop good practice in managing unwanted aspects. In your work setting you should try to see not only how other staff and parents deal with incidents, but also which methods seem to be effective with which children.

Observing and recording behaviour

An **event sample** is a useful way of recording negative behaviour as and when it occurs. This method involves creating a chart to note:

* time
* context (location, activity)
* people involved
* actions and language of the child or children
* actions and language of the adult
* child's response to adult/other children
* any other relevant information.

This provides the A-B-C information and helps to identify what, or who, may have led to each incident.

You may find that:

* particular pairings or groupings of children present problems

* some form of bullying is occurring
* there is confusion about what is expected – unclear rules
* large-group times (e.g. register, story, assembly) are often the 'trouble' times
* the child responds positively to one form of discipline or adult more readily than to another.

Your findings can help staff to understand when unwanted behaviour is likely to occur, and extra support – perhaps a talk with the child about what would be acceptable behaviour – or closer supervision can be given. They may also highlight differences in the way staff deal with it, which may be confusing for children. Adults can then meet and work out how best to help the child.

A **time sample** can be even more useful and provide information, not only about the unwanted behaviour but also about the occasions when a child has behaved well.

This method involves creating a similar chart but a record of what is happening is made at regular intervals – every 30 minutes, or whatever seems appropriate and practical. This method enables you to see if the positive behaviour was noticed, appreciated and praised or rewarded. If it was overlooked, the child may use unwanted behaviour to gain attention – of any kind!

Recording and sharing the information with other staff and parents helps everyone to agree on a realistic and practical course of action. Similar observations can be repeated at a later date to monitor progress and review strategies.

Serious incidents (for example, biting) should be recorded and reported to parents of the children involved. Parents of each child (or children) must be assured that these incidents are dealt with seriously and appropriately otherwise there is a risk that they will take issue with each other. They should be given

information that explains what happened so that they:

* do not feel the need to question their child, and
* are aware of the full facts rather than their child's viewpoint.

Confidentiality is vitally important, although the children themselves will probably name names!

Ways in which adults can contribute to children's behaviour

Behaviour is very closely linked to self-esteem – children who feel bad about themselves may not behave well. The poem reproduced in Unit 1 (page 14) sums up the positive and negative ways in which adults can contribute to children's development and behaviour.

Factors affecting behaviour

It is well known that behaviour is commonly affected by certain factors. Some factors stem from the children themselves:

* illness
* accident and injury
* tiredness.

Other factors result from their situations:

* arrival of a new baby
* moving house
* parental separation or divorce
* change of carer – either at home or in a setting
* loss or bereavement
* change of setting (e.g. transition from home to nursery or nursery to school).

Individual children will respond to these situations differently but **regression** is common (usually temporary) when they revert to behaviour that is immature for them. Events that they do not understand will leave them confused, leading to frustration and aggressive outbursts, or they may blame themselves, which could result in withdrawn behaviour and the development of unwanted habits through anxiety.

Generally, any factor that causes stress may result in the child:

* needing more comfort and attention
* being less sociable
* being unable to cope with tasks that they would normally manage
* being subject to mood swings
* being unable to concentrate (this includes listening to instructions) and less able to cope with challenging situations and difficulties.

How to manage behaviour: goals and boundaries

If children are to understand what is regarded as acceptable behaviour at home, in the work setting and in society, then they must be given very clear **guidelines**. Work settings will have a policy relating to behaviour and discipline, which all staff should follow and which is regularly reviewed. The policy will explain the rules that are applied and how children will be helped to understand, and learn to keep, them. In most cases the rules are simple and reflect the concerns for safety and for children to be considerate of others and their environment. They should be appropriate for the age and stage of development of the children and for the particular needs of the work setting.

Goals are the forms of behaviour that are encouraged, and cover physical, social and verbal aspects. They should be realistically set for the child's age and stage of development.

Examples of goals for a 4–5 year old are:

* to say 'please' and 'thank you'
* to share play equipment
* to tidy up
* to be quiet and listen for short periods (e.g. story or register time).

Boundaries are the limits within which behaviour is acceptable – they identify what may, and may not, be done or said. Children need to understand the consequences of failing to act within those boundaries. It is important that the boundaries are appropriate for the age and stage of development.

Examples of boundaries for 4–5 year olds are:

* that they may play outside – but must not tread on the flowerbeds
* that they may watch television – but only until tea is ready
* that they may use the dressing-up clothes – if they put them away when they have finished.

Promoting positive behaviour

* It is helpful to set '**positive**' rules rather than 'negative' ones.
* **Negative rules** tend to begin with the word '**Don't**' and tell children what they must **not do** but give them no guidance as to what they may or **should do**.
* **Consistency** in applying the boundaries is important, especially in the work setting where children need to relate to several adults. They will check that the rules have not changed and that they still apply whichever adult is present.
* If you are supervising an activity the children will expect you to apply the same rules as other staff. It undermines your own position if you allow unacceptable behaviour and another staff member has to discipline the children you are working with.

Managing behaviour

First of all it needs to be agreed in a work setting what behaviour is unwanted and then some decisions made as to how staff will manage it when it does arise. These should take account of **individual needs**, as children will respond in their own ways. Here are two examples.

1. In a school setting, staying in at playtime is punishment for some children but, for those who have poor social skills and find the playground rather intimidating, it can be a relief.
2. Some children enjoy tidying and helping the teacher because they might get more individual attention.

Theories about behaviour

1. **Albert Bandura** developed a '**social learning**' theory, which states that children learn about social behaviour by *watching* and *imitating* other people, especially those they admire. Children will learn negative behaviour as well as positive behaviour so the presence of good role models is very important.
2. **B.F. Skinner** developed a '**behaviourist**' theory, which states that children's behaviour is shaped by adults through *positive* and *negative reinforcement*.

These two theories have influenced current practice for managing and modifying (shaping or reforming) behaviour.

There are three main aspects of **behaviour modification**.

1. **Identifying positive** and **negative behaviour** – deciding what behaviour is to be encouraged and what is to be discouraged.
2. **Rewarding positive behaviour** – encouraging and promoting it through reward. There are different forms of reward:

    *   verbal praise (e.g. 'Well done')
    *   attention – this could be non-verbal (e.g. smile of approval, a nod)
    *   stars or points (for older children) leading to certificates or for group/team recognition
    *   sharing success by having other staff and parents told
    *   own choice of activity or story
    *   tangible rewards such as stickers.

These work on the principle of **positive reinforcement** – based on the idea that if children receive approval and/or a reward for behaving acceptably they are likely to want to repeat that behaviour. If one child is praised (e.g. for tidying up) others are often influenced to copy or join in so that they, too, will receive praise and attention. For young children the reward must be *immediate* so they understand the link between it and the positive behaviour. It is of little value to promise a treat or reward in the future. Similarly, star charts and collecting points are not appropriate for children younger 5 five years old.

3. **Discouraging negative behaviour** (according to this approach):
    *   **whenever possible such behaviour should be ignored** (bearing in mind safety or injury), although not if attention is drawn to it (perhaps by another child) as the message sent then is that it is acceptable
    *   giving **attention and praise** to another child who is behaving acceptably
    *   **distracting the child's attention** (particularly appropriate with younger children) or removing him/her to another activity or group

* **expressing disapproval** – verbally and/or non-verbally through body language, facial expression (frowning) and shaking of the head
* **imposing a punishment** – withdrawal of a privilege (e.g. watching a favourite TV programme).

These work on the principle of **negative reinforcement** – based on the idea that children will avoid repeating an unpleasant experience. If they behave unacceptably and earn the disapproval of an adult, or receive some sort of punishment, they will be less likely to repeat that behaviour. As they learn from watching others, older children may be deterred (put off) from behaving unacceptably by seeing someone else receive discipline. This approach encourages the adult to act immediately so young children understand the link between the unacceptable behaviour and the adult's response to it.

REMEMBER

Physical, or corporal, punishment is **illegal** in work settings and never allowed under any circumstances. This includes pulling a child by his/her elbow or arm, or grabbing him/her by the wrist. Intervention, to protect the child, others or property, should involve **minimal physical restraint**.

Using rewards

There are problems associated with rewards in that some children may behave in a particular way purely to receive the reward rather than from an understanding of the need to consider safety, others and their environment, or enjoying what they have achieved for its own sake. The *type* of reward also needs to be considered – for example, is it desirable for children to be given sweets as

rewards? Some parents may have strong views about this.

Rewards might work in the short term, but do not always succeed in the long term. They might even undermine lifelong learning by encouraging children to seek reward, rather than be disposed to learn because something is interesting.

Problem – or unwanted – behaviour

Attention-seeking, aggression (physical and verbal) towards others, and self-destructive behaviour need to be dealt with calmly.

Attention-seeking

Children will do just about anything to get the attention they crave from parents and carers. This is often shown through *disruptive* (making noises, not responding to an instruction) or *aggressive* behaviour, and needs managing as identified above. Sometimes children who are trying to please can be just as disruptive. Those who desperately want adults to notice them will call out, interrupt, ask questions and frequently push in front of other children to show something they have made or done. Children who seek attention challenge patience, but with a bit of reminding about turn-taking, and clear expectation that they will, they can learn to wait for their turn. It is important to give attention when they have waited appropriately so that they are encouraged to do so again.

Physical aggression

This usually results from strong feelings that are difficult to control. Whatever the cause – and it may be provocation – the adult should deal with it calmly and ensure that the needs of all the children involved are met. A child who has lost control frightens herself and the other children. Some work settings favour a 'time-out' approach; this involves the aggressive child being taken to an identified place away from the incident (e.g. a corner or chair). 'Time out' allows for a calming-down period and other children to be reassured. This method can work but needs positive follow-up by a staff member to explain that the behaviour was unacceptable, explain why and suggest how the child might have behaved otherwise (e.g. asked instead of snatched; listened to the apology for the model being broken). Unless this is done there is a danger that the chair or area becomes known to the children as the 'naughty chair' and staff begin to use it as a way of 'grounding' a child who is causing annoyance, without addressing the issues. Many adults do not like to use this approach for this reason.

Temper tantrums

These are usually associated with 2-year-olds, but can occur in older children. They may happen, particularly, when a child is ill or tired but often build from a confrontational incident when he or she is asked to do something, or not to do something and a 'battle of wills' begins! Temper tantrums often involve shouting and crying, refusal to cooperate and mounting anger – shown through kicking, hitting, screaming, stamping – and, on occasions, self-harm. In younger children tantrums can be over very quickly but in older ones can take longer to reach a peak and longer for the calming down afterwards.

Dealing with tantrums

* **Try to avoid them:** if you can anticipate them, try distracting the child with a game or another activity.
* **Try to ignore them:** apart from safety concerns try to give as little attention as possible during them.

* **Be consistent:** if children think, from past experience, that the adult will not keep the boundary firmly there, they will continue – clear boundaries are essential.
* **A firm hug** may help the child feel secure and under control until the child calms down – this is useful in situations where you cannot walk away.
* **Talk about them:** this may help older children to express their feelings calmly.
* **Provide experiences and activities** that the child finds interesting; this usually helps them to become involved in positive ways.

Do not give in and let the boundary go – this almost certainly leads to more rather than fewer tantrums because children are confused by inconsistency.

Self-destructive behaviour

This includes head-banging and forms of self-mutilation (e.g. tearing out hair, excessive nail-biting causing pain and bleeding). It usually signals some emotional difficulty that needs expert intervention. Staff and parents need to discuss their concerns and agree a common approach based on the advice they are given.

Unacceptable language

This includes swearing and name-calling, which often result from children repeating what they have heard themselves. Sometimes they are unaware that it is unacceptable in one setting but not another. In these cases they need to be told firmly not to say those words 'here' – you cannot legislate for language they may use at home, or criticise their families.

* Some children will deliberately use unacceptable language to shock or seek

attention. In these cases you should state the rule calmly and firmly.

* **Name-calling**, particularly if it is discriminatory (e.g. regarding race, creed, disability, family background, appearance) must always be challenged and dealt with firmly. Explain that it is hurtful and that we are all different. This behaviour is best combated through good example and through anti-discriminatory practices in the work setting, which will help children to value other people as individuals.

Sometimes the behaviour management strategies outlined above fail to be effective or are effective for only a short period of time. So when behaviour is inappropriate for the child's stage of development or is persistently challenging, there are other professionals who may be called upon to help all those involved. It is useful to attend meetings that allow everyone to contribute information about a child; these will help to create an overall view of progress, development and behaviour, and it is here that recorded observations will be especially useful.

Professionals who may become involved include:

* **health visitors** – who work primarily with children up to 5 years and their families, checking for healthy growth and development

* **physiotherapists** – who assess children's motor skills and development, and might be asked to advise on appropriate activities and equipment

* **speech therapists** – who assess mouth movement as well as speech/language itself, and might suggest ways of supporting children who experience communication difficulties

* **play therapists** – who have specialist training and work with children, using play, to help them feel emotionally secure

* **paediatricians** – who specialise in the care of children up to age 16, check for normal development and diagnose difficulties

* **educational psychologists** – who assess children who have special needs and give advice, particularly for those with emotional and behavioural difficulties

* **child psychiatrists** – who work with children and their families to help them to express their thoughts and feelings.

It is important to follow correct procedures for reporting incidents. Check that you know what they are in your work setting.

Case study 1: Andrew's behaviour

Andrew had recently started in the reception class and displayed negative behaviour in many ways and in many situations. On arrival in the playground in the mornings, with both his parents and younger sister, he would walk around poking and kicking other children as he went. This caused anger among other parents, upset among the children and ill-feeling towards his parents, who would shout at him before grabbing him, holding him by the hand and loudly telling him off. The staff discussed this with the parents and it was agreed that, in the short term, Andrew should be brought to school 10 minutes later than everyone else. Every morning the father would deliver him to the classroom door with the instruction 'Behave.'

Andrew always said that he would; however, he did not really understand what 'behave' meant in terms of his own actions. His teacher made a point of reminding him, throughout the day, of what behaviour was expected, and explained what that meant for him – for example, 'When I ask you to "sit nicely", this means sitting still without touching any other child or anything.' It was also an opportunity to reinforce the rule for other children. Improvement was very gradual. Only one aspect of behaviour was dealt with at a time. He was given one-to-one support when available, and observations were recorded to monitor progress and plan future strategies.

1. In pairs, produce some simple rules for 4–5 year olds in a reception class that give clear guidance about what they should do. For example DO walk instead of DON'T run.

Case study 2: Using rewards

In an infant school a new head teacher introduced the practice of listening to children read to her regularly. This involved children being sent individually to her office, where she would reward them with a jelly bear if they read well or tried hard. One mother was surprised, when talking to her daughter about the school day, that she was upset to have read to her class teacher instead of to the head teacher. The girl explained that everyone was asking to read to the head teacher and she was not chosen – so she missed out on a jelly bear!

The parent was alarmed that (a) sweets were being given as a reward without parents knowing, and (b) children were not rewarded by the experience itself and the head teacher's appreciation of children's efforts.

Unit 4

Children and Play

Contents

Unit 4 is divided into three sections:

Section 1: The importance of play

Section 2: The stages of play

Section 3: Planning activities for play in a range of settings and provision

Section 1
The importance of play

WHAT IS PLAY?

Through play, children bring together and organise their ideas, feelings, relationships and their physical life. It helps them to use what they know and to make sense of the world and people they meet. Play brings together:

* ideas and creativity
* feelings
* relationships
* physical coordination
* spiritual development.

Play helps children to use what they know and understand about the world and people they meet.

During play, children:

* get things under control so that they can face the world and deal with it
* get ready for the future
* think about things that have happened.

There are different ideas about how to develop play, but although there are wide cultural variations, all children seem to develop and learn through play, including children with severe disabilities.

Children who do not play find it difficult to learn (e.g. children in the Romanian orphanages were held back in learning about objects, ideas, feelings, relationships and people).

Your role will be important in providing opportunities that support and extend children's play.

The Charter of Children's Rights (1989) says that every child in the world should have the right to play.

Theories of play

Ideas about play are influenced by thinkers from the past and thinkers from around the world. A theory is something that helps us to explain and answer 'Why?' It helps us to look at the role of play in a child's development. The different theories of play emphasise different aspects. They all help us to learn more about children's play.

Friedrich Froebel (1782–1852)

Froebel was a forester and mathematician. He was the first person to write about the importance of the play in development and learning. He started a community school, where parents were welcome at any time. He trained his staff to observe and value children's play.

* He thought it was important to talk with parents and learn with them how to help children learn through their play.
* He designed a set of wooden blocks (Gifts), which are still used in early childhood settings today. He also designed many other kinds of play equipment (Occupations) and Movement Games (action songs and finger play rhymes and dancing) through which children learn by doing.
* He considered that relationships with other children were as important as relationships with adults, and he had a strong belief in the value of imaginative and symbolic play.
* He encouraged pretend play. He encouraged play with other children.
* He thought both indoor and outdoor play to be important.
* He helped children to make dens in the garden and to play with natural materials such as sand, water and wood.
* He believed that teachers should be sensitive and approachable, and that they

should have qualities that the children could respect and imitate.

He called his schools kindergartens (for children aged 2–8 years). Kindergarten means 'children's garden' in German. Even today there are kindergartens all over the world. Froebel has had a profound influence on early childhood education and care.

Maria Montessori (1880–1952)

Montessori was an Italian doctor who worked in the poorest areas of Rome in the 1900s. She did not believe that pretend play was important. She thought children wanted to do real things (e.g. not *play* at being cooks but to actually do some cooking). However, she did like Froebel's play equipment, and she designed more (didactic materials) to help them learn, for example, about shapes, weight, colour, size and numbers.

* She believed that all children have absorbent minds, and that the way in which children learn is different from the way in which an adult learns. She believed that they absorb information from the environment. Initially this learning is unconscious, but after the age of 3 the child absorbs information consciously. The ability to absorb language and to learn motor skills is initially without formal instruction but later they use language to question.
* She thought that children experience sensitive periods during which they are particularly receptive to developing specific skills. A child will develop a particular interest in one specific skill or action, which they will repeat time and time again.
* She thought that children should be guided by a trained adult to use her equipment until they could use it confidently on their own and independently.

A Montessori teacher plays a very different role from that of a teacher in mainstream school provision. The teacher, who is known as the directress, is seen to guide or direct the children, putting them in touch with their environment so that they can learn for themselves.

Montessori called her schools Children's Houses, and these are still to be found all over the world.

Rudolf Steiner (1861–1925)

Rudolf Steiner encouraged play through natural materials, such as clay, beeswax, silk scarves for dressing up and wooden blocks that are irregularly shaped.

* He believed singing and dancing were important, and that stories give children ideas for their play.
* He thought that education is an artistic process. He believed that there must be a balance between artistic, creative and practical experiences on the one hand, and academic activities on the other.
* He believed that children pass through three specific phases, as follows.

1. **The Period of Will** (0–7 years) – where the active aspect predominates. Within this period there are three stages: 0–3 years – the main features are walking, speech and the ability to think in words; 3–5 years – the development of the imagination and memory is important; 5 years onwards – the stimulation for play tends to come less from external objects but more from ideas generated within the children.
2. The **Period of the Heart** (7–14 years) – the feeling phase. The child is now ready for formal learning, although the role of the imagination is still very important.
3. The **Period of the Head** (14 years onwards) – the cognitive phase. The

adolescent theory is considered to be the period of thinking. At this stage children develop a healthy idealism, and may be very sensitive about their feelings.

Steiner's schools are called Waldorf Schools and are now the largest independent school system in the world, with many of the schools situated in North America and Australia.

Margaret McMillan (1860–1931)

Margaret McMillan (and her sister, Rachel) fought for the education of young children, to emphasise physical care and development. They campaigned and were successful in introducing free school meals under the Provision of School Meals Act 1906, and they introduced regular medical inspections for school children by opening the first clinic especially devoted to school children in 1908.

* McMillan believed that children cannot learn if they are undernourished, poorly clothed, sick or ill, with poor teeth, poor eyesight, ear infections, rickets, etc. (Recent reports emphasise that poor health and poverty are challenges still facing those who work with families in the UK today.)
* She believed that children learn by exploring and that they achieve their whole potential through play; she placed an emphasis on craft and water activities, singing and model-making.
* She believed that outdoor play and being taught in the fresh air was important; gardening was a regular activity.
* She stressed the importance of hygiene and cleanliness, and considered it to be her role to educate parents about how children should remain clean and hygienic.
* She thought that the role of the 'home' in supporting a child's learning capability was very important.

* She also stressed the importance of having trained teachers and she opened a special training school for the teachers in her schools. Children were taught in small groups, and McMillan expected teachers to be imaginative and inventive.
* She believed in very close **partnership with parents:** she encouraged parents to develop alongside their children, with adult classes in hobbies and languages made available to them.

The British nursery school, as envisaged by McMillan, has been admired and emulated across the world. McMillan Nursery schools have gardens, and are communities that welcome both parents and children.

Ideas about play from around the world

In Western Europe and the USA, children are often given toys to play with. Sometimes they are very expensive to buy. In other countries, specially designed toys may not be part of the way of life, and children will play mainly with natural materials, such as stones, twigs, sand, water and mud, and make their own pretend play.

In some cultures, adults think it is not a good idea to play with children. They let children play together and older children play with younger children (for example, Maori children in New Zealand). In other cultures, adults think adults (usually mothers) ought to play with their children and to teach them through their play.

How children become involved in their play and activities

Some theories emphasise the importance of childhood play because it encourages children to practise things they need to do later on in life. It helps them with the physical coordination of their bodies, objects and people.

Learning through practice play

There are two sides to practice play.

1. **The biological side of practice play:** studies of young animals playing show that, for example, lion cubs playing together quite naturally begin catching and chewing. This helps them to learn what they need to know later in order to hunt for their food and survive.
2. **The social/cultural aspect of practice play:** even newborn babies are very aware of other people. Children imitate people who are important role models for them.

Play and feelings

Some theories emphasise the importance of children's feelings. These are 'psychoanalytic' ideas about why children play.

The play scenarios children create deal with their feelings of happiness, sadness, anger, and so on, in an emotionally healthy way. Although this helps any child, therapists particularly emphasise sad and angry feelings through play for the children they work with.

Research shows that emotional health is helped through play, and leads to children developing resilience.

Play helps socially acceptable behaviour

Other theories show that children learn to think of others through their play. They learn to behave in ways that are socially acceptable as they play. This helps them to understand how other people feel and to develop

morally (to value and respect others, and to care about other people). This is called **theory of mind**.

Play helps thinking and ideas (concepts) to develop

There are three important theories about how play helps children to have ideas and learn to think. They are all useful for adults working with young children. Two of these theories emphasise social/cultural learning.

Both Vygotsky's and Bruner's theories show that other people are important in developing a child's play.

* **Vygotsky** was a psychologist in the 1930s who found that children do their best thinking when they play with others. This is because play helps them to feel in **control** of their ideas, and to make sense of things that have happened. Play helps children to **think ahead**.
* **Bruner** believes that play helps children to learn how adults do things in their culture. Adults observe children as they play and break things down into easily manageable steps for them. This is called **scaffolding the learning**.

The third theory (Piaget's theory) emphasises both biology and social/cultural learning. It is the most famous theory.

Piaget emphasised that children are active learners. They learn through their senses (seeing, touching, hearing, smelling, tasting) and through their own movement.

* Sometimes children will **play alone**.
* Sometimes they will **play with others** (children or adults).
* Children are like scientists, exploring their world and working at different levels about the world.

PIAGET'S STAGES OF PLAY

- **Babyhood (0–18 months)**: play involves sensory-motor behaviour (the senses and movement).
- **The early years of symbolic play (18 months–5 years)**: play involves making something stand for (represent) something else.

- **The school years (5–8 years)**: children move from play to taking part in games. They are able to play more cooperatively. The rules of games are quite different from the rules of play. In games the rules are given; in play children make up the rules as they go along.

✳ Although each of the stages builds on the one before, they also overlap. Modern research shows some children do things earlier, and some later, than others.

THE IMPORTANCE OF PLAY IN SUPPORTING ALL ASPECTS OF DEVELOPMENT

Knowing the way that play progresses as children grow older helps adults to plan appropriate play materials and play opportunities for different children according to their stage of development.

This is called knowing about progression in the development of play.

Play and the development of physical coordination

Children vary and develop at different rates. This depends partly on their biological stage. It also depends on where they grow up and what play opportunities and materials they are given. A child who has played with wooden blocks since toddler times might well be building towers that are castles by the age of 4 years. A child who has not had these experiences is unlikely to do this.

This shows that what children learn is influenced by how adults help their development. This is why **observing**

children as they play is important, especially if they have disabilities.

Section 2
The stages of play

It used to be thought that there were four stages of social play:

1. solitary play
2. parallel play
3. associative play
4. cooperative play.

Recent research shows that children do not develop as if they are climbing up a ladder. Instead, brain studies show that their play develops like a network. Sometimes they will play alone (solitary play). Sometimes they will play with others (parallel, associatively or cooperatively).

It will partly depend on their age, but it will also depend on their mood, others around them, where they are, and whether they are tired, hungry or comfortable.

It is certainly easier for toddlers and young children to play together in parallel, associatively or cooperatively if they are in a pair (two children). Larger groups are more of a challenge for young children. Gradually, three or four children might play cooperatively together. This tends to develop from 3 or 4 years of age.

PLAY AND THE DEVELOPMENT OF PHYSICAL COORDINATION

Sit (usually 6–9 months)	• Play with feet (put them in mouth) • Cruise around furniture	• Play with objects using a pincer movement (i.e. finger and thumb) • Transfer toys from one hand to the other • Enjoy dropping objects over the side of the high chair and look to see where they have gone • Play with objects by putting them into the mouth • Enjoy 'treasure baskets' (natural objects and household objects) *Provide:* • Cups, boxes, pots of different sizes
Crawl (usually 9–12 months)	• When sitting, the baby leans forward and picks up objects • Enjoy playing by crawling upstairs or onto low furniture • Love to bounce in time to music	• Pick things up with a pincer movement (finger and thumb) • Pull objects towards themselves • Can point at toys • Clasp hands and love to copy adults' actions in play • Love to play by throwing toys on purpose • Hold toys easily in hands • Put objects in and out of pots and boxes *Provide:* • Push and pull toys
Walk (but with sudden falling into a sitting position) (12–15 months)	• Can manage stairs with adult supervision • Can stand and kneel without support	• Begin to build towers with wooden blocks • Make lines of objects on the floor • Begin using books and turn several pages at a time • Use both hands but often prefer one • Lot of pointing • Pull toys along and push buttons *Provide:* • Board books and picture books with lines • Big empty cardboard boxes • Messy play with water paints and sand (be alert for physical safety)
Walk confidently (usually 18 months)	• Can kneel, squat, climb and carry things, can climb on chairs • Can twist around to sit • Can creep downstairs on tummy going backwards	• Pick up small objects and threads • Build towers • Scribble on paper • Push and pull toys • Enjoy banging toys (e.g. hammer and peg drums) *Provide:* • Large crayons and paper for drawing
Jump (usually 2 years)	• Can jump on the spot and run, and climb stairs two feet at a time • Kick but not good at catching ball • Enjoy space to run and play (trips to the park) • Enjoy climbing frames (supervised)	• Draw circles • Build tall towers • Pick up tiny objects • Turn the pages of books one at a time • Enjoy toys to ride and climb on • Enjoy messy play with water paints and sand pits *Provide:* • Duplo, jigsaws, crayons and paper, picture books, puppets, simple dressing-up clothes, hats, belts and shoes
Hop (usually 3 years)	• Jump from low steps • Walk forwards, backwards and sideways • Stand and walk on tiptoe • Stand on one foot	• Build taller and taller towers with blocks • Begin to use pencil grip • Paint and make lines and circles in drawings • Use play dough, sand for modelling, paint • Hold objects to explore

	• Try to hop • Use pedals on tricycle • Climb stairs one foot at a time	*Provide:* • Enjoy trip to the park, walks, library, swimming • Enjoy cooking, small world, gluing, pouring, cutting
Skip (usually 4 years)	• Balance (walking on a line) • Catch a ball, kick, throw and bounce • Bend at the waist to pick up objects from the floor • Climbing trees and frames • Can run up and down stairs one foot at a time	• Build tower with blocks that are taller and taller • Draw people, houses, etc. • Thread beads • Enjoy exercise, swimming, climbing (climbing frames and bikes) *Provide:* • Jigsaws, construction toys, wooden blocks, small world, glue and stick, paint, sand, water, clay, play dough, dressing-up clothes and home area play • Cooking (measuring, pouring and cutting)
Jump, hop, skip and run with coordination (usually 5 years)	• Use a variety of play equipment (slides, swings, climbing frames) • Enjoy ball games • Hop and run lightly on toes, and can move rhythmically to music • Well-developed sense of balance	• Sew large stitches • Draw with people, animals and places, etc. • Coordinate paint brushes and pencils, and a variety of tools • Enjoy outdoor activities (skipping ropes, football – both boys and girls enjoy these) • Make models, do jigsaws
Move with increased coordination and balance (usually 6–7 years)	• Can ride two-wheel bicycle • Hops easily with good balance • Can jump off apparatus at school	• Build play scenarios with wooden blocks • Draw play scenarios in drawings and paintings • Hold pencil as adults do • Enjoy ball games • Enjoy vigorous activity (riding a bike, swimming) (NB children should never be forced to take part, unless they want to) • Enjoy board games and computer games • Often (but not always) enjoys work being displayed on interest tables and walls (NB Children should never be forced to display their work)

Table 4.1: Play and the development of physical coordination

PLAYING ALONE

Solitary play: a child plays alone

From 6 months onwards

Solitary play is play that is undertaken alone, sometimes through choice and at other times because the child finds it hard to join in, or because of his or her developmental stage.

In the first stage of play, beginning at about 6 months, babies play alone. Babies and toddlers need time and space to play alone, but often appreciate having others around them as they do so. Playing alone:

* gives personal space and time to think, get to know yourself and like yourself
* when toddlers play alone, they seek interesting experiences, but need support when frustrated
* children of all ages engage in solitary play sometimes; playing alone enables older children to concentrate and practise their skills (e.g. when constructing a model)

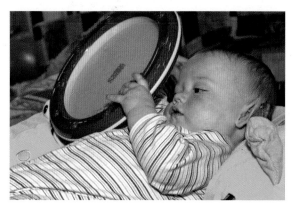

Fig 4.1. Baby playing alone

* it is important to protect the child's play space and toys from interference by other children
* children should be allowed to experience 'ownership' of toys and not be pushed to share before they are ready.

Example

A child might play alone – for example, with a doll's house – because they want to play out a story that they have in their head. Having other children join the play would stop them being able to do this.

Onlooker behaviour

From about 8 months to 3+ years

Onlooker 'play' is the passive observation of the play of others without actual participation. Before children begin to play with each other, they go through a brief stage of looking-on behaviour:

* children will stop what they are doing to watch and listen to what other children are doing
* older children may also watch others play if they are new to the group and don't yet feel ready to enter into the play

* even a child who is already secure in a group may engage in onlooker behaviour – taking a passive interest in what their friends are doing, but not joining in.

STAGES OF SOCIAL PLAY: CHILDREN PLAY TOGETHER

Parallel play

From 2 to 4+ years

Parallel play is when children play alongside each other but quite separately and without communicating with each other. Onlooker behaviour evolves into parallel – or side-by-side – play, which includes a lot of imitation and conversation back and forth between the players:

* during this stage, children like to have exactly the same toys as their peers do, but their own play space
* they are no longer content to play alone, but they are also not ready for the demands of sharing toys or taking turns
* older children also enjoy parallel play with their friends.

Example

Two children might both put dolls to bed in the home area. They don't take much notice of each other.

Associative play

Between 3½ and 5+ years

Associative play is when two or more children actively interact with one another by sharing or borrowing toys, while not doing the same things. Children playing at the **parallel stage** will begin to become aware of other children. They will often

Fig 4.2. Parallel play

Fig 4.3. Associative play

begin to communicate through talking to each other or by becoming aware of each other's games and by explaining to each other what they are doing:

* gradually one child will become involved in the other child's play; this is known as **associative** (or partnership) play
* language becomes much more important, imagination increases and dramatic themes begin to come into the play; this category of play may seem to be cooperative, but this is not the case – at this age, children are still too egocentric to have true cooperation.

Example

Two children might play so that one is the cook in the cafe and the other is the waitress. They don't seem to care that they have no customers.

Cooperative play

From age 4½ years

Cooperative play is when children begin to 'play' together – to share their play. They become more sociable and take on roles in the play. Children begin to be aware of the needs and the roles of their peers and gradually the play can become complex:

* rules are sometimes devised and some cooperative play will be revisited over several days
* cooperative play continues throughout middle childhood, where it evolves into more stylised games with rules
* in the early stages of cooperative play, the rules are not as important as the sense of belonging to a group and working towards a common goal.

Example of early (or simple) cooperative play

One child might be the baby and the other might be the parent, as they play going to the shops. They talk about their play ideas: 'you say "mum" and I say "yes, darling".'

Example of later (or complex) cooperative play

A group of children between 3 and 5 years old have been on an outing in the local market. When they return, the adult sets up a market stall. Some children become customers and buy things. Others sell things. John has a hearing impairment and uses sign language. Jack understands his sign to give him three oranges. Other children talk as they play: 'You come and bag these apples.'

Fig 4.4. Cooperative play

PLAY AND THE DEVELOPMENT OF THINKING (CONCEPTS)

Look at the box detailing Piaget's stages of cognitive development in play, on page 126.

The areas and types of play

The terms 'structured play' and 'free play' are rather old-fashioned ways of describing the way children learn through play. Research is showing that we need to think about these in a modern way.

Free play

Children lead their own play, and adults leave them to it. They might make a play scenario with toy cars, for example, and pretend they are playing garages.

Adults provide:

* play materials
* play opportunities, both indoors and outdoors.

Children choose what to do and are given plenty of free time to develop their play.

Structured play

Research is showing that there are two kinds of structured play, as described below.

Directly structured play

Adults guide and lead the play. The adult might set up a shop and show the children how to play in it, introducing shop vocabulary (words about shopping) and guiding the play story that develops.

Indirectly structured play

The adult structures the environment indoors and outdoors. The materials offered to the children are chosen and organised carefully. Children have plenty of time for play. The adult observes the children as they play, and joins in following the children's play scenario ideas. The adult does not take over but follows the children's ideas.

This is a bit like the way a conversation between people goes along. One person speaks and the other listens. Then the other person replies.

Indirectly structured play means that adults have to be sensitive to the child's play ideas. The adult is very important because they add ideas to help the child's play develop.

Creative play

Children must not be expected to 'make something'. Creative play is about experimenting with materials and music. It is not about producing things to go on display, or to be taken home; for example, when children are involved with messy finger play with paint, nothing is left at the end of the session once it has been cleared away.

Adults can encourage creative play by offering children a range of materials and play opportunities in dance, music, drawing, collage, painting, model-making and woodwork, sand (small world scenarios), water (small world scenarios) and miniature garden scenarios.

Creative play helps children to express their feelings and ideas about people, objects and events. It helps children to:

* be physically coordinated
* develop language
* develop ideas (concepts)
* develop relationships with people
* be more confident, and it boosts their self-esteem.

Drama and imaginative (or pretend) play

This is where children make play scenarios – for example, about a shop or a boat, a garage, an office or a swimming pool.

The important thing to remember about pretend play is that there will be nothing left to show anyone when the play finishes. Pretend play scenarios do not last. This is why it is difficult to explain to parents the importance of pretend play.

Some adults take video or photographs of children during their play, to try to capture it on film. They want to value pretend play as they do all the other learning that children do.

What to look out for in pretend play

* Children use play props – for example, they pretend a box is a fridge, or a stick is a spoon, or a daisy is a fried egg.
* They role play and pretend that they are someone else (e.g. the shopkeeper).
* When they pretend play together, cooperatively, this is called socio-dramatic play.
* Young children pretend play everyday situations: getting up, going to sleep, eating (just as the Teletubbies do).

* Gradually children develop their pretend play scenarios to include situations that are not everyday events and that they may only have heard about but not experienced. This is called fantasy play. They might pretend to go to the moon or go on an aeroplane. It is not impossible that these things will happen to them.
* Superhero play develops when they use unreal situations, like Superman or Power Rangers or cartoon characters.
* Children use imaginative play to act out situations that they have definitely experienced, like going to the supermarket.

For example, a group of children made a swimming pool out of wooden blocks. One of them pretended to be the lifeguard and rescued someone drowning. All the children had visited a swimming pool so this pretend play was based on a real experience.

Pretend play links with the Early Years Foundation Stage Profile and is part of all six areas of learning. Pretend play also links with all areas of a child's development:

* emotional development
* social development
* language development
* cognitive (thinking) development
* physical development.

Physical play and exercise

Physical play promotes a child's health. It links with all other areas of a child's development.

The brain works better if children have plenty of fresh air and exercise. That is why both indoor and outdoor play are very important.

Through physical play children learn to challenge gender stereotypes. Boys and girls can enjoy playing ball games (e.g. football play scenarios, running and climbing). Children need to be encouraged in these activities. It helps if they wear clothes and shoes that allow freedom of movement. Children also:

* learn through their **senses**
* coordinate their **movements**
* develop their **muscles**
* learn about pace and keeping going (**stamina**)
* learn how to use space in a **coordinated** way

* learn to challenge **gender stereotypes**.

Manipulative play

Children need plenty of opportunities to play using manipulative skills. This particularly encourages children to use their hands, which are very important in human development.

* Boys and girls can enjoy manipulative play.
* Manipulative play links with the Early Years Foundation Stage Framework, with the area of learning called Physical Development.

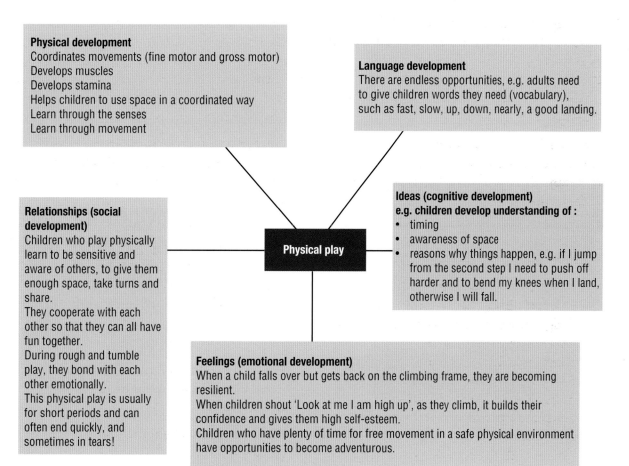

Physical development
Coordinates movements (fine motor and gross motor)
Develops muscles
Develops stamina
Helps children to use space in a coordinated way
Learn through the senses
Learn through movement

Language development
There are endless opportunities, e.g. adults need to give children words they need (vocabulary), such as fast, slow, up, down, nearly, a good landing.

Relationships (social development)
Children who play physically learn to be sensitive and aware of others, to give them enough space, take turns and share.
They cooperate with each other so that they can all have fun together.
During rough and tumble play, they bond with each other emotionally.
This physical play is usually for short periods and can often end quickly, and sometimes in tears!

Physical play

Ideas (cognitive development)
e.g. children develop understanding of :
* timing
* awareness of space
* reasons why things happen, e.g. if I jump from the second step I need to push off harder and to bend my knees when I land, otherwise I will fall.

Feelings (emotional development)
When a child falls over but gets back on the climbing frame, they are becoming resilient.
When children shout 'Look at me I am high up', as they climb, it builds their confidence and gives them high self-esteem.
Children who have plenty of time for free movement in a safe physical environment have opportunities to become adventurous.

Fig 4.5. Aspects of physical play

Relationships (social development)
Children talking about what they are doing with each other and passing each other materials they need – sharing and co-operating.
Children learn to challenge gender stereotypes.

Physical development
Using fingers and thumbs (pincer movements)
Hand–eye coordination
Develops hand muscles

Language development
Adults and children talk together as they use materials. Does it fit? Do you have enough? It's too big, will you pass me the scissors please?

Manipulative play

Ideas (cognitive development)
Children solve problems as they make models, paint, draw, etc. They think ahead, estimate sizes, use shapes and make choices. They develop ideas of their own.

Feelings (emotional development)
Helps resilience
Builds confidence and high self-esteem
Helps children to persevere (keep going)

Fig 4.6. Manipulative play

Fig 4.7. Child using fine manipulative skills and concentration

Section 3

Planning activities for play in a range of settings and provision

When planning play activities, adults should consider the following:

* the needs of the children
* the six areas of learning, and the relationships between them
* the setting
* the group
* the children and their contribution to the planning process
* the learning context – indoor and outdoor environment
* the local community.

EXAMPLE

Andrew enjoyed playing at making a waterfall in the water tray by pouring water out of a bottle from as high as he could reach up. Other children joined in.

Adults can develop this play by setting up more bottles and having two water trays. Then the activity won't become too crowded. They can set up the paddling pool outside to use as a big water tray, and let children use the hosepipe to fill it. Put guttering in the paddling pool to act as a water chute and provide jugs to pour water down the chutes. Spare clothes are needed in case children get wet. It is important to keep the floors indoors safe from becoming slippery with too much water. Always keep a mop and bucket near a water activity.

HOW TO PLAN

The best planning comes from knowing the children really well. This develops from using the **observations** adults make of children to plan the next step in their play.

Children need a variety of activities or experiences, using a range of resources, to enable them to learn and make progress in all areas of development. Planning what will be offered helps children to use a range of resources and materials. It encourages a 'balanced' day.

Having made decisions about what to provide it is then necessary to plan each activity/experience and consider the following factors:

* aim or purpose
* time needed/group size
* preparation in advance
* preparation at the time
* space/resources/safety
* suitability for age/stage of development
* supervision/adult role
* adaptation for a child with a special need
* consideration of equal opportunities issues
* opportunities for monitoring and assessing individual children.

Aim or purpose

As for observations, a clear aim is preferable to one that is too wide or vague – for example, 'To develop fine manipulative skills through putting a straw in a carton of drink' or 'To develop listening skills through a "sound" lotto game.'

Almost all activities have many benefits and will help development in more than one area. It is a good idea to identify the main purpose and mention briefly other aspects that are also likely to be involved.

Time needed/group size

Most settings have a daily routine with set times for:

* refreshment, sleep or rest
* outdoor or energetic activity
* assembly or group time, and
* start and finish times for sessions (these may vary for individual children in a nursery setting).

Knowing how long you are going to need to carry out an activity from start to finish for a group is very important. It helps to decide when it can be done and, if all children are to have the opportunity to do it, how many 'sessions' will be needed. Generally, the younger the children the fewer you would have in a group – perhaps for a 'messy' activity such as finger painting you may work with pairs or perhaps just one child. You need to allow time for clearing away, especially if the tables or the area are needed for another activity. Similarly, the children themselves may need to wash ready for lunch or get dressed for going outside/home.

Preparation/resources

In advance

1. The first step is to find out the setting's current topic or theme, if it has one, and discuss with your supervisor what activity might be appropriate.

2. You should then plan the activity, show the plan to your supervisor and, if it is suitable, agree when you may implement it. This should avoid a similar one being carried out by someone else the day before! At this stage you can ensure that the space you need (e.g. the book corner or the water tray) will be available. An activity that uses 'permanent' equipment (e.g. Lego, Stickle Bricks, puzzles) will need setting up – space, layout of equipment, seating if applicable. However, one that uses 'consumable materials' (i.e. ones that are used up and need replacing, such as paper, paint, glue) requires more consideration.

3. Make a comprehensive list of what you need – this should be detailed. For example, not just 'six sheets of paper' but six sheets of A3, black, sugar paper (i.e. state size, colour, type).

4. Check that your selected resources are available (another staff member may have reserved the last of the gold paper for a particular display or activity, so do not just go and help yourself!) and collect them in plenty of time. Some may need further

preparation – for example, cutting to a smaller size or particular shape, arranging in pots or tubs for easy access, and so on.

5. Check that:
   * (for very young children) there are no tiny pieces
   * materials are clean
   * materials are undamaged
   * there are no toxic substances/contents.

For preparation relating to food and cooking activities see Unit 8, pages 216–217.

At the time

Always allow time for preparation on the day – arrive early if necessary. Your supervisor will have made arrangements for you to take the agreed number of children at the agreed time. If you are not ready, someone else has to supervise those children and/or find them an alternative activity.

* **Remember to protect tables**, surfaces, children and their clothing appropriately.
* **Prepare sufficient quantities of paint, paper**, and so on, for the group size identified and have them conveniently to hand – you cannot leave a group of young children alone while you go to fetch more paper from the stock cupboard or to mix up more paint!

When planning your activity think about how you will introduce it – what will be your starting point? You might show the children the equipment and ask them about it, or remind them of a previous related experience.

Suitability for age/stage of development

Although you can use books to help you understand what is the 'expected' or 'norm' ability for the age range you are working with, it is more important to base your own planning on what you can see and have experienced in your particular work setting. If you have used your placement time effectively you will have helped with activities planned by other staff members and become familiar with the resources and with the children. Remember that children should be **active learners** and your plan should provide them with 'hands on' experience. Avoid activities that involve colouring in work sheets or 'sticking' ones that do not allow children to select their own materials and choose how to use the space.

Supervision/adult role

Your activity – perhaps a physical one involving large apparatus – may require more than one adult supervising. In this case it is important not only to check that there are sufficient adults available but also that any other adult knows your activity's aim and what is involved. If you have written a clear plan then it can be shared more easily. Try to think ahead about any aspects of your plan that may involve an adult in offering practical help to all children or an individual child.

Adaptation for a child with a special need/consideration of equal opportunities

As you will be planning for children in your work setting you will be aware of any children with special needs – whether the difficulty results from a physical condition, a sensory impairment, a learning disorder, or a behavioural or emotional problem. Take notice of the strategies used by other staff members to allow access to all activities and equipment. This may be as straightforward as ensuring that you make left-handed or 'dual-handed' scissors available or more challenging in adapting space and materials for a child whose

leg is in plaster. Try to think about adaptations for children with sensory impairment. Visually impaired children will depend heavily on hearing and touch so try to adapt resources or provide extra ones to support their learning (e.g. samples of materials mentioned in stories like 'The Three Little Pigs' – straw, sticks and bricks). Hearing impaired children will also benefit from learning through touch, but will need visual aids too – perhaps puppets or figures to demonstrate parts of a story or clear pictures sequenced to help with a cooking or construction task. Always make sure that you have the children's attention – touching a visually impaired child on the arm so it is clear she needs to listen and ensuring that when talking, or giving instructions, to a hearing impaired child she is able to see the speaker's face (see the section on effective communication, in Unit 5). Think about the equal opportunities issues dealt with in Unit 1 (e.g. gender and cultural stereotyping) and make sure that your resources promote **positive images**.

Opportunities for monitoring and assessing individual children

Your activity will offer opportunities for observing how children use equipment, listen to any instructions, talk about what they are doing and interact with each other. At the end of an activity make a note about any aspects that presented difficulties, caused frustration or were not sufficiently challenging. Make a note also of those in which the children were particularly successful. This helps staff to keep records, report progress to parents and plan for individual children's future needs.

Evaluating your plan

As well as recording the points mentioned above in relation to the children, you need to consider your own learning. You should try to judge how suitable your activity was and how it might be improved or altered. You can also reflect on your own ability to prepare, explain, support children and maintain behaviour. Refer to all the factors you had to consider, and identify which ones 'worked' (were appropriate) and which were less successful.

For example: would it have been more effective with thicker paint, coloured paper, fatter brushes? Did you allow enough/too much time? Was the cutting task too fiddly for the children to manage independently? – How could it have been improved? Do not be too dismayed if an activity seems to be a disaster, *but* make sure you understand *why* and what went wrong!

Planning activities to meet children's needs

When deciding what activities and experiences will be offered to children, staff in a work setting must consider safety, space, children's ages and stage of development, supervision, and availability of resources. Most work settings plan activities around well-chosen themes or topics. These are usually relevant to the children themselves and, perhaps, the time of year; common ones are 'Ourselves', 'Autumn', 'Festivals' (e.g. Christmas, Diwali, Hanukkah, Chinese New Year), 'Growth' and 'Nursery Rhymes'.

THE ROLE OF RISK AND CHALLENGE IN PLAY

There is a popular idea that learning through play means always having fun. Certainly, children will have plenty of fun as they learn through play. However, children also learn about sad and angry feelings. They are challenged to learn about difficult things such as:

* death
* being separated from people they love
* being hurt.

Learning through play is not just about having fun. Play is about learning for life.

KEEPING CHILDREN SAFE AS THEY LEARN THROUGH PLAY

Physical safety

Children who play in a physically safe environment are more likely to develop confidence, self-esteem and self-reliance. They are in a can-do situation. In modern life it is often dangerous for children to play outside in the street. It is therefore very important that when children attend group settings they can be physically safe.

Children with disabilities may find it more challenging to play, and will need careful help from others.

Safety should always be borne in mind when working with young children so that accidents are prevented. This is called risk assessment because adults are thinking ahead about possible physical danger to children. It is important to check materials such as pens, crayons and felt pens for the safety mark. Remember, children put objects into their mouths as part of the way they learn.

* Worn equipment should be mended or replaced.
* Equipment should be checked for splinters, sharp edges or peeling paint.
* At the end of each day all aprons should be checked and wiped clean.
* Tables need to be disinfected.
* Floors need sweeping and washing once the rooms have been tidied.
* Carpets need to be cleaned with a vacuum.

Setting up materials and equipment

* Check large apparatus such as climbing frames and trucks for safety catches and safety surfaces. Do the children have enough space to move about safely?
* Heavy objects should not be on shelves in case they fall on children.
* All fire exits must be kept clear at all times.
* Doors must not be left half open, especially if there are children with visual impairments, as they bump into them.
* Objects on shelves should not stick out at a child's head height in case they bump their heads.

Emotional safety

* Children need to feel emotionally safe or they will not be confident enough to play.
* They need to play with or near an adult, especially if they are just settling in or they have been upset.
* They may need to have a special friend with them in order to feel secure enough to play confidently.

Social safety

When children quarrel they often begin to shout at each other and even fight. Shouting means they are trying to put their feelings into words. Adults can help them by saying something like 'I think you are angry. What shall we do about it? Do you want the bike? When Mary has finished with it she will give you a turn.'

If children become very quiet they might be blocking the drains or something adults don't want them to do. Children need to be supervised carefully. It is important for adults never to sit with their back to the group, either indoors or outdoors.

If children rush about and become overexcited, it is sometimes best to join their play and help them to develop a storyline. Sometimes they may have lost their play ideas in the excitement.

VIOLENCE AND PLAY

In some settings, both war play and guns are banned. The thinking here is that this discourages children from becoming violent. Some adults think that children need to learn about the terribleness of violence in ways that are emotionally safe. Some adults think that children learn how to stop violence through play about violence.

In this approach, adults usually allow war play as long as these emotional safety rules are kept:

* children can play war only with children who have agreed to join this play scenario
* they cannot pretend to shoot at or pretend to kill children or adults who are not playing this war scenario
* they must stop if children decide they want to leave the play, or they don't like it
* adults usually join the play to help children think about pain, hurting people and the sadness of losing people they love, not having food to eat, being tired, being rough.

DEALING WITH SAD AND FRIGHTENING EVENTS IN PLAY

Children will see things on television and in videos that show wars, starvation, etc. They might want to use these ideas in their play scenarios as a way of helping them to understand these events.

* Children often think about monsters, giants, witches, ghosts, creatures from outer space. It is best if adults do not introduce these ideas into children's play. Children are usually **emotionally safe** if they do this for themselves. This is because if they create the monster, then the monster is under their control. They can decide how the monster behaves and when to stop the play.
* **Feeling in control** is important for children's emotional safety when they play with danger and fear. This is why **hospital play** is often important for children before and after a visit.
* A new baby in the family also brings fears, such as 'am I still loved?' and **play scenarios** help children to deal with this fear.

PROMOTING ANTI-DISCRIMINATORY PLAY

Children need to be helped not to develop ideas which are discriminatory or which **stereotype** people (think of other people in narrow ways).

* Play scenarios – for example, where Eskimos (now called Inuits) are stereotyped as still living in igloos, might lead children to think that is how such people live nowadays.
* Children see gender stereotypes on television and in videos. This often leads to superhero play:
  - boys will be macho men
  - girls will be glamorous sex symbols.

  This can be dealt with by helping children to decide as they play – for example, what does Superman eat for breakfast? When does he shop for his food? Who irons his shirts?

THE ROLE OF THE ADULT IN PROVIDING ACTIVITIES AND SUPPORTING CHILDREN

Adults need to choose play materials carefully and to create:

* play opportunities
* time to play
* space for play indoors and outdoors
* places for dens, physical play, manipulative play and creative play
* play props and clothes for dressing up and role play
* an adapted play environment for children with disabilities.

Adults who provide **open-ended** materials create more play possibilities for children. You should provide:

* recycled junk materials (string, boxes, wood)
* natural materials (clay, woodwork, sand, water, twigs, leaves, feathers)
* traditional areas (home area, wooden blocks, work shop area with scissors, glue, etc.).

Choosing materials and equipment to give children play opportunities

Children learn about play from natural and recycled materials, as well as specially designed toys and equipment. They need a balance – for example, wooden hollow blocks and cardboard boxes.

Natural materials

These should be attractively presented. They are important for children living in a modern world. Plastic is everywhere; natural materials help children to learn about sand, water, wood and clay. These show children how they can find materials for themselves. They are cheap to provide.

Recycled materials

These cost nothing to provide. Margarine tubs, bottle corks and plastic bottles, for example, need to be set out in attractive containers, easy to reach and use. Children need enough space and table room for creative play with these materials.

Commercially made equipment

This can be expensive and needs to be chosen carefully. Look at Unit 3, which emphasises the safety of equipment, non-toxic materials and cleanliness. Equipment is often pre-structured, which means that children can only use it in a narrow way. Open-ended equipment that can be used in a variety of ways is better value for money (e.g. wooden blocks, Lego, Duplo).

Children gain if there are plenty of these so that they can build exciting models. It is best to have all the same brand of wooden blocks, or Lego or Duplo, then these can be added to over the years.

* Check equipment for safety marks.
* Can it be cleaned easily?
* Can it be mended easily or are there replacement parts?
* Is it open-ended so that it can be used in many different ways (e.g. doll's house, farm, home area equipment, wooden blocks)?

THE INDOOR AND OUTDOOR AREAS

It is best not to change the room around too often because children take some time to find out where things are, both indoors and outdoors. Adults need to know about the child's development in play so that they, in their curriculum, can provide what is needed for play in their curriculum plan. Important points to consider when providing for children's play are:

* things should be set out so that they are interesting, with enough variety to keep stimulating the play
* the layout of the room should take account of different children's cultural experiences and heritage
* there should be specially adapted equipment for children with disabilities
* adults should think carefully about what materials to set out, and how to present them in order to encourage play.

Planning the indoor and outdoor areas

The materials that adults set up indoors should (whenever possible) be available outdoors in any group setting (see the Early Years Foundation Stage Guidance document). This means that children can learn as much outdoors as they do indoors. Examples include the following.

* **Climbing frames:** these need to be carefully designed to offer children plenty of challenges as safely as possible. One side of the frame might have evenly spaced rungs for children who are less experienced in climbing. The other side might have unevenly spaced rungs, which need more thinking by the child.
* **Tarmac:** an outdoor area needs some tarmac or tiled area so that in wet weather it is possible to run or walk about without muddy feet tramping back indoors.
* **Wild area:** many gardens now have a wild area, which has plants that

encourage butterflies, moths and birds. A bird table is also a source of great interest.

* **Grass:** outdoor areas also need grass where children can find worms, make daisy chains and blow dandelion clocks. A grassy slope can also provide rough-and-tumble play and roly-poly possibilities on a fine day.

* **Paddling pools:** these are suitable for fine days. When providing a pool, remember:

  - the pool must be constantly supervised; there should always be towels near it so that children do not become cold

  - to protect children's skin from sunburn – follow your setting's policy

  - that there are cultural sensitivities with regard to children taking off their clothes when using a pool; this needs to be carefully discussed between staff and parents before introducing children to a paddling pool

  - some children do not like to be splashed and this needs to be respected; perhaps there can be 10 minutes at the end of a session for 'splashy times' so that children who enjoy this can stay on in the pool and other children can get out if they want to; in this way children learn to respect each other's feelings.

* **Digging patches:** some outdoor areas provide digging patches and a vegetable planting area. Younger children tend to dig, carry earth about, find worms and tip water into holes (often 2 to 3 year olds). Older children (often aged 3–5 years) begin to understand the process of digging, planting, watering and growing. This shows in their play – they want to play farmers or gardeners, and a sandpit is often where they will choose to do this.

* **Bikes, carts and other wheeled equipment:** bikes are often the source of conflict among children. Some children always want to ride them. For this reason many settings now provide carts and different types of bikes and trikes, which two or three children can ride on and on which they can pull each other around. These are very useful in encouraging children to help each other so that they become a team. Adults often make special zones in the outdoor area where children can use bikes without knocking other people over.

THE EARLY YEARS FOUNDATION STAGE

The Early Years Foundation Stage applies to children from birth to 5 years of age. During this Foundation Stage, children might be attending a playgroup, pre-school, nursery school, nursery class, day care setting, reception class or private nursery, or be with a childminder or nanny.

Well-planned play, both indoors and outdoors, is an important part of the Early Years Foundation Stage; it helps children to reach the early learning goals by the time they enter Year 1, Key Stage 1 of the National Curriculum.

There are six areas of learning:

1. Personal, Social and Emotional Development
2. Communication, Language and Literacy
3. Problem Solving, Reasoning and Numeracy
4. Knowledge and Understanding of the World
5. Physical Development
6. Creative Development.

PROVIDING WELL-PLANNED PLAY FOR THE EARLY YEARS FOUNDATION STAGE

The following pages look more closely at seven different types of play provision and at the way they link to the six areas of learning and development in this Stage. These areas are:

1. wooden block play
2. sand and water play
3. home area
4. dressing-up clothes
5. small world play
6. clay, dough and mud patches
7. painting and drawing.

Wooden block play

Indoors

Wooden blocks are best if they are free standing. They never wear out and can easily be reconditioned (sanded). There are three kinds of blocks:

1. unit blocks
2. mini hollow bricks
3. large hollow bricks.

All of these link with each other. To use wooden blocks, children need:

* enough space to build
* to play with the blocks away from 'traffic' of people walking through the area
* to have the blocks set out on shelves with outlines of shapes showing each type of block, so that children know where different types of blocks should be stored – children need to see them and to choose which they will use
* a complete set of blocks (and not to lose any!); they should be easily tidied away
* to have blocks available each day.

Outdoors

Blocks could also be milk crates or wooden boxes, which can be stored outside along the wall and used each day. Children can make stepping stones and build with them.

Safety

Children must not build too high unless supervised (except when using soft foam blocks), in case blocks fall on them. Look at the section on general safety on pages 100–102 to see whether you have missed things you need to remember when you are working with wooden blocks with the children.

Progression in block play

* At **1 to 2 years:** children mainly build towers and put blocks in rows.
* At **2 to 3 years**: children make enclosures, towers get taller and they put blocks in rows. Balance is important now. They sometimes call their models something (e.g. a house).
* At **3 to 5 years:** children begin to put together a variety of patterns. They begin to create play scenarios with more complicated stories. They make many patterns and quite difficult balancing is achieved. They are interested in how to balance and build blocks.
* At **5 to 7 years:** the stories and buildings become very complex and are highly coordinated.

Construction

Construction is similar to block play except that all the pieces connect with each other, whereas blocks balance. Ideally, a variety of construction sets should be available (e.g. Lego, Duplo, Stickle Bricks, Construct-O-Straws). However, it is important that whatever sets you have should contain

Wooden block play

Personal, Social and Emotional Development
- Interested, excited, motivated to learn
- Try out new ideas and activities
- Select blocks they want to use without help and feel valued
- Sensitive to others; share and take turns
- Make good relationships with other children and adults

Communication Language and Literacy
- Talk as they build
- Listen to each other
- Make up play scenarios with stories
- Make comments and ask questions
- Increase vocabulary about blocks (it's taller, could you pass me the cylinder, please?)

Problem Solving, Reasoning and Numeracy
- Use number ideas
- Use maths language: talk about shapes and sizes of blocks
- Solve practical problems – is this too tall?
- Space awareness about blocks

Knowledge and Understanding of the World
- Find out about materials – wooden blocks, foam blocks
- Ask questions about how to do things with blocks
- Think about how wooden blocks are made from trees
- Building and constructing with blocks

Physical Development
- Use blocks with confidence and safety
- Use a range of wooden blocks, hollow and unit blocks to develop fine and gross motor skills
- Balance blocks with increasing control
- Aware of space and of others using the block play area

Creative Development
- Explore shape, form, texture and space of wooden blocks
- Use senses and movement to explore blocks
- Use imagination to make play scenarios
- Design and make constructions (children use their own ideas)

enough pieces to interest a group of children. Younger children find Duplo easier than Lego because the pieces are larger and easier to hold as they develop muscle control in their hands. By then they have developed their pincer movement and enjoy practising using it.

Sand and water play

Indoors

Sand can be offered in a commercial sand tray, in seed boxes from a garden shop or in washing-up bowls on tables. It can be poured on to a plastic mat and used as a 'beach' experience with shells, buckets, spades and pebbles. The mat can be rolled up at the end of the session and the sand poured into a sand tray to use again.

* There should always be both wet and dry sand on offer (e.g. dry sand in bowls on tables, or wet sand in a sand tray.
* Provide jugs, scoops, funnels, sponges, small world scenarios, farms, tubes, spades, small buckets and rakes.
* Miniature gardens can be made by adding twigs, moss, and leaves.

Outdoors

Sand and water play outside is similar to indoors. However, the following equipment can also be used outdoors:

* hoses
* watering cans
* water-washable paint for use on the tarmac (using buckets of water and giant brushes)
* large, covered sand pit where several children can play.

Safety

Make sure that sand and water play is carefully supervised.

* Be alert, as children can drown in very shallow water, get sand in their eyes or slip on wet floors.
* Outdoor sand pits need covers to keep animals and insects out.
* Place the indoor water tray near to the sink (because it's heavy and in case people slip).
* Change the water every day.
* Always sweep the floor after sand play.
* Use a mop to ensure floors are not slippery after water play.

Progression in sand and water play

* At **1 to 2 years:** children begin by pouring and carrying water and sand, and by putting these materials in and out of containers.
* At **3 to 5 years:** children begin to enjoy practical problems, and to solve them as they develop their learning (e.g. how to make a strong jet of water, how to make sand keep its shape).
* At **5 to 7 years:** children's play scenarios have more of a story than before. They use a variety of play people and cooperate more with other children.

Home area

Indoors

The home area is one of the most important areas in early childhood settings. The home area should ideally have:

* some things in it that are like those in the child's home (e.g. cups, cooking pots)
* some things that are from other cultures (e.g. a wok, chopsticks)
* a proper place for everything, and children should be encouraged to tidy up carefully
* a large dresser – with hooks for cups, and cupboards to store dishes and saucepans
* big, middle-sized and small dolls, representing children of different cultures

Sand and water play

Personal, Social and Emotional Development
- Interested, excited, motivated to learn
- Confidently play, try out new ideas
- Concentrate, aware of what they need
- Take turns and share
- Choose sand and water on their own – no help
- Make good relationships with other children and adults

Communication Language and Literacy
- Enjoy listening to others
- use action words – filling, pouring, spilling, etc.
- Talk to others as they play
- Explore sounds of water – splash, drip, etc.
- Learn words about sand and water – dry, wet, cold, warm, etc.

Problem Solving, Reasoning and Numeracy
- Use maths language; capacity – e.g. how many cups to fill this jug?
- Solve practical problems, e.g. pouring water through a funnel
- Make patterns and shapes in the sand

Knowledge and Understanding of the World
- Use the senses to investigate – differences between wet and dry sand
- Ask questions about what is happening
- Choose tools – watering can for plants, spade for digging
- Find out about the environment – water pipes for skins, sand found on beaches

Physical Development
- Use sand and water with confidence, safely
- Move with control and coordination, aware of space, how many can use area easily
- Use large sandpits and paddling pools, supervised
- Swimming (gross motor skills)
- Small trays with sand (fine motor skills)

Creative Development
- Ask questions – how does water fill a space?
- Pour water and dry sand, using senses to feel the texture of sand and water
- See, smell, listen to sounds of water
- Make play scenarios, express ideas, feelings and thoughts

Home area

Personal, Social and Emotional Development
- Interested, excited, motivated to learn
- Confidently play, try out new ideas
- Concentrate, have play scenarios of their own
- Take turns and sharing
- Aware of which cups and pots to use for cooking
- Make good relationships with others

Communication Language and Literacy
- Enjoy talking and listening to other children as they play
- Enjoy making stories and acting out ones they know
- Think about ideas, feelings, events
- Learn new words about the home area, e.g. saucepan, cooker, wok

Problem Solving, Reasoning and Numeracy
- Use numbers ideas, e.g. No. 5 on the gas cooker, four places at the table, three beds
- Use shapes; a plate is a circle

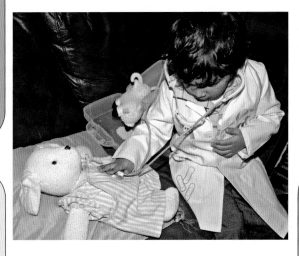

Knowledge and Understanding of the World
- Find out about materials – e.g. how plastic snaps or bends, metal gets hot and cold
- Ask questions about what is happening
- Choose utensils – pan for frying, pram for pushing, etc.

Physical Development
- Use equipment with more coordination and control
- Stir the pot, turn the knobs, lift the dishes – manipulative skills
- Use a range of materials – cutlery, crockery, bedclothes, dressing and undressing dolls

Creative Development
- Express and communicate ideas, thoughts and feelings
- Use a range of objects in the home area, e.g. putting dolls to bed, preparing food
- Role play with families

* a cooker (this can be homemade – e.g. from a cardboard box)
* wooden boxes, which can be used as beds, tables, chairs
* food can be pre-structured (plastic fruit), transformable (dough), real food (a salad) or pretend
* clothes can be kept in a chest of drawers, labelled with pictures and words
* magazines, notepads and writing implements can be put by the telephone, and perhaps a bookcase with books
* adaptations for children with disabilities (e.g. a child who is a wheelchair user will need a low table so that they can use the bowls and plates).

Outdoors

The home area outside is a den. Children at home enjoy playing in outside dens.

* Old furniture can be used outside to make a home area. An old airer (clothes horse) with a sheet or blanket over it makes good walls.
* Children can make pretend food using sand, water and messy materials.
* A rug can be put in the den and furniture can be made by collecting spare cardboard boxes (e.g. they can become tables or beds for dolls).
* Cushions can make seats or beds.
* A box on its side can become a cupboard with flaps as the cupboard doors.
* Cups and saucers can be made out of old yoghurt pots and margarine containers.

Safety

* Wooden equipment should be checked regularly for rough edges and splinters.
* Cutlery must be carefully introduced. Ask your supervisor for advice.
* Glass and china break easily and should not be used in the home area.

Progression in home area play

* At **1 to 2 years:** children carry materials – pots, pans, dolls, etc. – about; put them in and out of boxes, prams; puts them in rows.
* At **2 to 3 years:** they begin to make play scenarios, often about food.
* At **3 to 5 years:** more of the story develops, about a wider range of events and people.

Dressing-up clothes

Indoors and outdoors

Children wear dressing-up clothes indoors, but enjoy wearing them outdoors too.

* The clothes need to be simple and flexible in use.
* A basic cape, some basic hats (including 'uniform' hats such as a fire-fighter's helmet), scarves and drapes, sari, tunic, shoes and baggy trousers help children in role playing. They need to reflect different cultures.
* Fastenings should be varied to give children different experiences of connecting clothes together (e.g. zips, buttons, tying bows, buckles and velcro).
* The clothes need to be hanging on a rack, with separate boxes for shoes and hats. A large safety mirror at child height is useful.

Safety

* There should be no strings, ribbons or purses on strings around the neck, which might strangle a child.
* Beware of children tripping over clothes that are too long.
* Make sure children wear suitable footwear (e.g. no high heels when playing on climbing frames or running out of doors).
* Clothes should be washed regularly.

Dressing-up clothes

Personal, Social and Emotional Development
- Dress and undress
- Choose clothes to wear
- Show a range of feelings
- Make a good relationship with other children and adults
- Respect their own and other cultures

Communication Language and Literacy
- Enjoy listening to and telling stories in role play
- Talk to others as they play
- Make up play stories and act out some already known
- Take turns and share with others

Problem Solving, Reasoning and Numeracy
- Use numbers ideas – four buttons, two shoes, one hat

Knowledge and Understanding of the World
- Choose clothes suitable for their role play

Physical Development
- Use different fastenings on clothes – zips, buttons, velcro etc. – development of manipulative skills
- Move with confidence and control

Creative Development
- Choose colours and textures – wool, nylon, glitter
- Make play scenarios, express ideas, feelings, relationships and thoughts through role play

Progression in dressing-up clothes play

* At **1 to 2 years:** children wear hats and shoes.
* At **2 to 3 years:** children wear hats, shoes, capes and scarves.
* At **3 to 5 years:** children are more adventurous – they begin to wear whole outfits and want more accuracy to look right for the role they play.

Small world play

Garages, farms, zoos, space scenes, domestic, hospitals, boats and castles all feature in small world play.

Indoors

Children can easily create play scenarios with pretend people, and make up imaginative stories using small world materials to help them. These are best set out on a floor mat or carpet, or in a sand tray (see 'Sand and water play').

* Miniature gardens make a good play scene; these can be made in seed trays from garden centres and put on tables.
* Children can make their own gardens and make up stories using them – pots of moss, gravel, twigs, pebbles and feathers.
* They can also make paths, trees, grass and hills.
* Older children begin to use doll's houses, garages and castles.

Outdoors

Small world materials are easily lost outside.

Safety

Check that the pieces are not so small that a younger child might choke on them.

Progression in play

* At **1 to 2 years:** children mainly put toys in rows and make constructions.
* At **2 to 4 years:** they make more complex constructions (e.g. a house; simple everyday stories).
* At **4 to 6 years:** children use play scenarios (e.g. going shopping) and make up a story with different people (e.g. hospital scenes, outer space, garage scenes).

Clay, dough and mud patches

Indoors

Children often do not make anything in particular because this is creative play. There is no need to have any sort of result or finished product. It is important not to force children into this.

Storing clay

Clay can be brown or grey. It is stored by rolling it into a ball, the size of a large orange, pressing a thumb into it, pouring water into the hole, and covering the hole full of water with clay. It should then be stored in a bin with a well-fitting lid.

Outdoors

A mud patch for digging is a popular area outdoors. Spades and rakes with short handles are useful. Children love to bury things and fill holes with water. They enjoy planting flowers and vegetables.

Safety

* Dough must be made using salt and cream of tartar if it is to be stored and used more than once.
* Deter children from putting the dough in their mouths. Be extra vigilant with

Small world play

Personal, Social and Emotional Development
- Interested, excited, motivated to learn
- Concentrate and try out new ideas
- Know which equipment they might need to use
- Take turns, share and play with others
- show a range of feelings as they create their play scenarios
- Show they understand how other people feel through the people in their play stories

Communication Language and Literacy
Enjoy listening to and talking with their friends as they play
Make up their own stories and re-tell some they know as they play with small world materials
Extend vocabulary, especially by grouping and naming

Problem Solving, Reasoning and Numeracy
- Show an interest in shape and space by making arrangements with objects (e.g. a square field to make a farm)
- Use size language such as 'big' and 'little'
- Use words about position in space ('the cow is next to the sheep')
- Solve practical problems (e.g. the house falls over so prop it up against a wall)

Knowledge and Understanding of the World
Observe, find out about and identify features in the place they live and the natural world
Find out about small world materials and see how things work and can be changed
Show curiosity, observe and manipulate objects

Physical Development
- Manipulate materials and objects by picking up, releasing, arranging, threading and posting them
- Use small world materials in a coordinated way with fine motor skills and a range of play scenarios

Creative Development
- Make play scenarios, express ideas, feelings and thoughts
- Engage in imaginative and role play based on own first-hand experiences
- Play alongside other children who are engaged in the same theme
- Think about the countryside (farm) and wildlife (elephants, zebras, etc.)

Clay, dough and mud patches

Personal, Social and Emotional Development
- Interested, excited, motivated to learn
- Confidently try out new ideas with clay
- Concentrate, aware of what they need, e.g. rolling pins or hands
- Think of others by taking turns and sharing
- Make good relationships with other children and adults
- Understand other people will respect them

Communication Language and Literacy
- Enjoy listening and talking to each other
- Learn new words – soft, hard, rolling pin
- Make play scenarios with stories
- Make comments and ask questions

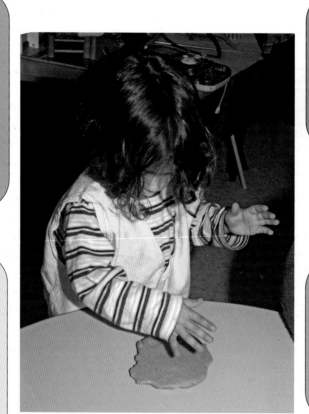

Problem Solving, Reasoning and Numeracy
- Use numbers ideas – 'I am making six cakes' or 'I have got more than you'
- Concepts of size and weight
- Make patterns and shapes

Knowledge and Understanding of the World
- Use the senses to find out about dough, clay and plasticine
- Look at the differences between materials
- Ask questions and make models
- Choose tools – rollers, containers
- Find out about the environment

Physical Development
- Use the clay with coordination
- Use the tools with confidence
- Develop manipulative skills – punching, pinching, pulling, rolling, squashing, etc.

Creative Development
- Explore (through the senses) texture, shape and form of clay and dough
- Make designs – which do not have to be a product to keep or to display

children who have coeliac disease as they must not consume any gluten (present in ordinary flour).

Progression in play

* At **1 to 3 years:** children bash and bang clay.
* At **3 to 5 years:** they learn to pinch, pull and roll it as well:
  - they can make shapes
  - they choose their tools or use their hands more carefully
  - they begin to design and make models, which they sometimes like to keep and display, but not often.

Painting and drawing

Indoors

For drawing: children need a variety of materials to draw with (fat and thin felt pens, chubby crayons, pastels, chalks, charcoal and pencils). They also need paper of different sizes, textures, shapes and colours; paper should be attractively set out and stored on shelves or in boxes or trays.

For painting: provide a variety of paints – freshly mixed every day – and brushes, clean water, non-spillable paint containers, and pots to mix colours.

* Children need a range of paintbrushes (thick, middle and thin), ideally made from good-quality hog's hair. Poor-quality brushes lead to poor-quality paintings and are frustrating to use.
* Flat tables are easier for younger children to use than easels.
* Children should choose which paper and tools to use.
* A well-designed paint dryer, which stacks paintings while allowing them to dry, is ideal, but you can spread paintings out on the floor under a radiator – or

hang with pegs to dry from a washing line.

* Mixing colours: it is best only to provide primary colours (red, blue and yellow paints) and to make shades by adding white or black to lighten or darken the colours:
  - red + blue = purple
  - red + yellow = orange
  - blue + yellow = green
  - red + white = pink
  - all colours mixed together = brown
* Children can mix their own colours if these are presented in large tins in the middle of the table, with a spoon in each tin. Patty pan pallets can be used for mixing, and water can be scooped with a small ladle from a large bowl in the centre into small, easily manageable jugs. In this way, children can pour small amounts, and learn to mix the colours and shades of paint they need with a paintbrush.
* Children need encouragement to wear aprons. Those they step into using their arms first are the most popular, as aprons over the head can be frightening for very young children.
* If children want to keep their paintings or drawings they need to be kept in a safe place. They might like to see them displayed on the wall. They must have the right to say if they do not want this.
* Painting is a messy activity, which is probably why it is not always done in the home. Protect the floor, easels and tables with newspaper.
* Young children should always be given the opportunity to express themselves through painting, undisturbed by adults. Adults should never interrupt, ask questions about the child's painting or make their own suggestions; these actions will discourage creativity and may stop the children from valuing their own work.

Painting and drawing

Personal, Social and Emotional Development
- Interested, excited, motivated to learn
- Find out how to use different pens, chalks, crayons – with new ideas as they do so
- Concentrate, knowing which colours or materials they need
- Take turns and share; respect what other children draw or paint
- Choose what to draw, when to draw and how to draw

Communication Language and Literacy
- Enjoy talking about their drawings and paintings
- Organise materials and ideas, feelings and events
- Learn new words about drawing and painting
- Show interest in having their name written on their drawings – may have a go at doing this themselves – or ask an adult to do this for them
- Hold a pencil, however they like and how it feels comfortable
- By Key Stage I learn to hold pencil correctly

Problem Solving, Reasoning and Numeracy
- Use numbers ideas in their drawings, i.e. two legs, two eyes, three bears, four sides on the house
- Make patterns and learn new words to define them, e.g. round, square, zig-zag

Physical Development
- Use crayons, paints, etc. confidently and safely
- Aware of the space they need when drawing, e.g. not jogging each other
- Use a wide range of drawing tools and a wide choice of paints (different colours and thicknesses)
- Handle pencils and paint brushes with increasing control

Knowledge and Understanding of the World
- Investigate paint and different drawing pencils, chalks, felt pens, crayons
- Observe living things, objects and events they decide they will draw
- Decide which tools to paint or draw with
- Know about their own culture and draw their experiences

Creative Development
- Explore colour, texture, shape, form and space in paintings and drawings
- Respond to how paint feels (e.g. finger painting) or chalks
- Use their imagination as they make patterns, pictures and scribbles of their choice

* Many children are not interested in the product of their paintings. At this stage they are interested in the process.

Safety

* Children should be discouraged from walking around with pencils or brushes in their mouths – in case they fall and injure themselves or someone else.
* Mop up any major water spills quickly to avoid floors becoming slippery.

HOW TO ENCOURAGE EXPLORATION AND INVESTIGATION THROUGH PLAY

Babies and young children learn about their world through their senses and by exploring objects around them. Their interaction with a wide range of objects helps them to develop the basic concepts of shape, colour, size, weight, texture, sound and many others. As mentioned in relation to displays, providing children with interesting objects in their environment is an important way to encourage curiosity, experimentation and problem-solving skills.

Providing interest objects

Safety must be the first consideration.

Avoid objects that:

* are damaged (unless they are natural objects)
* are made from toxic materials
* are too fragile to be handled
* are too heavy
* have small pieces

Choose objects that:

* are appropriate for the age/stage of children
* link to a topic/theme or concept

* are sufficiently robust for children to handle
* can be investigated through the senses.

If you choose to provide objects that may be delicate (e.g. a wasps' nest, pine cones or shells) then it is important to set some guidelines for handling them. If they really are too fragile then allow children to use magnifying glasses to look at them or to touch the object while it is under the control of an adult. Even quite young children will understand this if they are given an explanation.

* Using simple pictorial signs (e.g. of a hand with a tick through it or a hand with a large cross through it) to indicate whether objects may be handled or not will be clearer than a written sign saying 'Do not touch'.
* Objects from the past can stimulate children's interest and help them develop an understanding of history. For example, collections of electrical appliances – irons, kettles, toasters, radios, etc. – can be used to help them relate their grandparents' and parents' lives to their own experiences.
* Objects that represent everyday aspects of other cultures can provide the same links. Encouraging children to bring objects from home is an ideal way of maintaining positive links with their families, raising self-esteem and valuing their home life.

Ideas for collections of objects

* **Natural objects:** leaves, nuts, seeds, flowers, twigs, pieces of bark, stones, pebbles, shells.
* **Shiny objects:** safety mirrors (card), spoons, foil wrappers, 'silver' or 'gold' items.
* **Different materials:** soft ones (e.g. velvet, fur (artificial), cotton wool,

velour, towelling); rough ones (e.g. sandpaper, sacking, brick, brushes with stiff bristles).

* **Items connected with a season:** for example, clothing, related activities (buckets and spades, sunglasses or umbrellas, etc.).
* **Items from home connected to a theme:** baby toys, photos, favourite books, etc.

ORGANISING THE PLAY ENVIRONMENT

Children need both outdoor and indoor play from an early age. Many of the materials can be set out both indoors and outdoors. Babies and toddlers benefit from:

* **personal spaces** – e.g. toddlers can sit on a mat with objects for **heuristic play** (play with objects made up of everyday items, such as paper plate, bath sponge, nail brush, spoon); check these for safety
* **interesting sounds** (sturdy musical instruments)
* **books** that can be chewed and sucked
* **comfortable flooring** to crawl over, which is a mixture of carpets and other surfaces
* **outdoor play** – exploring grass to fall on and fall over on for beginning walkers
* **stable furniture** to pull themselves up and cruise between
* **push and pull toys**
* **messy play** with paints, water, sand, dough
* **wooden building blocks**
* **large foam building blocks**
* **toys** that are good to hold, shake and bang.

Most 2 year olds will enjoy being in these areas most of the time. However, they will need especially alert adults to support their play so that they feel secure, have a sense of well-being and remain confident. It is important to have a range of provisions. In this way the adult can find something to suit younger or less experienced children, or can help a child with a disability to use the areas.

This is called an **inclusive** approach. It means the general play environment is planned to be suitable for a variety of play needs, ages and stages, as well as children with disabilities.

PROVIDING INCLUSIVE PLAY OPPORTUNITIES

Children 2 to 3 years:

* are easily frustrated, however they can concentrate well if they are allowed to make choices and decide what they do; otherwise, their concentration will last for only a few minutes
* enjoy using wheeled trucks to sit in and be pulled along, and to sit on and scoot with feet on the ground
* will not share easily with other children, so there need to be enough boxes, hats, toy cars, tea set pieces, wooden blocks, and so on, or there will be fights.

Children 3 to 5 years:

* will use the area without so much adult support; even so, adults will need to make sure that children feel confident as they move about indoors and outdoors
* enjoy using tricycles with pedals; a few children may manage to use two-wheeled bicycles
* a child who is a wheelchair user can join in wheeled play in the zone where children have space to go fast and feel freedom of movement together
* it is important to think about progression in play, so that you challenge children to learn through their play

* there need to be zones where children have enough space to use wheeled toys safely
* other areas need to be available where children can play without these so that they don't have to worry about being knocked over; this means dividing the outdoor area into wheeled truck zones and other areas where children are not allowed to take wheeled trucks or bikes.

HOW PLAY DEVELOPS WITH ADULT SUPPORT

In most of Europe children's play is supported, encouraged and extended with the help of adults throughout the first eight years of life. This is because play is an important and central way in which children learn.

* From **birth to 2 years** the foundations of imaginative play are being laid.
* From **2 to 3 years** children need to stay near their special adults. Some early years settings make sure that each child has an adult or **key person** who stays especially alert to their needs.
* Between **2 and 4 years** imaginative play develops. Children in most parts of the world use the theme of food preparation in their play. They begin to pretend to be other people (role play) and they make up stories that they act out. Their play stories are often about everyday living, although monsters do appear quite often. Their play has simple themes, and children find it hard to play these out in large groups. They find it easier in pairs, or when playing alone with small world (for instance, doll's house, farm, garage or zoo).
* Between **3 and 5 years** children are beginning to have friends who they enjoy playing with. If their special friend is away, they may not be so confident

about playing as they are when their friend is there.
* From **5 to 8 years** play will flourish if it is encouraged to do so. The characters children pretend to be go beyond everyday life, and are often from story books or TV programmes, and so are the storylines (narratives) the children develop. They begin to be able to play out their themes in a larger group (often of three or four children) with lots of chasing about, leading and following each other. Play shows increasingly elaborate themes that are about very important areas, such as evil. They love to play goodies and baddies, kind or cruel people, and monsters that invade or ghosts that haunt. This is because, by this stage of development in their play, they can begin to move from the here and now (the present time) and go beyond to thinking about time in the past or future. Themes include the following.
* **'Here and now'** play themes cover settings from hospitals, clinics, libraries, outings on boats and to parks, stories in books, shopping and markets.
* **Beyond the here and now in time and space themes** include 'the olden days' such as King Arthur, Captain Hook, Princesses and Princes, exploring outer space or rainforests, or deserts, shipwrecks on islands, and so on.

Physical play also develops so that children become more coordinated and can play on two-wheeled bikes, rollerblades or with skipping ropes. Because they have more control of their bodies, they can play on more elaborate bits of equipment. This is why they introduce writing and cards into their play; for example, in offices, shops or hairdressing salons. Children at this age need to feel in control of the equipment they use when they play.

Unit 5

Communication and Professional Skills within Child Care and Education

Contents

Unit 5 is divided into three sections:

Section 1: How to develop effective communication skills

Section 2: The development of professional skills

Section 3: Employment opportunities and routes of progression

Section 1

How to develop effective communication skills

The cornerstone of work in child care and education is effective communication – or interpersonal interaction. You need to be able to communicate effectively with a wide range of other people:

* **children**
* children's **parents, families** and **carers**
* **colleagues and managers**
* different **professionals** (e.g. teachers, doctors, nurses, social workers).

These may be **one-to-one** interactions, with a child or a parent, or **group** interactions, such as activities with children, case conferences and staff meetings.

Good communication involves **listening, questioning, understanding** and **responding**.

It is important to remember that there is more to communication than the words being spoken. It also involves:

* **facial expressions**
* **body language** (posture and actions or gestures), which helps to convey meaning
* **tone of voice**, which can, in itself, alter the meaning of what has been said (e.g. the tone used to say our name instantly tells us whether we are in trouble, being appealed to or just having our attention drawn – particularly if it is our parent talking!)
* **pauses**
* **turn-taking**.

It is thought that more than 70 per cent of messages are conveyed through non-verbal ways.

It is also important to:

* take account of culture and context – for example, where English is an additional language
* build a rapport by showing understanding, respect and honesty.

DEVELOPING GOOD COMMUNICATION SKILLS

The most important skill that will improve communication is that of being approachable, and of being a 'good listener'. Some people are easy to talk to, while others seem to put up a barrier. There are people who possess these skills naturally, but don't despair if you're not one of them! It is possible to learn the skills that will improve your ability to communicate with other people. These include:

* respect for other people's beliefs and views
* establishing boundaries by managing expectations
* showing interest in the individual
* using appropriate body language
* active listening
* conveying warmth
* conveying understanding
* conveying sincerity
* conveying the positive value of others
* seeking feedback, paraphrasing and reflection.

Respect for other people's beliefs and views

We all have different ideas about how we conduct our lives. It is inevitable that each early years practitioner will encounter many people with vastly different backgrounds, beliefs and outlooks on life. Regardless of your own views, you should always respect the views of others. This involves:

* not passing judgement on the way other people live
* avoiding stereotyping people on the basis of age, sex or ethnicity (or colour)
* not trying to impose your views onto others.

Only if people feel that their individual values and beliefs are respected will they develop the confidence to express themselves freely and to make choices.

Establishing boundaries

All organisations operate within some set of boundaries or limits, which determines the extent of their willingness and ability to respond. People generally feel very uneasy and anxious if they don't know exactly what is expected of them. Think about situations at school or college when you felt uncomfortable in a lesson or lecture – perhaps because you were not sure if you were going to be chosen to answer a question. If you had been fully prepared, you would not have felt quite so anxious. Establishing boundaries within early years settings might include:

* an explanation of policies and procedures (e.g. arrangements on trips and outings)
* acceptable behaviour and ways of dealing with unacceptable behaviour
* your role in preserving confidentiality.

Showing interest in the individual

It is vital to try to establish a **rapport** with children and their parents, and with work colleagues. This can be achieved by:

* being patient and showing that you have time to listen to their views

* listening carefully to them
* trying to remember their names, likes, dislikes and personal preferences
* asking relevant questions and not suddenly changing the subject
* using **body language** effectively
* sharing personal information (i.e. information about you and your family) when it would contribute to their feeling comfortable with you.

Using appropriate body language

How you sit and use gestures will make a great difference to your interactions with others. To put someone more at ease, adopt an **open posture**: sit with your arms apart, hands open, legs uncrossed and slightly apart, leaning forward – with your body fully facing the other person. This shows that you are ready to communicate and that you are interested in what the other person has to say.

Active listening

On the whole we are poor listeners. Research shows that we tend to listen in 30-second spurts before losing attention. We tend only to hear items that we are interested in and not attend to others. If we are bored and if we dislike the speaker's personality, mannerisms, accent or appearance, we may 'switch off' and follow more interesting thoughts of our own.

Active listening – the listening required in any care relationship – calls for concentration; it is hard work and tiring. The following skills are crucial to active listening.

* **Eye contact:** typically, the interviewee, the person talking, looks away at times, then looks back now and then to check that the interviewer is still attending. The

listener's eye contact tends to be stronger.

*   **Posture:** the listener should keep the body and hands neat and relaxed. An occasional nod acts as positive reinforcement (i.e. it can encourage the other person when he or she is saying something useful or helpful).
*   **Interview skills:** the '5Wh test' is a useful standby formula to obtain information in a fact-finding interview. This acronym stands for sentences that start with 'Wh':
    *   Why? (use this sparingly)
    *   Who?
    *   What?
    *   When?
    *   Where?
    *   How? (a sixth useful question).

Sensitive use of these key words can draw out a lot of basic information.

Example

A parent tells you that they are worried because their child refuses to eat properly at home. Try asking: *What* is the problem? *When* did it start? *Who* could help? *Where* should we begin to sort it out? *How* have you managed so far?

Conveying warmth

Conveying warmth in the initial stages of an interview or meeting is very important. The person may have personal information to reveal and may well decide not to do so if the early years practitioner is in any way cold and rejecting.

Warmth may be conveyed *non-verbally* by:

*   a warm smile (facial expression)
*   open, welcoming gestures
*   a friendly tone of voice
*   a confident manner
*   your general appearance.

Conveying understanding

An early years practitioner conveys understanding through empathy, acceptance and a non-judgemental attitude. These are all-important values that underpin child care and education.

Understanding is also conveyed where the practitioner shows knowledge and acceptance of the particular physical, intellectual and social needs of the individual.

Conveying sincerity

Warmth, understanding and sincerity are all conveyed primarily by the use of **eye contact**, which shows interest and attention. Sincerity is also conveyed by reassuring the person that all information is strictly confidential.

Conveying the positive value of others

Healthy personal development occurs through forming relationships that provide us with affection, love or respect from others. Such positive regard is *unconditional*: it does not matter how badly we behave, we are still loved just for being ourselves. If we *do* receive unconditional positive regard then we would also give *ourselves* unconditional positive regard – in other words, we will have high **self-esteem** or self-worth. If our parents love us *conditionally*, perhaps only showing affection when we behave well or do well at school, we will constantly seek approval from others as we grow into adulthood.

Conveying the positive value of others may be done by using the following *non-verbal* signals:

*   smiling
*   calm movements

* listening skills
* eye contact
* open gestures.

Both verbally and non-verbally the positive value of others may be shown through:

* empathy
* freedom from any type of stereotyping or discrimination
* conveying warmth, understanding and sincerity
* assurance of confidentiality, with its boundaries explained
* acceptance and a non–judgemental attitude
* respect for the individual.

Seeking feedback, paraphrasing and reflection

(Please see Section 2, pages 171–172, for information on reflective practice.)

EMPATHETIC LISTENING

Empathy means being able to 'project' yourself into the other person's situation and experience, in order to understand them as fully as possible. Early years practitioners need to be able to listen with sympathy and understanding, and give support at the appropriate time. They also need to be able to encourage people who lack confidence that other people will value what they say.

COMMUNICATING WITH OTHERS

Communicating with parents

You will find that there are many occasions when you are responsible for passing information clearly to parents. But parents will want to talk, as well as listen, to you. You will need to develop listening skills. Try to set a particular time for parents so that they do not take your attention when you are involved with the children. For some parents this can be very difficult to arrange, especially if they are working.

Communicating with children

How parents and other significant adults speak to children is extremely important. When talking with children, we tend to:

* emphasise key words
* slow our speech down
* repeat phrases if the child has not understood
* add gestures and expressions to help them understand the meaning.

This is an example of 'scaffolding' children's learning. When talking with babies, adults often talk in 'motherese' or 'parentese'; this means they speak slowly, in a higher-pitched voice than usual, and use a lot of repetition (e.g. 'cootchie, cootchie coo'). Many people use this sort of 'baby talk' unconsciously when talking to very young babies – and often to their pets too!

Good communication helps children develop confidence, feelings of self-worth and good relationships with others. It also helps them grow into adults who have good feelings about themselves and others.

It must be a **two-way process**. It is not just about you telling children something or giving advice, but rather listening to their viewpoints and accepting their emotions.

NON-VERBAL COMMUNICATION: HOW CHILDREN COMMUNICATE WITHOUT WORDS

From birth, babies are primed to learn; they learn about **body language** and non-verbal cues by observing and imitating other

GUIDELINES FOR COMMUNICATING WELL WITH PARENTS

- Maintaining eye contact helps you to give your full attention to a parent.
- Remember that your body language shows how you really feel.
- Try not to interrupt when someone is talking to you. Nod and smile instead.
- Every so often, summarise the main points of a discussion, so that you are both clear about what has been said.
- If you do not know the answer to a parent's question, say so, and that you will find out. Then, do not forget to do this!
- Remember that different cultures have different traditions. Touching and certain gestures might be seen as insulting by some parents, so be careful.
- If the parent speaks a different language from you, use photographs and visual aids. Talk slowly and clearly.

- If the parent has a hearing impairment, use sign language or visual aids.
- When you are talking together, bear in mind whether this is the parent's first child or whether they have had other children already.
- Remember that if the parents have a child with a disability, they may need to see you more often to discuss the child's progress.
- If the parent has a disability, make sure that when you sit together you are at the same level.
- Occasionally, parents might become upset and will shout at you. If this happens, do not shout back. Simply talk quietly and calmly, and show that you are listening to them.
- Never gossip.

people. One of the first conscious facial expressions learned by a baby is the **smile**; this is because adults tend to smile at infants a great deal. Other baby body language includes:

* kicking and waving arms to show happiness
* turning away – and even shuddering – from an unpleasant taste
* banging on a high chair to get attention
* peering around the sofa to persuade the adult to play a game of hide and seek.

The range of gestures and expressions used before verbal communication takes over expands as the child becomes more mobile and inquisitive.

Toddlers

Examples of body language used by **toddlers** include:

* pointing
* touching
* reaching out a hand
* making eye contact
* shaking or nodding the head
* pushing something or someone away
* pulling something or someone closer.

Although this sort of body language is used with adults and with other children, it tends to be more obvious and forceful with other toddlers. For example, if Cara, aged 2, wants the toy that Anna is playing with, she will probably simply walk over and take it away from her!

Children aged 3 years to school age

Children show the same sort of non-verbal behaviour as before, but they develop their communication further by adding in **words**. For example, they may:

* point to a toy and ask to play with it rather than simply taking it
* move towards someone who is hanging back and invite him or her to come and join in their play
* hug other children and squeal excitedly
* sulk and pout to show their disappointment or anger.

Children still rely a great deal on body language – as do adults – but they are now able to combine verbal *and* non-verbal methods to express themselves and get what they want.

INTERPRETING CHILDREN'S BODY LANGUAGE

Young children often express themselves physically when they don't have enough words to say what they want or need. When children are frustrated or excited their body language takes over. For example:

* a child attempting to tell a lie will have trouble making eye contact; they may hang their head, or otherwise appear unsure of themselves
* a child who is feeling frustrated or misunderstood may cry, hit out at others, or show some other expression of aggravation and frustration
* a child who is very excited about a forthcoming event may jump up and down or rush around.

How you can help

You need to pay close attention to your *own* non-verbal messages and adapt them accordingly to best meet the needs of children. You can help children in the following ways.

* **Making eye contact:** give your attention to the child, and use a friendly facial expression; this will make the child

feel that he or she is important to you, and that you are respectful of his or her needs.
* **Teaching them how to manage their emotions**, control their impulses and express feelings of anger with words.
* **Talking them gently through** the experience when they have just had a tantrum.
* **Questioning the child sensitively:** try to find out what he or she was feeling. You could ask 'Did you feel sad?', 'Were you frightened?' or 'Were you angry?' Children need to be taught how to 'label' and manage their feelings – especially anger.
* **Get down to their level:** if the child has been aggressive – punching, biting or kicking others – try to prompt them to think about how they would feel if someone else had done the same thing to them.

ACTIVITIES WHICH ENCOURAGE CHILDREN TO LISTEN AND TO TALK

Children need to be encouraged to **learn through play** and to focus on a task rather than on practising a language item. They need:

* to enjoy themselves
* to pretend
* to feel they can speak the language quickly.

The following activities all encourage children to listen and talk to others.

Role play

Children enjoy being someone else and acting out a situation – for example, at the shop, at the Post Office, driving a car. Children naturally use role play in their own language situations.

GUIDELINES: HOW TO COMMUNICATE WITH CHILDREN

- Make **eye contact** and show that you are listening – it is very difficult to have a conversation with someone who never looks at you! When talking with very young children, it is usually necessary to stoop down to their level or to sit at a table with them.

- **Listen carefully** to the child's own spoken language and use it as a basis for conversation – very young children tend to use one or two words to mean any of a number of things (e.g. 'drink' can mean 'This is my drink', 'I want a drink', 'Where is my drink?' or 'You have got a drink').

- **Repeat** the child's words in a correct form or a complete sentence. This checks understanding and provides the child with an accurate model for the future. For example, young children often use speech such as 'feeded' instead of 'fed', 'runned' instead of 'ran'. In checking what they mean the adult should use the correct term. For example, *Child:* 'I feeded carrots to my rabbit' *Adult:* 'Oh, you fed your rabbit some carrots.'

- **Be a good role model**, speak clearly yourself and use correct grammar and patterns of speech.

- **Use open-ended questions:** encourage children to speak by asking 'open' questions that require an answer in phrases and/or sentences rather than a simple 'yes' or 'no'. For example, 'Tell me about your party' instead of 'Did you have a good time at your party?' This opens up opportunities for the child to talk about a range of different things or one single event of his/her own choice – you can always ask more questions as the conversation progresses to check the information, supply additional vocabulary and correct grammar.

- **Use prompts:** these invite the child to say more, and to share ideas and feelings. They also tell the child that you are really listening and interested, that her ideas are important, and that you accept her and respect what she is saying. Examples of prompts are 'Oh, I see', 'Tell me more', 'That's interesting.'

- **Listen attentively:** get rid of distractions and pay attention to what the child is saying. At times, adults may need to stop whatever they are doing and listen to the child. It is difficult to pay close attention to what the child is saying if you are busy trying to read at the same time.

- **Respond sensitively:** remember the importance of **non-verbal communication**. Watch out for when a child seems upset or looks sad – say, 'You seem upset – do you want to tell me about it?'

- **Say 'please' and 'thank you' to children:** children deserve the common courtesies that we – as adults – use with each other. Children will learn by imitating the speech and behaviour of adults.

- **Use kind words to help promote self-esteem:** kind words give children more self-confidence and help them to behave better, try harder and achieve more. They communicate love and respect, and also create an atmosphere in which problems can be discussed openly and understandings can be reached. For example, the child has spilt her orange juice on the floor. You could say, 'Don't be so clumsy! Just look at the mess you made.' But it would be better to say, 'Here's a cloth. Please wipe the juice up' and, later, 'Thank you for doing such a good job of cleaning the floor.'

- **Don't use unkind words which put children down:** unkind words make the child feel bad, and they prevent good communication. Avoid unkind words which:
  - *ridicule* the child (e.g. 'You're acting just like a baby')
  - *shame* the child (e.g. 'I'm so ashamed of you')

– *label* the child (e.g. 'You're a naughty boy').

Unkind words, spoken without thinking of their results, make the child feel disliked and result in low self-esteem. More importantly, unkind words do not help – they only make matters worse.

- **Always be positive:** tell children what *to do* instead of what *not to do*. For example, instead of 'Don't slam the door!' try 'Please shut the door quietly.' Instead of 'Don't spill your drink!' say 'Try holding your beaker with both hands.'

Story telling

This is a natural way to help increase a child's vocabulary. Choose stories with repetition like 'The Three Little Pigs' or 'The Very Hungry Caterpillar'.

Puppets and props

Children often use puppets or dolls to express themselves verbally, and props like masks or dressing-up clothes help them to act out roles in their own pretend play.

Games and puzzles

Children quickly learn to use the language necessary to take part in simple games, such as 'I spy' or 'Spot the difference'.

Songs and rhymes

These help children to learn new words in an enjoyable way.

FACTORS THAT PARTICULARLY AFFECT LANGUAGE DEVELOPMENT AND/OR COMMUNICATION

These include:

* any hearing impairments – permanent or temporary

* physical impairments such as cleft palate and hare lip
* stammers and stutters
* other medical conditions that affect other aspects of development and, as a consequence, a child's confidence or self-esteem
* disorders that affect learning, such as autism
* an additional language – children's home language must be valued; adults should recognise that these children are, most likely, competent communicators at home and need support to develop an additional vocabulary that, for the very young child, may apply only in the early childhood setting
* lack of language input (conversations) with an interested adult or good role model
* emotional factors that can result in shyness, low self-esteem and a lack of confidence.

SPEAKING AND LISTENING ACTIVITIES IN GROUP SETTINGS

These range from individual conversations between adult and child to whole class/group 'news' times. In addition, there are many games and activities that provide ideal opportunities for children to use and

As you may expect, young children *understand* more than they can *express* themselves. They may be able to follow simple instructions (especially if they are accompanied by a gesture, like pointing), such as 'Give daddy a kiss' or 'Fetch your teddy' long before they can use sentences themselves. They learn new words – initially the names of objects and important people – by listening carefully and copying. Many words that have unstressed syllables – such as 'important' and 'computer' – are learned as 'portant' and 'puter' because these are the sounds that they are able to hear easily.

practise their speaking and listening skills. For very young children, sharing rhymes – traditional nursery, finger and action – songs and books with an adult is both valuable and enjoyable.

As language develops and listening skills develop, older children will be able to play games that involve 'active' listening, such as those listed below.

* **'What (or who) am I?'** This involves the adult (or a child – perhaps with help) giving clues until the animal/person/object is identified. For example, 'I have sharp teeth. I have a long tail. I have a striped coat. I eat meat.' Answer: a tiger or a tabby cat.

* **Taped sounds:** these can be environmental (kettle boiling, doorbell, someone eating crisps) or related to a particular topic (farm animals, pet animals, machines) or be of familiar people's voices.

* **Taped voices:** reception or Year 1 children tape their own voices giving clues about themselves but without saying who they are. For example, 'I have brown eyes. I have two brothers. I have a Lion King lunchbox. I have short, dark hair. Who am I?' This activity is best done with a small group so they are not guessing from among the whole class! They find it difficult not to say their names but love hearing themselves and

their friends. The enjoyment factor makes it valuable and ensures concentrated listening once the excitement has died down.

* **Feely box:** use varied objects for children to feel (without being able to see) and encourage them to describe the shape, size, texture, surface, etc. This can be topic-related (e.g. fruit or solid shapes). A very good activity for extending children's vocabulary.

* **'Snowball'** games that involve active listening and memory. For example, 'I went to market and I bought . . .'. There are many versions of this. It can be used for number (1 cabbage, 2 bananas, 3 flannels, etc.) or to reinforce the alphabet (an apple, a budgie, a crane . . .) or topic related (food items, transport items, clothing, etc.).

* **Chinese whispers:** this is appropriate for older children, who are more able to wait patiently for their turn.

* **Circle activities:** in which children and adult/s sit in a circle and a 'special' object is held by the person who is speaking. Rules are that only the person holding the object is allowed to speak – the object is passed around in turn or to whoever wants to say something (adult supervision needed!). Alternatively a large ball can be rolled across the circle and the person rolling the ball makes his/her contribution (this can be on a

theme – favourite foods/colours/games, etc.) and the person who receives the ball makes the next contribution.

These activities encourage children to take turns, to use language to express their thoughts, feelings and ideas, and to gain confidence as communicators. The circle activities are particularly good for encouraging shy or withdrawn children who may not otherwise get a word in – literally!

MULTI-AGENCY WORKING

Multi-agency working is about different services, agencies and teams of professionals and other staff working together to provide the services that fully meet the needs of children, young people and their parents or carers.? Practitioners share a sense of team identity and are generally line-managed by the team leader, though they may maintain links with their home agencies through supervision and training. Features of multi-agency teams include:

* there is a dedicated team leader
* there is a good mix of education, health, social care, youth justice and youth work staff
* the people who work in the team think of themselves as team members; they are recruited or seconded into the team, either full- or part-time
* the team engages in work with universal services and at a range of levels – not just with individual children and young people, but also small-group, family and whole-school work
* the team is likely to share a base, though some staff may continue to work from their home agencies
* there are regular team meetings to discuss case working as well as administrative issues.

One example of a multi-agency team is a BEST.

Behaviour and Education Support Teams (BESTs)

These are multi-agency teams bringing together a complementary mix of professionals from the fields of health, social care and education. The aim of a BEST is to promote emotional well-being, positive behaviour and school attendance, by identifying and supporting those with, or at risk of developing, emotional and behavioural problems. BESTs:

* work with children and young people aged 5–18, their families and schools, to intervene early and prevent problems developing further
* work in targeted primary and secondary schools, and in the community, alongside a range of other support structures and services
* have a minimum of four to five staff members, who between them have a complementary mix of education, social care and health skills in order to meet the multi-faceted needs of children, young people and their parents.

A typical team may include the following professionals:

* behaviour support staff
* clinical psychologists
* education welfare officers
* educational psychologists
* health visitors
* primary mental health workers
* school nurses
* social workers/family workers
* speech and language therapists.

Schools with BESTs include those with high proportions of pupils with, or at risk of developing, behavioural problems, usually demonstrated in levels of exclusion and attendance.

Another example of multi-agency working is **Early Support** – services for disabled children in early years. Early Support is the central government mechanism for achieving better-coordinated family-focused services for very young disabled children (under 3) and their families. Families receive coordinated support through key worker systems, better sharing of information between agencies, family support plans and family-held records.

To work successfully on a multi-agency basis you need to:

* be clear about your own role
* be aware of the roles of other professionals
* be confident about your own standards and targets, and
* be respectful of those that apply to other services.

Each profession has its own jargon and set of rules. You do not need to know about these in depth, but should always be willing to learn from other professionals and to respect the contribution of others working with children, young people and families.

THE IMPORTANCE OF CONFIDENTIALITY

Confidentiality is very important when working in early years settings. You will be entrusted with personal information about children and their families, and it is important that you do not abuse this trust. You should never gossip about parents or their children, and never discuss one parent with another.

Sharing information

Some information *does* have to be shared, but only with your line manager. For example, if you suspect there may be a child protection issue, this should be shared with your line manager in strictest confidence. Parents need

to be aware of this policy from the outset of your partnership so that they understand that, although they may tell you things in confidence, you may have to share the information with your line manager. It is not fair to encourage parents to talk about confidential things with you unless they first understand this.

Some information has to be shared with the whole staff team, such as information about diet, allergy and if the child is being collected by someone else. Make sure parents are clear about the sort of information that *cannot* be confidential.

Section 2

The development of professional skills

PERSONAL AND PROFESSIONAL DEVELOPMENT

There are many skills involved in working with and caring for children and young people that all adults need. These include:

* experience and the support to reflect and learn from experience
* confidence and the ability to respond in the best possible ways to individual children
* really knowing about the child, trusting that knowledge and the judgements that are based on it
* being prepared to learn from the child – for example, by listening to what a child tells you and observing what they do.

Working in the field of child care and education can be physically and emotionally exhausting, and professionals will need to consolidate their skills and develop the ability to be **reflective** in their practice. You also need to be able to give and receive feedback; this is a skill that needs to be practised in order for it to be effective for both parties.

THE IMPORTANCE OF SETTING TARGETS

Setting targets – or goals – as part of a learning **Action Plan** will help you to get more involved in your learning. Remember, your targets are personal – they may be quite different from those of others in your class.

Learning targets can help you to:

* decide what is most important to you in your learning
* fit your studies in with your other commitments
* decide on how you will study
* become an active learner
* think about your personal and professional development.

Your learning targets should:

* include a **time-scale** to show when they should be completed; you could identify a final goal and then break down the steps towards achieving that goal into **short-term** and **medium-term** targets
* identify **success criteria** – to show how you will know when have achieved a target

* be **realistic**
* be **relevant to you**.

HOW TO KEEP A PLACEMENT DIARY

The practice evidence diary for this CACHE Level 2 course is very important. Your tutor will explain how to complete the practical tasks in the Diary – all of which relate directly to the **practice evidence records** (PERs), which you will use to show competence in your placements.

There are **four** Diary tasks for Unit 3, **three** for Unit 4 and **one** for Unit 6. The Practice Evidence Diary will give you the opportunity to demonstrate your skills in evaluation and reflection. It will also give you the opportunity to show your understanding of the practical skills you have gained in placement.

Evaluating your own performance

Self-evaluation is important because it helps you to improve your own practice and to modify plans to meet the learning needs of the children.

Reflective practice

You should get used to reviewing and reflecting on your experiences as part of

ACTIVITY: USING TARGETS FOR PERSONAL AND PROFESSIONAL DEVELOPMENT

1. Write down in two or three sentences what you hope to achieve through your course and how you see it helping you in the future.
2. What do you want to be able to do, think, feel, understand or know?
3. How would this learning be recognised by others?
4. What are the steps you need to take to reach the end result?
5. Now write your Action Plan and learning targets based on these ideas and using the notes above as a guide.

your everyday learning. In this way, each experience – whether positive or negative – will contribute to your development and personal growth. Ways to reflect include:

* setting yourself some goals or targets when you start studying, and using your tutor's and your placement supervisor's feedback to monitor your progress
* working out what you've achieved and what you still need to work on
* making a record of your thoughts and reflections to help you to keep track of your ideas and see how far they've developed over a period of time
* recording your thoughts on any difficulties or challenges you are facing
* talking things through with another person, such as another student or a trusted friend.

Using **reflective practice** will help you to review and evaluate your own practice. Reflective general and specific questions will help to organise this evaluation. For example:

* Was your contribution to the planning meeting appropriate?
* Did you achieve your targets? If not, was it because the targets were unrealistic?
* What other methods could be used?
* How can I improve my practice?
* Who can I ask for advice and support?
* How can I help a child to settle in again after his hospital stay?
* What is making a child behave inappropriately at mealtimes?

Using feedback to improve your practice

Feedback is structured information that one person offers to another, about the impact of their actions or behaviour – in other words, how you are doing in your study or work role. It is vital to the success of most workplace tasks, and is an activity we engage in on a daily basis. Feedback should not be confused with *criticism*, which is often an unprepared reaction to people who aren't behaving in the way you want them to; criticism can make the recipient feel undervalued or angry – both unproductive emotions.

The information you hear when receiving feedback from others may be new – and even surprising. You may react with strong emotion. Good feedback is an offer of information, not a diagnosis of your character or potential, so you should not react angrily or 'take it too personally'.

Receiving feedback can:

* help you become aware of how you are getting on – the good and the bad, what's working and what isn't
* give you some ideas to help you plan your own development, in order to reach your full potential
* give you a 'reality check' – you can compare how you think you are, with what other people tell you.

Feedback from a number of different people helps you make a balanced decision about the information you are hearing. (Remember – not everyone has good feedback skills; you are likely to get a mixed quality of feedback – some perceptive and supportive, some critical and unspecific.)

PLANNING AND KEEPING ACCURATE RECORDS

You may be asked to plan an activity to implement in your work setting – for example, a story-telling session using props (see page 167 for ideas and guidance). Some work settings involve the whole team in planning a curriculum for the children; these plans can be made for the whole term, for three or four weeks, or even on a daily basis. Records are kept in all work settings; these

GUIDELINES FOR RECEIVING FEEDBACK

1. **Ask questions:** state what you want feedback about. Be specific about what you want to know. Give the speaker time to think about what they want to say.
2. **Listen:** listen attentively – don't interrupt or digress. Ask for clarification if you're not sure you've understood what you've heard. Try not to be defensive or to reject the information. You need to listen, but not necessarily to agree. Take notes of what is said.
3. **Check:** check what you've heard. Repeat back what they have said and ask for

examples of what the speaker means. Give your reactions to the feedback or ask for time to think about it if necessary. Ask for suggestions on what might work better.

4. **Reflect:** feedback is information for you to use – it is not a requirement to change. If you are unsure about the soundness of the feedback, check it out with other people. Work out the options open to you and decide what you want to do. It is up to you to **evaluate** how accurate and how useful the feedback is.

may be general information and attendance records or more detailed records about each child's progress. You need to be aware of your role in completing records, such as the Accident Report Book (see Unit 3).

ACCESSING SUPPORT TO REVIEW YOUR PROGRESS AND ACHIEVEMENTS

Work with an appropriate person, such as your tutor or placement supervisor, to give your opinions and develop an **individual learning plan** that includes:

* **targets** that clearly show what you want to achieve in your learning, work or personal life, and how you will know if you have met these
* the **actions** you will take (action points) and dates for completing them (deadlines) to help you meet each target
* how to get the support you need, including who will review your progress, and where and when this will take place.

Your **tutor** will help you to discuss your progress; he or she will enable you to reflect

on *what* you learned, *how* you learned, and *what* has gone well and what has not gone so well. You should also aim to:

* **identify the targets** you have met, by checking your plan to see if you have done what you set out to do
* **identify your achievements** – check what you need to do to improve your performance (the quality of your work, and the way you work)
* **use ways of learning** suggested by your tutor or supervisor, making changes, when needed, to improve your performance.

The effect of your own background, life history and experiences on your practice

Your **personal development** includes your own 'growth' as a person.

* Your experiences at work and at home can change your attitudes, priorities and ambitions.
* Changes in home circumstances influence decisions you make about your work – for example, the hours you work,

where you work and the level of responsibility you take on. If you are without family responsibilities you may welcome the extra challenge of a training course to develop your career. However, if you have to strike a balance between career and home life and additional time is not available for training then this might seem a burden.

* Sometimes a personal interest will influence the course of your professional development. You may, personally, become interested in working with children with physical difficulties – perhaps you have become involved with the disabled child of friends – and would like to find a job in that field. The opportunity to gain experience or training would benefit you both personally and professionally.

An important part of your personal development is self-awareness. **Self-awareness** means:

* knowing who you are and what you enjoy doing
* being able to recognise your skills, strengths and weaknesses
* being able to recognise your effect on other people.

Key areas for self-awareness include our personality traits, personal values, habits and emotions.

Self-awareness helps you exploit your strengths and cope with your weaknesses. The process of being self-aware can be uncomfortable when you realise that something you have done or said has had a negative impact on someone else. However, unless we face such self-awareness we can never really develop and improve our practice. What is important here is that you have a network of **colleagues** that you can call upon for support and guidance should you require it.

Self-awareness is also crucial for developing good interpersonal skills and building effective relationships with children and their families. Additionally, being self-aware allows you to identify your own **learning needs** and the ways in which they can be met – and then it is involved in your **evaluation** of whether those needs have been met.

It is also important that we be **non-judgemental**. It is easy to criticise others and to believe that you would approach things in a better way. However, parents can learn to trust you only if they know that you are not judging their actions.

Section 3
Employment opportunities and routes of progression

WHERE NOW? CAREER PROGRESSION

You will have worked hard to obtain the Level 2 Award/Certificate/Diploma in Child Care and Education and can then look forward to developing your career with children. This is called professional development and is important because it:

* enables you to develop greater knowledge and understanding in connection with your work
* offers opportunities to improve skills or gain new ones
* can enable you to experience new situations
* can prepare you for different roles and responsibilities.

You may decide to progress to the **CACHE Level 3 Diploma in Child Care and**

THE PUBLIC SECTOR		
Local Education Authority	**Local Government Services**	**Health Authority**
Areas of work Nursery schools State nurseries Infant, lower and primary schools Schools for children with special needs	**Areas of work** Family Centres Children's Centres (run by Social Services) Holiday Playschemes	**Areas of work** Health visiting in the community Hospitals Hospital crèches and nurseries Adventure Centres and One O'clock Clubs
Types of job Nursery trained teacher Nursery assistant Classroom assistant Special needs classroom assistant	**Types of job** Nursery assistant in Family Centres and Children's Day Care Nurseries Playworker in Holiday Playschemes and Adventure Centres	**Types of job** Health visitor assistant in clinics and in clients' homes Play assistant in hospital children's units Nursery assistant in crèches and nurseries

THE VOLUNTARY SECTOR	
Areas of work Pre-school playgroups After-school clubs Holiday playschemes Nurseries	**Types of job** Nursery assistants After-school club assistants Holiday playscheme workers Playworkers

THE PRIVATE SECTOR	
Areas of work Day nurseries Nursery schools Crèches (in workplaces, shopping centres or sports and leisure centres) Holiday companies: e.g. ski chalets, watersports, cruise ships, hotels Families	**Types of job** Nursery assistants Playworkers or ski nannies Mother's help (looking after children and doing housework) Au pair – usually unqualified in child care; often young people from aboard who live with a family and offer child care services Nanny – usually qualified in child care; may live with the family or live out

Table 5.1: Working in the public, voluntary and private sectors

Education or a **Playwork** course. Some aspects of professional development are dealt with through **training courses**, often organised and paid for by your employer. You may receive the training from a member of your own staff or visit a college or recognised training organisation on a part–time basis. Courses can cover anything from dealing with a particular medical condition to developing ways of improving assessment and record-keeping. It is also important to keep abreast of all the changes in child care practice by reading the relevant journals, such as *Nursery World*, *Early Years Educator* (*EYE*), *Child Education* and *Professional Nanny*.

CACHE Level 2 qualifications provide a stepping stone to Level 3 qualifications. They show that you have a good knowledge and

are applying for, or that demonstrate your flexibility or personal strengths. Any part-time employment, even if it is not related to child care, may show that you have worked as part of a team, been punctual and reliable, handled money and been given responsibility – all of which may be important in a work setting.

There is no single way or format although it is usual to begin with personal details. One suggested example is shown opposite in Fig 5.1, but your tutor will help you compile yours and it may follow a different format.

In addition to the information shown in the example you may indicate your gender (there are many 'unisex' names, e.g. Ashley), state that you are a non-smoker and say whether or not you can drive a car (e.g. 'Full, clean, driving licence since . . . [date when test passed]').

Many employers ask for a letter of application to accompany the CV. It is from these two documents that they decide which applicants to interview for the vacancy. It is important to put time and effort into your application so that you have a chance to 'sell yourself' at an interview.

The interview

Employers have checked through applications and will interview those whom they believe have the right qualifications for the job. However, they are looking for 'the right person' for their particular team of staff, so the interview gives them the opportunity to find out more about you. They are investing their time hoping to complete their team and want all the applicants to do themselves justice. They are not going to ask you 'catch' questions. Similarly, it is your opportunity to find out more about the work setting and the staff, and to decide if they suit you!

* Try to dress neatly, but appropriately for the work setting.

* Check the address and that you know how to get there. Make the journey beforehand if possible, to judge how long it will take.
* Ensure you arrive in plenty of time.
* Try to take notice of what is going on while you are waiting – it may help you make relevant comments or ask appropriate questions during the interview.
* Take placement reports (PDPs), PER and any photographs or samples of children's work to show if there is time.
* During the interview, sit comfortably without slouching.
* Look directly at the interviewer/s when answering questions.
* Try to avoid mumbling and fidgeting (e.g. pushing hair back or fiddling with clothing).
* Refer to your own experiences, giving examples (whenever they are relevant) to demonstrate your understanding.

When writing your letter of application:

* make sure you know the closing date for applications (if there is one)
* use good-quality, plain, A4 paper
* do rough drafts first before copying out in your neatest handwriting, or
* draft it on a word processor, save and edit (use a spell-check) before printing
* always keep a copy of your letter and application form (especially if you are applying for several posts with different employers)
* check you address it to the right person using the correct title ('Madam', or 'Dear Sir'); if you do not know the person's name (e.g. where the advertisement asks you to apply to the manager), end your letter 'Yours faithfully'; address 'Dear Mrs Taylor' (or whatever, if you know the title and name) and end with 'Yours sincerely'; if you only have the full name for a female, e.g. Wendy Taylor, you could address her as 'Dear Ms Taylor'

CURRICULUM VITAE

Name:	Mark Williams	**Date of Birth:** 04/04/1991	
Address:	10 Station Road	**Tel. No:** 01444 765432	
	Castletown		
	Hamptonshire	**Nationality:** Welsh	
	CW1 IAB	**Martital status:** Single	

National Insurance No: AB 1234 5678

Education

September 2007–June 2008: Castletown College of Further Education, College Road, Castletown CW1 7GT

Course: **CACHE Level 2 Diploma in Child Care and Education**

Placement Experience:

September–December 2007	Park Infant School	Age 4/6 yrs	36 days
January–April 2008	Sunny Day Nursery	Age 1/3 yrs	39 days
April–June 2008	Family home	Age 1–4+yrs	20 days

Sept 2002–June 2007: Castletown Community School, Main Road, Castletown CW2 2YZ

Qualifications – GCSE

Subject	Board	Date	Grade
English Language	AQA	June 07	C
English Literature	AQA	June 07	D
Mathematics	OCR	June 07	E
Science (Dual award)	OCR	June 07	E
Technology (Food)	OCR	June 07	C
French	AQA	June 07	F
Drama	AQA	June 07	C
Geography	OCR	June 07	D
History	OCR	June 07	E
Art	OCR	June 07	E

In addition: Duke of Edinburgh bronze award – June 2006; St John Ambulance – Basic First Aid Certificate – April 2007

Work Experience
March 2007 – 2 weeks at Castletown Family Centre Nursery

Employment

September 2007 to date:	Castletown Pet Shop (Saturdays only)	Caring for pets, operating cash machine, dealing with customers.
March 2007 to date:	Mr and Mrs Smith	Casual babysitting for 3 children aged 9, 6 and 4 years.

Interests and hobbies:
I am involved in the local theatre group productions and am also interested in animal welfare.
I help with the St John Ambulance 'Badgers'.

Referees
Ms A. Tutor (personal tutor), Castletown College of Further Education, College Road, Castletown, Hamptonshire CW1 7GT Tel: 01444 987654
Mr H. Jones (St John Ambulance leader), 45 High Street, Castletown, Hamptonshire CW2 8JA Tel: 01444 654321

Fig 5.1. Curriculum vitae

* remember to refer to the post for which you are applying, and state where you saw the advertisement
* explain why you are interested in the post (look carefully at the details and information you have been sent)
* refer to aspects of your course and previous experience which are relevant to the job
* explain how your personal qualities make you suitable for the job
* sign your letter and print your name and title (e.g. Mark Williams, Mr) underneath
* include a stamped SAE if you want an acknowledgement for your application (this helps to prevent you worrying about whether they have received it if you hear nothing for a while!)
* post your application in good time for the closing date.

Some questions that may be asked at interview for a post in a school nursery unit

* As a newly qualified nursery assistant can you tell us about your placement experience with 3 to 5 year olds?

* Describe a planned activity that you thought was successful.
* What do you particularly enjoy about working with this age range?
* What strategies might you use to deal with incidents of unwanted behaviour?
* What personal qualities do you think you have to make you a successful early years worker?
* What do you feel are your particular strengths?
* How do you think you would fit into our team?
* Thinking about confidentiality – children often share their concerns with us. How would you deal with this?
* Would you tell us more about the interests you have listed in your CV?
* Have you any questions?

ACTIVITY: WORKING AS A CHILD CARE PRACTITIONER

1. Make a list of what you consider to be the most important qualities a child care and education practitioner should possess.
2. Explain what type of professional development a child care and education practitioner might expect in his/her first year of employment.
3. Create your own list of ten 'top tips' that you think would be helpful to a child care and education practitioner about to begin his/her first job.

Unit 6

The Child Care Practitioner in the Workplace

Contents

This unit involves your **practical** work with children. You will learn about the professional standards of the practitioner and how to apply these. You will also get the opportunity to observe the ways in which children develop, and to carry out planned play activities.

ACHIEVING UNIT 6

You need to complete three parts in order to achieve Unit 6. These are:

1. placement summary
2. practice evidence records (PERs)
3. professional development profiles (PDPs).

Placement summary

This provides an accurate record of your work placements and must be filled in when you have completed each practical placement.

Practice evidence records (PERs)

When you receive your *Candidate Handbook* at the start of the course, take a look at the **practice evidence records (PERs)** at the end of the book – but don't be alarmed by them! Your tutor will explain what is required of you on placement and will also tell you about the **professional development profiles (PDPs)**. You will receive plenty of support from your tutor and your placements to enable you to complete the necessary paperwork.

* Practice evidence records describe the skills and tasks that you must show you are able to carry out competently (capably and effectively).
* You must show your competence in practical skills in both core age ranges (1 to 3 years 11 months, and 4 to 7 years 11 months).
* There may also be the opportunity to gain experience with babies (birth to 1 year) and with older children (8 to 16 years).
* When you are in your placement you will learn how to do practical things (e.g. set out play materials, supervise outdoor play, prepare snacks), but the

underpinning knowledge – in this book – explains why they are done that way.
* Your placement supervisor, tutor or teacher will sign each practice evidence statement when they are satisfied that you are competent in the particular task or skill described.

Your Practice Evidence Diary

You will also be expected to complete a **Practice Evidence Diary**. Your tutor or teacher will explain how to complete the diary, which can also form a useful part of your portfolio when you continue your career with children. The diary will provide evidence of your ability to evaluate and **reflect** upon your practice through a given task. Each task will have a sheet to be filled in. You are not expected to produce large amounts of written material as these tasks are not assignments and do not have to be referenced.

Professional development profiles (PDPs)

There are nine sections in a professional development profile (PDP). You need to gain a Pass in each section to achieve a satisfactory PDP. If you do not achieve a satisfactory PDP, you will be **referred**. Each placement supervisor will complete a final PDP towards the end of your placement, indicating a Pass or Refer, and will provide comments for each statement. You should make sure that you discuss the outcome with your supervisor and ask how you can improve your work, particularly if you are referred.

In order to achieve an overall Pass in the PDPs you need to complete **two** PDPs satisfactorily (a Pass in each of the nine sections). Each PDP must be completed over a period of at least 20 days, unless it was achieved in a birth to 1 year environment. If, at the end of your course of study, you have not achieved a Pass in the required number of PDPs you will be required to undertake an additional training placement of 25 days for each outstanding PDP.

THE CACHE STATEMENT OF VALUES

The CACHE Statement of Values is a useful tool for checking that you are upholding important child care values (see box).

PLANNING FOR YOUR WORK PLACEMENT

Being well organised will make the many separate demands of the course easier to cope with. Your training placement time is very precious and you need to ensure that the course work you carry out is spread across the whole age range – your tutor will probably set each task to be implemented within a particular setting. It is easy to put off doing an activity because your supervisor has arranged something else for you to do, or because you delay asking when would be convenient. The result can be lack of evidence for your PER! Planning how you can achieve what is required and discussing it in advance with your supervisor will help you to 'pace' yourself. This requires you to know what is needed. A **record sheet** can help you keep track of tasks as they are set and, importantly, ensures that you remember any pieces that have been given a referral grade and need resubmitting. Avoid allowing a 'backlog' of work to build up during the early part of the course as assignments and the MCQ paper loom menacingly from the mid-point onwards.

Be positive

It is important to view your experiences positively, including those at placements where you may have felt unsettled. Every work setting will be different, depending on staff, premises, function, attitude, outlook and, of course, the children! There is plenty to learn from those who have experience and are willing to share their expertise with you and offer advice. You will have the

---

THE CACHE STATEMENT OF VALUES

You must ensure that you:
- Put the child first by:
  - ensuring the child's welfare and safety
  - showing compassion and sensitivity
  - respecting the child as an individual
  - upholding the child's rights and dignity
  - enabling the child to achieve their full learning potential.
- Never use physical punishment.
- Respect the parent, or those in a parenting role, as the primary carer and educator of the child.

- Respect the contribution and expertise of staff in the child care and education field, and other professionals with whom they may be involved.
- Respect the customs, values and spiritual beliefs of the child and their family.
- Uphold CACHE's Diversity Statement.
- Honour the confidentiality of information relating to the child and their family, unless its disclosure is required by law or is in the best interest of the child.

opportunity to decide if you have a preferred age range – this may be useful when you seek employment.

Similarly, you may feel more comfortable and confident in some staff teams than others. It may be because of organisational factors or attitudes – try to analyse what makes the difference and to reflect upon your experiences. Unit 1 provides further information on:

* how to **prepare for your work placements**

* **how and when to observe children**, and

* how to **reflect upon your experiences**.

If you are following the career path that is right for you, then it is very likely (and preferable) that you enjoy your training placement time more than your study centre time! If this is not the case, think carefully about your choices for now and the future. This is one field in which you definitely cannot achieve through written work alone.

Unit 7

Working with Children from Birth to Age 5 Years

Contents

Unit 7 is divided into four sections:

Section 1: Promoting children's welfare in a range of settings

Section 2: Working with parents as part of a team

Section 3: Working with other professionals and agencies

Section 4: Your role in supporting a diverse and inclusive environment

Section 1

Promoting children's welfare in a range of settings

Children and their families need an environment that is not only safe, healthy and hygienic, but also reassuring and welcoming. To provide for all children's needs (i.e. their physical needs, intellectual and language needs, emotional and social needs), the early years environment should:

* take account of each child's individual needs, and provide for them appropriately
* be stimulating – it should offer a wide range of activities that encourage experimentation and problem-solving
* provide opportunities for all types of play.

THE DIFFERENCES BETWEEN SETTINGS

In Unit 1, the range of settings was described. The way in which a safe, nurturing environment is provided will vary according to the type of setting. Examples include the following.

* **The home environment:** children who are cared for at home (by a nanny) or in a childminder's home (a **home learning environment**) may not have access to special child-sized equipment or the wide range of activities that can be provided in a purpose-built nursery setting. (*Private sector*)
* **Pre-school or playgroups:** staff may have to clear away every item of equipment after each session because the hall or room is used by other groups –

for example, when the sessions take place in a village hall. (*Mostly private or voluntary sector*)
* **Purpose-built nurseries and infant schools:** these usually have child-sized chairs, basins, lavatories and low tables. Such provision makes the environment safer and allows children greater independence. (*Public – or state – sector*)

THE IMPORTANCE OF PROMOTING CHILDREN'S WELFARE IN A RANGE OF SETTINGS

Maintaining the environment so that it is safe, hygienic, reassuring and attractive is part of *everyone's* role, wherever children are being cared for.

In a nursery setting

Jobs may be shared out on a **rota** basis (e.g. cleaning toilets, preparing snacks, washing and sterilising equipment). However, it is every individual's responsibility to deal with any health and/or safety hazard that arises. This may be something quite straightforward, such as mopping up a spillage, or more serious, such as clearing away glass from a broken window. Immediate steps should be taken to make the surrounding area safe by clearing away fragments, keeping children away and then reporting the situation to the appropriate person.

In the home

Whether working with a childminder or in the child's home, you are expected to be alert to any potential hazards in the child's environment – for example, stairs without safety gates, access to outside, family pets, sharp corners on tables.

Where children are able to see that the care of their environment is important and shared between all adults they are provided with **positive role models** to influence their own attitudes.

Children learn about themselves, others and the world through play. As adults, it is our responsibility to make sure play is as safe as possible. You have an important role in ensuring that the environment where children play, learn and are cared for is as safe as possible.

HOW YOU CAN HELP TO PROMOTE A REASSURING AND SECURE ENVIRONMENT FOR YOUNG CHILDREN

You can help to promote a sense of belonging by:

* greeting children individually by name and with a smile when they arrive
* marking their coat pegs with their names and their photographs
* naming their displayed work
* ensuring that their cultural backgrounds are represented in the home corner, in books, displays and interest tables
* providing routines for children – children like their environment to be predictable; they feel more secure and comfortable when their day has some sort of shape to it; most early years settings have a daily routine, with fixed times for meals, snack times and outdoor play.

Helping children to feel valued

Children and their families need to feel that they matter and that they are valued for themselves. You can help by:

* establishing a good relationship with parents; always welcoming and listening to them

* squatting down or bending down to the children's level when you are talking with them
* praising, appreciating and encouraging children
* being responsive to children's needs
* using positive images in the setting
* providing support for children who may be experiencing strong feelings (e.g. when settling in to a new nursery, or when they are angry or jealous)
* encouraging children who use them to bring in their comfort objects (e.g. a favourite teddy or a piece of blanket)
* encouraging the development of self-reliance and independence
* ensuring that children who have special needs are provided with appropriate equipment and support.

ADAPTING ENVIRONMENTS TO MEET THE DIVERSE NEEDS OF CHILDREN

Children with particular needs should have the same opportunities for playing and learning as other children. Early years settings may need to adapt their room layout to improve access – for example, for children who use wheelchairs or for children with visual impairment. They may need to work with parents to find out how the child can be encouraged to participate fully with other children within the nursery or school. Any setting must take into account the particular needs of each child – in addition to the basic care needs of all children. This might involve:

* providing ramps for wheelchair users
* providing thick pencils and brushes for children with poor fine motor skills
* positioning children so that they learn effectively – for example, by making sure the light falls on the adult's face, so that a child wearing a hearing aid is able to lip

read and a child with a visual impairment can use any residual eyesight to see facial expressions

* adapting standard equipment – for example, by having a tray on the table so that objects stay on the table, and a child with a visual impairment does not 'lose' objects that fall off
* providing the opportunity to learn sign languages – for example, Makaton or PECS (see Unit 9, page 239)
* helping children to maintain good posture, appropriate muscle tone and ease of movement, and promoting skills in independent mobility
* helping children to manage eating and drinking; there is a wide range of specialist aids for eating and drinking, such as angled spoons and suction plates
* promoting relaxation and support to help children manage stress and anxiety; some settings use a sensory room, but a quiet, comfortable area will benefit all children.

The physical layout of the environment

Creating a comfortable, child-friendly environment means planning both the **physical layout** and the **organisation of activities**. It involves:

* considering health and safety before anything else – for example, fire exits and doors should be kept clear at all times
* giving children the maximum space and freedom to explore; rooms should be large enough to accommodate the numbers of children and be uncluttered
* ensuring that the room temperature is pleasant – neither too hot nor too cold (between 18°C and 21°C)
* making maximum use of natural light; rooms should be bright, airy and well lit

* enabling access to outdoors; this should not be restricted to certain times and seasons
* ensuring displays are clearly visible and interest tables are at child height where possible, and include items that can be safely handled and explored
* available space being divided appropriately to suit the range of activities offered.

There are certain aspects of arranging the space that are decided already by some fixed features. These include the following.

* **The position of electric sockets:** this will dictate, to a certain extent, where you can site the computer, and where you can use a television/video recorder. Remember, it is dangerous to have wires and leads trailing across the floor. There may need to be similar consideration for audio/tape players.
* **Washable flooring** is likely to be near the sinks and taps; therefore messy activities – such as water play, painting and clay modelling – need to be arranged in this area.
* **Carpeted area:** quieter activities and the book 'corner' will be best suited to a carpeted area, although a natural light source is important. Equipment should be stored close to the area where it will be used – construction resources and 'small world' may be in tubs or crates near a large carpeted floor space where children can spread out. Pencils, paper, puzzles and table-top games need to be near tables and chairs.

The needs of adults working with children should also be provided for; adults need to feel comfortable to work effectively. For example:

* furniture should be arranged to allow supervision without excessive walking
* materials should be stored conveniently and be easily accessible

* furniture should be designed to be flexible – easy to rearrange
* equipment provided should be designed to avoid excessive lifting (e.g. nappy-changing units with steps, or cots with drop sides – travel cots are sometimes chosen for ease of storage, but these can cause backache in practitioners as the child has to be lifted from floor level)
* seating for adults – gliders, settees, and rockers are perfect for bonding with babies; there should also be chairs that are low, yet scaled to fit adults, so staff can interact at the child's level.

Furniture

Chairs must be stable and allow children to have their feet on the floor so that they feel comfortable and secure. This firm base strengthens control of their upper bodies. Height-adjustable tables are also useful in a setting with varying sizes of children. In addition:

* they can be altered for a child who is standing or sitting for a particular activity

* they are useful in after-school settings or for children with special needs (some tables are kidney-shaped, allowing the practitioner to reach each child easily).

The **furniture** in any early years setting should:

* be appropriately child-sized – in all dimensions
* comply with safety standards with regard to materials
* be well designed to suit its intended purpose or function
* be stable, but not too heavy – this allows items to be moved to create flexibility in layout
* be hard-wearing
* be easily washed/cleaned
* have safe 'corners' (rounded or moulded) and edges
* be attractive – perhaps through use of colour.

Provision of equipment

Always remember that you, the practitioner, are the child's most valuable resource. (One

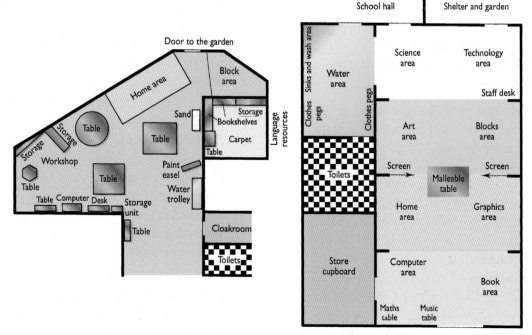

Fig 7.1a. James Lee Nursery School   Fig 7.1b. Eastwood Nursery School

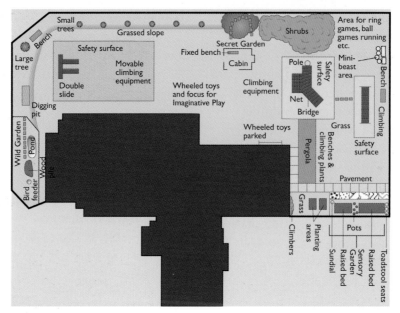

Fig 7.1c. The garden at Eastwood

of the principles that underpins the Birth to Three Matters Framework is that 'Caring adults count more than resources or equipment.') Most early years settings provide a wide variety of equipment, as listed below.

* **Sand** – wet and dry, and equipment in boxes on shelves nearby, labelled and with a picture of contents; these may be 'themed' (e.g. things with holes in/clear plastic/red items).
* **Water:** activities that require water or hand-washing should be near the sink and with aprons nearby. Equipment can be stored as for sand.
* **Clay and play dough:** cool, airtight storage; selection of utensils for mark-making, moulding, cutting.
* **A quiet area:** for looking at books and reading stories, doing floor puzzles; ideally carpeted and with floor cushions.
* **Puzzles, small blocks and table-top games:** stored accessibly close to tables and carpeted area.
* **Technology:** computer, weighing balance, calculators, tape recorders, etc.
* **Cookery:** with measuring equipment, bowls, spoons and baking trays.

* **Art work:** with tabards/aprons, brushes, paints and other materials within easy reach.
* **Domestic play:** with dolls, cots, telephones, kitchen equipment, etc.
* **Make-believe play:** box of dressing-up clothes – these should be versatile and have simple fastenings.
* **Small world toys:** animals, cars, people, farms, dinosaurs, train and track, etc.
* **Construction:** blocks for building, small construction blocks (e.g. Duplo, Mobilo, Stickle Bricks); a woodwork area.
* **Writing/graphics:** with a variety of paper and different kinds of pencils and pens.
* **Workshop:** with found materials (e.g. cardboard from boxes, egg boxes), glue, scissors, masking tape, etc.
* **Interest table:** with interesting objects for children to handle.
* **Growing and living things:** fish aquarium, wormery, growing mustard and cress, etc.; ensure conditions suit (e.g. away from direct sunlight).

A variety of **outdoor** play equipment is needed, as listed below.

* **Outdoor space:** with safe equipment for climbing and swinging, a safety floor surface, wheeled toys, balls and bean bags.
* **Garden:** plants and a growing area, a wild area to encourage butterflies, a mud patch for digging.

Supervision is important and separate areas indoors can be divided at child height so that children can focus attention and not be distracted, yet still be overseen by an adult. Storage units, low-level screens and display surfaces can all be used to divide space effectively without 'shutting off' some activities. The 'role play' area can get quite noisy and needs to be set up away from similar activities – 'small world' play, train track, construction, etc. In school settings, particularly, where there will be more 'directed' and 'structured' activities, this can lead to rising noise levels and cause disruption.

The different ways to display children's work

Work settings would be dull and uninteresting places without displays. They can give a lot of information to children, parents and visitors about the setting's values and curriculum. Displays are created for a range of purposes and, sometimes, for different audiences. Most settings have a notice or display board for parents and carers, usually sited near the entrance. This is used to update general information and news about usual routine and forthcoming events. Often there will be named photographs of staff members and, perhaps, the week's menus.

Most displays reflect the activities and learning that take place.

* Some will be used as **learning resources** – alphabet and number friezes, days of the week, word banks (lists of commonly used words to consolidate reading and support writing, particularly in school settings), children's birthdays, and so on – and remain on display indefinitely.
* Others will be of **work done by the children** themselves, showing their ideas, of their own or about a topic or different materials (e.g. string painting, finger painting, collage). These displays show that we value all the children's efforts.

Creating attractive displays needs careful consideration and can be time consuming. Factors to take into account include:

* size of space available
* themes/materials/colour schemes of adjacent displays
* location of space (some are very tricky, having thermostat controls or pipes in awkward places, or involve going round corners!)
* availability of materials
* age and stage of development of children – this affects content and also what kinds of labels/titles/lettering you use.

Different types of display

Wall display

The most usual type of display found in early years settings is a straightforward wall display. Boards of varying shapes and sizes are often placed on otherwise plain walls so that displays can be created and changed frequently to provide interest.

Window display

The use of windows for displays is also common. Paint (with a little washing-up liquid added so it can be washed off easily) is used to create colourful window displays – often of well-known characters from cartoons, stories or television, or of animals or seasonal pictures. Sometimes pieces of art or craft work may also be attached to windows, particularly if the materials lend themselves to having light behind them (e.g. 'stained glass' windows or tissue paper pictures). Remember that the sunlight will fade the colours after a short time.

'Mobile' or 'hanging' display

Mobile or hanging displays can be used effectively, especially in very large rooms. Hanging or suspending shapes or pictures from a hoop or the ceiling needs careful thought. For them to be at an appropriate height for the children may cause difficulties for staff! Also you may have to consider security or alarm systems that can be set off by moving objects. Such displays can be useful in identifying particular areas of a work setting (e.g. story characters over the book area, solid or flat shapes over the maths or numeracy area).

Table-top display

Table-top displays (sometimes referred to as **interactive displays**) give you the opportunity to use objects or artefacts that will engage the children's interest. Interest objects should be attractively and appealingly displayed to encourage children to interact with them. Posing a question (e.g. 'How many blue shapes can you find?') will invite children to use the display as an extra activity (if working with very young children then you must explain what they might do and, perhaps, take them to the display and handle the objects with them). These displays are often accompanied by an upright board or display space, which can be used for interesting pictures, photographs or posters and your own titles to add interest. Older children may appreciate related fact and story books to use for research.

Fig 7.2. Types of display

THE BASIC PHYSICAL AND HEALTH NEEDS OF CHILDREN FROM BIRTH TO AGE 5 YEARS

To achieve and maintain healthy growth and development (that is, physical, intellectual, social and emotional), certain basic needs must be fulfilled. These basic needs are:

* food
* shelter, warmth, clothing
* cleanliness
* fresh air and sunlight
* sleep, rest and activity
* love and consistent and continuous affection
* protection from infection and injury
* stimulation
* social contacts
* security.

It is difficult to separate these basic needs in practical care, as they all contribute to the holistic development of a healthy child. (The care of children from birth to age 5 is covered in Unit 2, Section 4.)

Section 2

Working with parents as part of a team

Parents or guardians and their families occupy a central position in children's lives:

* they provide their child with what they need to develop and grow, and are the people who know their child the best.

Your role: you must never try to take over this central role inappropriately. Instead, listen to parents and families as the true 'experts' in their own children's care.

* Parents and guardians start off in an unequal relationship with child care staff. Some get very anxious – they may never have been separated from their child before, or may speak a different language from that used in the child care setting.

Your role: you need to be able to see things from their point of view and do everything possible to make them feel welcome.

* A crucial part of making families feel welcome and part of the child care setting is respecting their traditions and child care practices.

Your role: always listen to any specific wishes, and comply with them whenever possible.

* There are differences between the relationship that a parent has with their child and the relationship you have with that child.

Your role: try to keep a little distance, while working in a warm, sensitive way. You should not develop a deeply emotional attachment.

* What carers, parents and guardians *do* all have in common is their desire for the best for the child.

Your role: the best approach is to think of yourself as a resource and source of support for parents. You can offer ideas, but don't insist on, or be judgemental about, the way that they bring up their children. Share information about children's development and progress openly with their parents or guardians. This encourages a spirit of collaboration which will ensure that the child gets the best and most consistent care. It also builds trust between the early years practitioner and parents or guardians.

THE ROLE OF THE KEY PRACTITIONER (OR KEY PERSON)

The advantages of having a **key person** or practitioner are that children feel happier and more secure. They also gain in confidence and independence skills; this enables them to explore and to try out new things. Having a key person in group settings is particularly important for babies and young children; but even when children are older and can hold special people in mind for longer, there is still a need for them to have a key person to depend on in the setting, such as their teacher or a teaching assistant.

A key person:

* helps the baby or child to become familiar with the setting and to feel confident and safe within it
* develops a genuine bond with children and offers a settled, close relationship

* meets the needs of each child in their care, and responds sensitively to their feelings, ideas and behaviour
* talks to parents to make sure that the child is being cared for appropriately for each family.

The key person's relationship with parents

Some parents may worry that the close emotional relationship their child has with a key person in the setting might undermine their own relationship with their child. They should be reassured that nobody can take their place in their child's life. Studies in **attachment** have shown that babies and young children in 'group' care benefit greatly from having their own familiar key person. Careful records of the child's development and progress are created and shared by parents, the child, the key person and other professionals as necessary.

Nurseries and other group settings should ensure that:

* staffing rotas are based on when a key person is available for each child
* there is a *second* key person for children so that when the main key person is away there is a familiar and trusted person who knows the child well
* there is planned time for each key person to work with parents so that they really know and understand the children in their key group
* as children move between settings, they are helped to become familiar with their new key person
* a key person does not become over-attached to a child; also they should reassure parents who worry that children may be more attached to staff than to them.

THE LINES OF REPORTING AND RECORDING TO MANAGEMENT IN A PROFESSIONAL MANNER

It is vital that all practitioners know the **lines of reporting** and how to obtain clarification of their own role and responsibility. If you don't feel confident in carrying out a particular task, either because you don't fully understand it or because you have not been adequately trained, then you have a responsibility to state your concerns and ask for guidance.

Section 3
Working with other professionals and agencies

Multi-agency working is about different services, agencies and teams of professionals and other staff working together to provide the services that fully meet the needs of children, young people and their parents or carers. Through Sure Start and the Change for Children programme, there has been an increase in the range of multi-agency services available to children and families. For example:

* integrated working within children's centres and extended schools
* multi-agency teams supporting small groups of schools.

As an early years practitioner, you will work closely with your colleagues in the setting and will liaise with parents of the children in your care. You may also be involved in the network of relationships between staff at the setting and other professionals from outside agencies. These include the following.

* **Health service professionals:** doctors, health visitors, paediatricians,

physiotherapists, occupational therapists, school nurses, speech and language therapists, psychologists, play workers, hospital play specialists and play therapists.

* **Social service professionals:** social workers, specialist social workers in mental health, sensory disabilities, physical disabilities, children and families.
* **Local education authority professionals:** support teachers, special needs advisers, specialist teachers, education welfare officers.
* **Charities and voluntary organisations:** for example, Portage workers, National Autistic Society, RNIB (Royal National Institute for the Blind), NDCS (National Deaf Children's Society), SCOPE (about cerebral palsy) and many others. There are many other local support groups, including Gingerbread, which works on behalf of lone parents, and Contact A Family, which provides independent information, advice and support to parents of children with disabilities or special needs.

(For more information on working with other professionals, see Unit 5, Section 1, and Unit 9.)

Section 4

Your role in supporting a diverse and inclusive environment

THE RIGHTS OF CHILDREN AND THEIR FAMILIES

Children are entitled to basic human rights such as food, health care, a safe home and protection from abuse. However, children are

a special case because they cannot always stand up for themselves. They need a *special* set of rights that take account of their vulnerability, and ensure that adults take responsibility for their protection and development.

The rights embodied by the **UN Convention on the Rights of the Child** that particularly relate to early years care and education are as follows.

* Children have the right to be with their family or with those who will care best for them.
* Children have the right to enough food and clean water for their needs.
* Children have the right to an adequate standard of living.
* Children have the right to health care.
* Children have the right to play.
* Children have the right to be kept safe and not hurt or neglected.
* Disabled children have the right to special care and training.
* Children have the right to free education.

THE CAUSES AND EFFECTS OF DISCRIMINATION IN A MULTICULTURAL SOCIETY

What is discrimination?

Discrimination occurs when someone is treated less favourably, usually because of a negative view of some of their characteristics. This negative – or pejorative – view is based on stereotypical assumptions that do not have a factual basis.

Types of discrimination

The most obvious types of discrimination occur as a result of the stereotypes described in Unit 1: racism, sexism, ageism and disablism. Children may also discriminate against other children on account of their differences. This often takes the form of **name-calling** and **teasing**, and may be directed at children who are either fatter or thinner than others in the group, or who wear different clothes.

Sometimes discrimination is **institutionalised**. This means that the particular institution is not organised to meet the needs of all the people within it; in other words, the structures are not in place to prevent discrimination taking place. Examples include:

* institutional racism within the police force; many more black youths are still stopped by the police than are white youths
* children with impairments or learning difficulties are not provided with the equipment or resources to enable them to take a full part in the school or nursery curriculum
* adults who use wheelchairs may not be allowed access to cinemas or theatres, because of lack of suitable adaptations to comply with fire regulations
* the needs of children from minority religious or cultural groups are not recognised within the nursery or school.

Direct discrimination occurs when someone is treated less favourably on specific racial or other grounds than other people are, or would be, treated in similar circumstances. For example, if an Asian woman is turned down for a job as a shop assistant and told there are no vacancies, then a white woman with equivalent qualifications is offered the job a short while later, the Asian woman has been **directly** discriminated against.

Indirect discrimination occurs when a condition or requirement is applied equally to people of all racial or other groups, but far fewer people of a particular group are able to comply with it. Such indirect discrimination is against the law when it cannot be justified other than on racial or other grounds. For example, if an employer requires job applicants to have a qualification in a particular subject, but will only consider people whose degree is from a British university, this condition could amount to indirect discrimination.

The effects of discrimination on children's development

The early childhood setting – nursery, playgroup or nursery school – is often the first experience beyond their immediate family and friendship group that the child joins. When they join any wider setting, children need:

* to feel valued for themselves – as individuals
* to feel a part of things, and a sense of belonging
* to feel accepted by others
* to develop a sense of self-worth (i.e. to feel that they matter to other people).

Discrimination of any kind prevents them from developing a feeling of self-worth or **self-esteem**. The effects of being discriminated against can last the whole of a child's life. In particular, they may:

* **be unable to fulfil their potential**, because they are made to feel that their efforts are not valued or recognised by others
* **find it hard to form relationships** with others because of lack of self-worth or self-esteem
* be so affected by the **stereotypes or labels** applied to them that they start to believe in them and so behave in accordance with others' expectations; this then becomes a **self-fulfilling prophecy** – for example, if a child is

repeatedly told that he is clumsy, he may act in a clumsy way even when quite capable of acting otherwise

* **feel shame about their own cultural background**
* **feel that they are in some way to blame** for their unfair treatment and so withdraw into themselves
* **lack confidence in trying new activities** if their attempts are always ridiculed or put down
* **be aggressive towards others**; distress or anger can prevent children from playing cooperatively with other children.

Disability and discrimination

Children who are disabled (and their families) may be discriminated against in particular ways.

* They may face difficulty gaining access to shops. Most large stores have easy entrance arrangements, but smaller shops prevent access by wheelchair (and often by large pushchairs and prams, too).
* Children who look different often face more discrimination because the disability is seen first rather than the child; for example, they may be stared at and hear remarks about themselves when out with their families. Disabled children have even been barred from cafés and restaurants because of their differences.
* Children who look just like any other child may have a 'hidden' disability, such as autism, attention deficit hyperactivity disorder (ADHD) or deafness. Their behaviour may attract disapproval when out in public and the family will feel under attack.
* They may have financial difficulties. There are always extra financial costs involved in bringing up a disabled child in the family – for example, mobility costs, the costs of giving full-time care,

and perhaps extra laundry costs. Parents may have to rely on state benefits to enable them to give their child the care they need.

* Parents who are caring for a disabled child may not have the time or energy to give equivalent attention to any other child in the family. This could restrict the other child's development.
* Parents often have to struggle 'against the odds' to obtain the best treatment and resources for their child. Many parents find it difficult to have to ask for help all the time; others find the process very tiring. (For example, the process of **statementing** can take many months or even years – see Unit 9.)

Your role in challenging discrimination

The first step in being able to challenge discrimination is to identify when it is taking place. The most obvious and common form of indirect discrimination is when **labels** are applied to children. You may believe in private, for example, that Mark is a 'spoilt' child who gets away with the sort of behaviour that you personally think is unacceptable. It would be unnatural not to have an opinion on such matters. However, you should not initiate or join in any discussion that results in Mark being labelled as a 'difficult' or 'spoilt' child. Equally, you will find some children more likeable than others; again this is quite natural. What is important is that you are fair in your treatment of all the children in your care. You should treat them all equally and with respect.

Remember the poem on page 14 of Unit 1, 'Children learn what they live', and try to develop **positive attitudes** towards all the children you meet, so that they cannot feel the effects of discrimination. It is only natural to like some children better than others, but our behaviour should always reflect the principle that all children are entitled to the same love and respect.

It is important to support an environment that is **inclusive** – that is, it includes *everyone* – and that promotes cultural diversity. Some practical ways of encouraging cultural diversity are by:

* providing a range of activities that celebrate these differences (e.g. to make children aware of what is involved in celebrations of religious festivals such as Diwali and Chinese New Year, as well as Christmas and Easter, whether or not there are children in the nursery who celebrate these occasions)
* promoting a multicultural approach to food provision; for example, parents could be invited into the setting to cook authentic national and regional dishes – Caribbean food, Yorkshire pudding as a dessert, Welsh griddle cakes, Irish Bara Brith, Asian sweets . . . the list is endless!
* encouraging self-expression in solo and in group activities; for example, by providing 'tools' for cooking and eating from other cultures – woks, chopsticks, griddles, etc.
* celebrating the diversity of language; use body language, gesture, pictures and actions to convey messages to children whose home language is not English.

HOW TO ENCOURAGE DIVERSITY AND INCLUSIVE PRACTICE

Every child needs to be included and to have full access to the curriculum, regardless of their ethnic background, culture, language, gender or economic background. Some practical ways of valuing and encouraging diversity are listed below.

* **Provide positive images:** books and displays should use positive images of children with disabilities and from different cultures. Children also need positive images of gender roles (e.g. men caring for small children and women mending the car).
* **Arrange activities to encourage children with special needs to participate fully with other children:** this might mean providing ramps for wheelchair users, or working with parents to find comfortable ways for a child to sit (e.g. a corner with two walls for support, a chair with a seat belt, or a wheelchair with a large tray across the arms).
* **Learn a sign language**, such as Makaton or Signalong, to help communicate with a child who has a hearing impairment or a learning difficulty.

Planning activities which promote equality of opportunity

Every child needs to feel accepted, and to feel that they belong in the setting. Try to find out as much as possible about different cultures, religions and special needs. Activities should be planned which enable children:

* to feel valued as individuals
* to explore a wide range of everyday experiences from different cultures and backgrounds
* to express their feelings.

Make sure that the books, posters and other resources include positive images of minority ethnic groups and children with impairments, and that gender roles are non-stereotyped and reflect the diversity of family life. Specific activities may include the following.

* Play with malleable materials such as play dough, sand or clay; drawing, painting and craft activities help children

to express their feelings and are non-sexist activities; include examples from different cultures (e.g. papier mâché, origami, weaving).

* Provision of toys that offer a range of play opportunities rather than those that are aimed particularly at one sex or the other (e.g. provide a wide variety of dressing-up clothes that can be used by girls and boys). Include dress from different cultures and make sure that superhero outfits are available for either sex (e.g. Superwoman as well as Superman, Wonderwoman and Batman).

* Extension of the home corner to provide a wide range of play situations (e.g. a home corner plus an office or shop, or a boat).

* Using books and telling stories in different languages: invite someone whose first language is not English to come and read a popular story book – such as 'Goldilocks and the Three Bears' – in their language to the whole group; then repeat the session using the English text, again to the whole group.

* Playing music from a variety of cultures (e.g. sitar music, pan pipes, bagpipes), and encouraging children to listen or to dance to the sounds.

* Planning a display and interest table around one of the major festivals from different cultures (e.g. Diwali, Hanukkah, Easter, Chinese New Year).

* Using posters that show everyday things from different countries (e.g. musical instruments, fruit and vegetables, transport and wildlife).

* Organising the home corner to include a variety of equipment commonly found in homes in different cultures (e.g. tandoor, wok, chopsticks).

* Providing dolls and other playthings that accurately reflect a variety of skin tones and features.

* Arranging cookery activities using recipes from other cultures and in different languages; contact the relevant organisations to find out how to promote cooking skills for children with special needs.

See Unit 9 for discussion of promoting individual children's needs and how you can support children with additional needs.

ACTIVITY: EXPLORING ASSUMPTIONS AND STEREOTYPES

The following adjectives are often used to describe children:

bossy	noisy	shy
energetic	competitive	helpful
aggressive	lively	gentle
warm	moody	quiet
kind	babyish	emotional
strong	lazy	sissy
clinging	cheeky	

1. Use the headings **girls**, **boys** and **either boys or girls** to create three columns.

Then put the adjectives from the list into the appropriate column, according to whether you think they describe girls, boys or either girls or boys. Compare your lists with those of a friend.

* How similar were your choices? Discuss the similarities and the differences.
* Discuss reasons why some adjectives are so closely related to gender.
* Do your lists really apply to all the children you work with or know?

Play Activity for Children from Birth to Age 16 Years

Contents

Unit 8 is divided into three sections:

Section 1: The diverse play needs of children

Section 2: How to support play opportunities

Section 3: The role of the adult in providing play activity for children

The diverse play needs of children
THE STAGES OF PLAY

(The stages of play in young children are described in Unit 4.)

In later childhood and early adolescence, children's play becomes more organised and structured as their enthusiasm for logical thinking shows itself through **games with rules** and in **team sports**.

Winning becomes important as they begin to understand that winning means following the rules. This is the age when team sports become important. However, even when teenagers are just 'hanging out' together, they are learning – sharing information and knowledge, and gaining a better understanding of social relationships.

As children enter their teenage years, they rarely refer to what they do outside school hours as playing; however, older children do need to play, just as much as do the under-5s. Many children from about 11 years and older have little opportunity for play. When school time is over, their leisure time is often taken up with household chores, sports activities, reading, using the computer or watching TV or DVDs. Research has shown that older children also need time to **play**. They need free time – when nothing is planned or scheduled, nothing demanded, and during which they are discouraged from watching TV or using the computer.

Play-based learning activities provide many different ways for children to learn a variety of different skills and concepts; they also enable children to feel competent about their ability to learn.

The interests of children from birth to age 16 years

Babies (from birth to 18 months) are totally dependent on caring adults to provide them with new play experiences; they show an interest in:

* watching movement and listening to rhythmic sounds
* holding rattles, chiming balls and musical toys
* exploring textures – for example, on an activity mat
* playing with stacking beakers and bricks
* exploring objects with their hands and their mouth
* active play with a caring adult
* making noises by banging toys
* playing with empty cardboard boxes
* looking at picture books.

Children aged 1½ to 3 years have an increasing desire for independence; they show interest in:

* playing with things that screw and unscrew
* paints and crayons
* sand and water play
* playing with balls – rolling, kicking and throwing.

Fig 8.1. Babies enjoy picture books

Towards the end of this period, they show interest in:

* toys to ride and climb on
* matching and sorting games
* simple jigsaw puzzles
* puppet play and action rhymes
* musical games
* jumping, running and physical games
* role play.

Children aged 3 to 5 play with other children; they show an interest in:

* playing outdoors
* active pretend play with other children
* jigsaw puzzles and making models
* simple craft activities and playing with dough
* playing on the floor with bricks, trains, dolls and boxes, alone and with others
* acting out puppet shows
* imaginative play.

Children aged 5 to 8 are learning self-control and enjoy showing what they can do; they show an interest in:

* team games and games with rules
* complicated games on the floor with small world objects
* more elaborate pretend play with others
* playing cooperatively with other children
* fantasy play
* activities that involve precise movements – such as hopscotch or skipping games.

Children aged 8 to 12 usually have at least one special friend, but also like to belong to a group; they show interest in:

* being physically active outdoors
* cooperative and competitive games
* reading fictional stories, magazines and 'how-to' project books
* games with rules – traditional board games such as draughts and chess, word games, card games and quiz-type

games – as well as the more complex fantasy games
* craft activities and making things from construction kits
* making collections.

Adolescents (12 to 16 years) are becoming increasingly independent from their parents; they show an interest in:

* developing their own ideas and values – often becoming concerned about social issues such as global warming and poverty
* being with their friends; at first they socialise in mixed-gender groups – this gives way to one-to-one friendships and romances
* music, sports, computing and computer games
* role models – particularly media personalities – pop stars, sports stars and film stars.

The importance of consulting with children about their play environments

Children and young people have the right to be consulted and involved in decision-making about the type of play provision they have. Involving children in making decisions is important because it helps them to develop:

* **independence**, which increases their feeling of confidence in their own abilities
* **a sense of being in control** of their own environment
* **trust** – knowing that adults trust their judgement and opinions
* **self-help skills** – for example, knowing that the adult will be patient in letting the child dress himself, even if it takes a long time and several attempts.

Teenagers would probably not refer to their social activities as 'play', but surveys of the views of children and young people show that they want:

* opportunities to be physically active – indoors and outdoors
* the chance to meet with their friends
* the chance to be somewhere quiet
* choice and variety.

Young people have also identified the following barriers to their play:

* fears for their safety, especially from bullying
* traffic
* dirty and/or rundown play areas and parks
* lack of choice
* play provision that is too far away.

How to recognise the individual play needs of children

What are play needs?

Play needs are individual to each child and are directly related to the age, stage of development and interests of the child. **Play needs** include opportunities to:

* play in safe places
* use a variety of objects and materials
* learn about the physical environment
* develop empathy (being able to imagine what someone else feels or thinks)
* take control of their own learning – at their own pace
* develop relationships with others – both other children and adults
* explore their own feelings – and learn how to control them

Adults often make assumptions about the play needs of children and these are not always an accurate reflection of what children both want (play preferences) and need (play needs).

Observing children during their play and **discussing their play preferences** with them will help to ensure that each child's play needs are met.

Section 2
How to support play opportunities

PLAY SETTINGS AND RESOURCES

Children play in a great variety of settings, including their homes, nurseries, schools and playgroups. **Playworkers** work with school-aged children in *out-of-school* settings. Different playwork settings are run in different ways, but all aim to give the children and young people choices about how they spend their leisure time. Playworkers work in a range of settings, both statutory and voluntary, which aim to provide for children's play, such as those in the examples listed below.

* **Breakfast clubs (8–9 a.m.):** parents bring children to the club; children can have breakfast; staff take children to school; some activities may be provided.
* **After-school clubs (3–6 p.m.):** these cater for 4–14 year olds; parents book children in; clubs collect children from school; parents collect children from club; most clubs organise a refreshment break during the session.
* **Playbus:** open access; the bus goes to clubs, groups, play areas or other appropriate places; the children may come and go at will; activities can be organised; in some cases, the bus staff may organise something that is open only to members of a group or club.

* **Play centre/youth groups:** can cater for a variety of age ranges (e.g. 8–14 years, 11–14 years, 13–18 years, up to 25 years); venues vary from purpose-built buildings to village halls, church rooms and schools; opening times vary from one day to every day of the week.
* **Adventure playgrounds:** open access; children can come and go at will; children do not need to be booked in and out of the playground; the staff supervise outdoor activities and equipment; outdoor play equipment is often designed and built by the children; some activities may be available indoors, often led by the children.
* **Holiday play schemes:** usually for 4–14 year olds, but some may be open to older children; play schemes can be run by a variety of organisations – for example, the Church, voluntary organisations and uniformed groups; the times of opening and the number of days per week vary between schemes.

Playworkers may also work in a number of more *specialised* settings in which providing for play has been recognised as an important way of supporting children. For example:

* hospitals
* refuges
* family services.

Not all settings fit with these descriptions. For example, some after-school clubs may be open access; playbuses may run activities in a variety of settings, including open-access play in public parks or after-school clubs in village halls; some adventure playgrounds run sessions like after-school clubs.

Some disabled children using play settings need additional support; others who need extra help at school might not need it in a supervised play setting.

Playworkers are responsible for enabling or facilitating **play opportunities**. They should do everything possible to ensure that children have choice and control of their own play. The degree of 'enabling' a playworker might do depends on the needs, personality, age and ability of the child or children – or even just the mood of the children on a particular day. Playworkers:

* offer a **range of activities**, including creative activities, sporty games, drama, den building, cooking
* provide children with a **safe place to play**, socialise, try out new things or just spend quiet time; safety in a play setting does not mean that children are not able to take risks; playing safely means that the playworker has thought about protecting the children from harm – for example, providing 'crash' mats for a made-up climbing game or helping the children work out their own safety rules.

Play rangers

Play rangers are adults who are trained in 'supporting children's outdoor play in public parks, housing estates, village greens and other open spaces'. The concept was set up in 2001 and there are now play ranger schemes in many parts of the UK – usually funded by local authorities. All sessions are **open access** and led by what the children want to do; they can drift in and away as they wish. Play rangers:

* provide simple raw materials, such as ropes for a swing, tools or dressing-up clothes, which can be transformed by children's imagination, and help to get things started
* usually work with children aged from 5 to 13; but in practice, 3 year olds turn up with older siblings, and older teenagers return to the play areas with younger children

* encourage families and the wider community to join in
* are not limited by bad weather – activities are provided under a temporary cover.

Resources for play

We all need to practise skills to become competent, but life would be boring and repetitive if we always had to do things in the same way. Children need to be given plenty of opportunities to practise their newly developing skills, and to express their thoughts, feelings and ideas in different contexts. This means that there should always be a wide range of resources from which children can choose. These include the following.

* **The outdoor environment** (e.g. gardening, parks and wildlife): to promote physical development and their understanding of the natural world.
* **Natural materials** (e.g. sand, water, flour): to promote exploration and investigation.
* **Recycled materials** (e.g. cardboard, plastic, clean clothing): for constructing models, dressing-up activities.
* **Commercially produced items** (e.g. Lego construction kits, wooden blocks and climbing equipment): to promote exploratory play.
* **Space for play**: for children to use their imagination in games that require few props (e.g. making a den from a table and a cloth).

Good use of resources

A painting or drawing activity that will allow them to develop their fine manipulative skills can be varied by using:

* different-quality paper (e.g. sugar, cartridge, 'newsprint')

* paper of different colours
* different sizes of paper
* different media (e.g. pastels, wax crayons, colouring crayons, chalk)
* paint (e.g. ready-mixed, powder, thick, thin, fluorescent, pearlised)
* different techniques (e.g. finger, bubble, printing, marble-rolling, string).

While using such a variety the children are also learning about textures, which are appropriate materials to express an idea, colours and developing concepts about materials – how runny paint 'behaves', how chalk smudges, and so on. Other types of activity – construction, water, sand, small world, role play and the like. – can easily be varied to broaden children's experience.

PROMOTING INCLUSIVE PLAY

Boys often seem to dominate outside play and the use of equipment. As children become more aware of their gender, and of other people's expectations of their behaviour, they might reject activities they once liked and choose instead more 'gender-appropriate' activities. For example, girls might choose skipping games, while boys may prefer a game of football.

In order to challenge these stereotypes and to ensure equal opportunities are offered to every child, follow the guidelines presented here.

For more information on inclusive play, see Unit 4, page 156.

PLAYING GAMES WITH CHILDREN

The term 'game' covers a wide range of activity – from simple 'round-and-round-the-garden' played with babies, to complex games with special equipment and rules. Many games offer an enjoyable way of

GUIDELINES ON PROMOTING INCLUSIVE PRACTICE: EQUAL OPPORTUNITIES FOR EVERY CHILD

- **Avoid having expectations** of children's physical abilities based on stereotypes.
Example: 'You're a big strong boy, Tom, please carry that chair inside for me.'
- Ensure that the provision of play does not reinforce stereotypes.
Example: Allow only the girls to use the wheeled toys and bikes for one session.
- **Be a good role model.** You should be fully involved in children's physical play, rather than passively supervising. Show children that you are enjoying the session.
- **Be observant.** Take note of the child who seems reluctant to try new equipment, and offer gentle encouragement.
- Be aware of the use of **gender-specific terminology**.
Example: Fireman; instead use 'fire-fighter'.
- **Be sensitive to requests for privacy** when changing for school PE lessons.
- **Respect dress codes** based on religious beliefs, ensuring safety guidelines are still followed.
- **Children with special needs** may need different equipment – according to the special need they have – or they may need it to be adapted; for example, by fitting velcro straps to bike pedals. Other ideas include:
  - providing soft foam-filled blocks, soft balls, bean-bags and plastic bats; these can often be obtained from a charity or from a toy library
  - planning activities to encourage exercise and movement of all body parts; an occupational therapist or play specialist can offer valuable advice.

developing both knowledge and understanding and practical skills.

Babies and very young children enjoy one-to-one games that adults initiate. At this early stage they are not socially ready to join with other children and still spend much of their time exploring their world and objects in it. Games are a useful form of play as most can be adapted to include a wide range of abilities and preferences.

Playing games with rules

As children develop intellectually they can begin to cope with games involving colour matching and recognition, shape matching and recognition, counting, sequencing and memory. Their increasing ability to copy those around them means that they can follow simple rules, although taking turns and waiting patiently often causes problems!

Games that actively involve them can promote development in all areas. Ring and action games can help coordination, decision-making, language, rhythm and social skills of turn-taking and sharing. Where some children are chosen and others are not (e.g. 'The farmer's in his den') they learn an important lesson of consideration for others and discover that they, themselves, cannot always be first but will get a turn at some point.

Table-top games

Table-top games introduce children to rules and special equipment, and can be used to teach and consolidate basic concepts. The best games available are those that offer versatility – the possibility of adaptation for differing abilities and stages of development.

Ages 3–5 years

In these early stages children cope well with games that have a definite ending – with or without a 'winner'. This can be when a picture has been completed or a playing board has been filled. In most instances, although the first player to complete may be the 'winner', games are usually continued until all players have finished. It is the skill of the adult to maintain everyone's interest and involve children in each other's success.

Lotto games are among the most versatile as they:

* can be based on a wide range of topics, such as number (numerals, patterns, objects), shapes, colours, words, seasons, weather, transport
* have individual baseboards appropriate to young children
* can be adapted to suit needs of individual children
* can be for two to four (sometimes six) players
* can easily be made
* may have different versions (see below).

To create versatility a single baseboard may have two, or three, sets of cards. For example a lotto game to promote number may have baseboards with pictures of objects – one apple, two boots, three fish, etc. One set of cards could have exactly the same set of pictures for direct matching, another set could have the numerals, or number symbols – 1, 2, 3, etc. – and yet a third might have the number words – one, two, three, etc. The cards can be used for simple snap or pairs-type games, or for labelling sets of objects that children have sorted. Other lotto-type games may include baseboards

with a single picture, which require pieces to be collected (e.g. body parts/coloured balloons).

Other popular games are dominoes and pairs. For both these games **adult supervision** is important.

* **Dominoes**: children need to be constantly reminded of the choices, which can change at each turn.
* **Pairs**: young children tend to move the cards from their original places and the 'memory' element is lost. (These games can also last too long and result in children losing their concentration and enthusiasm.)

Age 5–8 years

At this stage children are able to share a playing board or area, and games involving throwing a die or dice, counting on or back with the winner being the first to the finish are popular. There is a wide range available; some games will also develop **reading skills** as there are instructions to be followed on the board.

* Be aware of the needs of the children you are working with; think carefully before you introduce a 100-square board for snakes and ladders: it will be too long a game for the younger end of this age range, and the direction changes – left to right and then back again – are confusing.
* If your game involves visual matching then make sure your pictures are identical (use wrapping paper or photocopied images) rather than 'nearly the same'.
* **Age-related**: try to think about children's interests (e.g. book or television characters). You should state the age for which you consider the game to be suitable, provide storage and attractive packaging.

ACTIVITY: MAKE A TABLE-TOP GAME

Design and make a table-top game for use with an individual child or small group of children of your chosen age from the range 3–8 years. In designing and making your game consider the following factors:

- age/stage of development
- clear objectives or purpose
- subject matter or content
- safety
- number of players
- rules
- attractiveness and appeal
- presentation
- storage/packaging.

Remember to make your pieces an appropriate size, durable (laminate or cover with sticky-back plastic), colourful and attractive.

---

* **Provide simple rules**: rules should be clearly presented so that any adult wishing to use the game would understand what the main aim was (e.g. to develop children's memory/counting/shape recognition), and step-by-step playing instructions should be included. Explain how to play alternative versions, if applicable.

* **Try it out**: when you have made the game you should try it out with the correct-age children in your work setting. Evaluate it by identifying whether:

  (a) it achieved your stated objectives
  (b) the children enjoyed it
  (c) they understood what they had to do
  (d) it maintained everyone's interest
  (e) there were any difficulties
  (f) there are any changes that could improve it.

ACTIVITY: PLAY AND LEARNING

1. Look at the following list of activities.

   - sand play
   - board game
   - painting
   - home play
   - story-telling
   - natural materials play
   - cooking
   - drawing
   - dressing up
   - poetry
   - clay
   - ring (or circle) game
   - modelling
   - water play
   - listening game
   - adventure playground
   - outdoor game
   - making music
   - role-play
   - songs
   - dough
   - drama activity/mime
   - finger rhymes
   - table-top game with rules

2. Choose **one** of the following age ranges:

   1 to 2 years
   2 to 4 years
   4 to 7 years
   8 to 11 years
   12 to 16 years

3. Select **three** of the listed activities that you have identified as particularly appropriate for that age range.
4. For **each** of the **three** activities describe:
   - what equipment and resources you would provide
   - the health and safety aspects you would need to consider
   - how you would prepare your equipment and the immediate environment
   - what the children will actually be doing and what experiences you want them to have
   - what language you would want to encourage or introduce; for example, new vocabulary – names of objects and/or descriptive terms, such as hot/cold, wet/dry, etc.
   - how you will provide for different cultural backgrounds
   - how you will provide for children who have particular needs.

Competitive games

Apart from the games described already, school-aged children are beginning to become involved in team games – perhaps in PE lessons – and the element of competition increases. However, many still find it difficult to 'lose' and need sensitive handling. Success and failure are facts of life and everybody experiences both at some time or another. Children can be helped to deal with their feelings through games in a safe and reassuring context.

Competitive games can:

* encourage children to try harder, concentrate more, foster determination
* help children understand that 'luck' often plays a part in success and failure
* promote positive attitudes towards cooperative and collaborative working
* help children recognise their own particular talents and those of others
* enable children to experience success and a sense of achievement
* enable children to experience 'losing' and to recognise the talents of others
* teach children the importance of rules and 'fair play'
* help children accept that there may be the ultimate decision of an umpire or referee, against which there is no appeal.

Drawbacks can be that children:

* who seem never to win may lose confidence and self-esteem
* may believe that winning is the most important thing
* may not be given opportunities to express their feelings of disappointment (e.g. being told to be a 'good loser')
* blame other team members for failure.

HOW TO USE MUSIC, MOVEMENT, RHYTHM AND GAMES TO PROMOTE PLAY

Musical activities

Although different cultures have their own traditions, music is a 'universal' language and is, therefore, accessible to everyone. Our bodies have a natural rhythm – the heartbeat and pulse – and even those with hearing impairments can be aware of rhythms and vibrations caused by sound.

Nursery, finger and action rhymes are often the first songs that children participate in, and each family will use its own favourites. Work settings usually introduce an even wider repertoire to children. These rhymes help to develop children's sense of rhythm as well as increasing their vocabulary and, perhaps, encouraging their number skills (counting up and down) or naming of body parts, and so on.

There is a range of musical activities that are appropriate.

Listening to music – live or taped

Try to introduce a wide range, including music from different cultures – oriental, folk tunes, pan pipes from South America, unaccompanied vocal music from other continents, as well as military band music and western styles. The extracts should not be too long and you can encourage active listening by asking them to focus on one aspect – the tempo (speed), the tune or the rhythm.

Singing

This can be well-known rhymes or games that involve the children in imitating a short tune sung by an adult (or – with older, confident children – a child). Regular singing games develop children's listening skills and ability to discriminate sound – particularly helping them to 'pitch' a note more accurately.

Playing instruments

This involves many skills – physical, listening, social and intellectual. The best and most available instruments are our own bodies. Body percussion involves hitting, flicking, tapping, thumping etc. different parts of the body to produce a wide range of sounds – try chests, fingernails, teeth, cheeks with mouths open . . . in fact, anything – not forgetting the human voice! Children learn to control their movements to create loud and soft sounds, fast and slow rhythms.

Any bought instruments available should be of good quality and produce pleasing

sounds – cheap ones are not sufficiently durable and often create a poor sound. Although tuned percussion (i.e. xylophone, glockenspiel, metallophone) are likely to be found in schools, individual, child-friendly instruments are better for younger children who may not be ready to share. A good range could include untuned percussion – tulip blocks, cabasa, guiro (or scraper), maracas, tambour (hand-held drum), tambourine (like a tambour, but with metal discs around the side), castanets (on a hand-held stick), claves (or rhythm sticks), click-clacks, bongo drums – as well as Indian bells, triangle and beater, individual chime bars and beaters, cow bells and hand-held bells. A group of instruments can be placed in a 'sound' corner for children to experiment with on their own or in pairs – perhaps all 'wooden' instruments on one occasion or 'ones that are struck with a beater' another time.

Playing musical instruments in a group

Large group sessions can be difficult to organise, but some **simple rules** can make them enjoyable for all and worthwhile.

*   **Sitting in a circle** and reinforcing the names of instruments as they are given out helps to keep things under control. Even 3-year-olds can understand that they must leave their instrument on the floor in front of them until asked to pick it up, although this is not easy in the first instance.
*   **Having a go**: it is usually a good idea to allow children to 'have a go' with their instruments before doing a more focused activity. The whole point of the games is for children to experience music-making so there must be plenty of playing and experimenting, and not too much sitting around waiting!

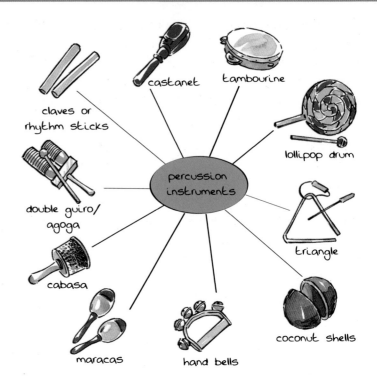

Fig 8.2. Percussion instruments

* **Taking turns to listen** to each child make as many different sounds on her instrument in as many ways as she can is a good way of building her confidence and understanding that there is no right or wrong way.
* **Offer choices**: children can then choose the sounds they like best. Similarly, work can focus on dynamics – loud and soft – and children can be asked to play as loudly as they can and as quietly as they can. Which instruments were difficult to do this with? Why?
* **Taking turns to play**: another activity involves each child having an instrument – this time make sure there are some that resonate (i.e. go on sounding after they have been played or struck) as well as the wooden percussion instruments. Going around the group, one child plays her instrument and the next child cannot play until the sound has died away. Discuss which instruments had 'long' sounds and which 'short' ones.

Moving to music

This allows children to respond creatively to different sounds and rhythms. A wide variety should be available, as for listening. Circle singing games such as 'The farmer's in his den', 'Ring-a-ring o' roses' and 'Here we go round the mulberry bush' all encourage children to move in time with the pulse or beat.

Composing music

Choosing sounds and putting them together in patterns around silence to create their own tunes and rhythms can develop listening and intellectual skills. (There are many useful books available with suggestions for games and activities.)

Using home-made instruments

This adds variety and interest. The most successful of these are shakers made from 'found materials' using different containers –

tins, plastic pots, boxes (these must be clean and have close-fitting lids) – and choosing contents that will produce interesting sounds. These could be rice grains, lentils, chickpeas, black-eyed beans, runner bean seeds, dried pasta, stones or sand.

Under supervision children can experiment and choose the contents, the amount and the container. If they are to be used continually it is a good idea to glue the lids on to avoid the danger of children putting small items in their mouths. They can also be decorated or covered in patterned sticky-backed plastic.

THE OPPORTUNITIES FOR DRAMA AND IMAGINATIVE PLAY IN A VARIETY OF SETTINGS

In imaginative play, children use their own real-life experiences and rearrange them. It provides opportunities for children to express emotions, such as jealousy, frustration or anger, in a safe and unthreatening way. Imaginative play links with:

* creative play
* role play
* dramatic play
* domestic play
* fantasy play
* play with dolls and small world objects.

Activities to promote imaginative play

These include the following.

Role play (or pretend play)

Children act out roles, usually pretending to be parents or characters from TV programmes or books. They benefit from having access to a home area, with scaled-down cooker, table and chairs, and so on.

Small world play

Small-scale models of people, animals, cars, doll's houses and fake food are useful in imaginative play; children are familiar with these objects and playing with them helps them to relax and also to extend their language skills.

Dressing-up activities

Playing with dressing-up clothes stimulates imaginative play, and pretending to be an adult (parent, superhero, king or queen) allows children to feel in control and empathise with others.

Play with puppets and dolls

Puppets and dolls (or teddies) can often help a withdrawn or shy child to voice their hidden feelings – by using the puppet's voice. This type of play may also help children to vent their powerful emotions (e.g. jealousy of a new baby) by shouting at, say, a teddy.

WAYS TO SUPPORT CHILDREN TO EXPRESS THEIR CREATIVITY

Creative play is about experimenting with materials and music. It is not about producing things to go on display or to be taken home. For example, when children are involved with messy finger play with paint, nothing is left at the end of the session once it has been cleared away – there is no end product to be seen.

Activities to promote creative play include:

* dance
* music
* collage
* drawing and painting
* model-making and woodwork
* sand (small world scenarios)

ACTIVITY: OBSERVING CHILDREN DURING PHYSICAL ACTIVITY

Select one child to observe during a period of physical activity (e.g. a gym or dance class, outdoor play with climbing equipment, or ball games). Devise a checklist (see Unit 2 for guidelines on making observations) to record the child's use of:

- gross motor skills (e.g. running, squatting, climbing)

- fine motor skills (e.g. throwing and catching a ball, picking up equipment and carrying objects).

Write a conclusion to show how the particular session of physical activity benefited the individual child; note if there were ways that the session could be extended to improve the development of these skills.

---

different materials in interesting and enjoyable ways.

Activities to promote exploratory play include:

- water play
- sand play
- clay and play dough
- drawing and painting
- cooking
- making music.

(For more information on these categories of play, see Unit 4, pages 144–156.)

Learning through cooking activities

Almost all children have some experience of cooking or, at the very least, food preparation, in their own homes. This experience can range from watching tins being opened and the contents heated, seeing fruit being peeled and cut, or bread being put in a toaster and then spread, to a full-scale three-course meal (or more) being cooked. All cultures have their own food traditions, and cooking activities with young children provide an ideal opportunity to introduce and celebrate their diversity and richness.

Mealtimes are, for most of us, social occasions that involve sharing, turn-taking

and an understanding of acceptable behaviour: 'table manners'! Apart from allowing children to develop these social skills, cooking activities are valuable in promoting **scientific understanding** in terms of materials and their properties and processes of change – both physical and chemical.

- **Physical changes** are those that can be reversed (e.g. water, when frozen, becomes ice but, when allowed to thaw, returns to its original state – water).
- **Chemical changes** are those that have brought about a change in the substance that cannot be reversed (e.g. a piece of bread once toasted will not return to its original state when left to cool, or cheese that has been heated and become melted will not return to its original form or texture even if it retains its essential flavour).

Most importantly, children are learning these fascinating facts in the context of an everyday activity.

Safety and hygiene are paramount considerations when planning and implementing such activities. Some people have food allergies that must be taken into account when planning what foodstuffs will be used. Less obvious may be skin conditions

GUIDELINES FOR COOKING WITH CHILDREN

- Always prepare surfaces with anti-bacterial spray and clean cloths.
- Always ensure children have washed their hands and scrubbed their fingernails.
- Always provide protective clothing and, if necessary, roll up long sleeves.
- Always tie back long hair.
- Always check equipment for damage.
- Always follow the safety procedures and policies of the work setting.

- Always ensure adequate supervision.
- Always remind children not to cough over food or put their fingers or utensils in their mouths when handling food.
- Always check the use-by dates of food items and store them correctly.
- Always check for 'E' numbers and artificial ingredients in bought food items.

(e.g. eczema), which may be painful particularly if in contact with fruit juices or, sometimes, soaps and washing-up liquids. Some thought at the planning stage should enable you to check with parents and take the necessary steps (e.g. thin disposable gloves) to involve all the children.

As you make these preparations for the activity you can use them to develop children's understanding and awareness of hygiene. Whenever possible you should provide a set of equipment, appropriately sized, for each child and ensure that the finished product is given to the child who made it.

Strangely enough, cooking activities do not always need to involve using a cooker or even a microwave oven! Figure 8.3 highlights a wide range of processes that offer opportunities to use food with children. For some you need only the food and basic utensils (e.g. for spreading, decorating biscuits, preparing fruit salad); for others the use of a kettle or access to hot water may be sufficient. Use of a refrigerator will be needed for others.

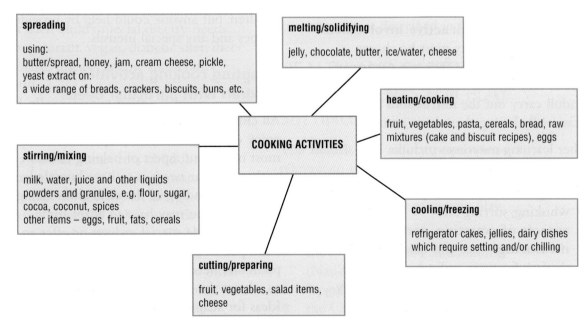

spreading

using:
butter/spread, honey, jam, cream cheese, pickle, yeast extract on:
a wide range of breads, crackers, biscuits, buns, etc.

melting/solidifying

jelly, chocolate, butter, ice/water, cheese

heating/cooking

fruit, vegetables, pasta, cereals, bread, raw mixtures (cake and biscuit recipes), eggs

COOKING ACTIVITIES

stirring/mixing

milk, water, juice and other liquids
powders and granules, e.g. flour, sugar, cocoa, coconut, spices
other items – eggs, fruit, fats, cereals

cooling/freezing

refrigerator cakes, jellies, dairy dishes which require setting and/or chilling

cutting/preparing

fruit, vegetables, salad items, cheese

Fig 8.3. Cooking activities

* the Regulation of Care (Scotland) Act 2001.

The policies and procedures of a range of settings

All play settings must have policies with clear procedures to show how to implement them. These vary from setting to setting, but generally include the following areas:

* health and safety, including safety on outings, safety when escorting children to and from the setting, risk assessment, etc.
* child protection
* fire alarms and emergency procedures
* dealing with accidents and injuries
* health and hygiene.

Figure 8.4 shows a sample 'Policy on Managing Accidents and Incidents'.

HOW TO ENCOURAGE CHILDREN TO DIRECT THEIR OWN PLAY

Children of school age are expected to be given responsibility, and choice in play, according to their age. The play environment must support this by providing:

* a stimulating play environment, which also promotes their physical safety and emotional well-being
* a wide range of opportunities for play, including an element of challenge and reasonable risk-taking

* minimal adult supervision – so that the child feels in control
* opportunities to choose whether or not they want to be involved in certain play activities
* access to a wide range of materials and the freedom to choose how they use the resources, which will allow them to direct – or determine – their own play
* group activities that are not too large so that children feel pressured and unable to enjoy the activity.

Section 3

The role of the adult in providing play activity for children

WORKING WITH COLLEAGUES IN THE PROMOTION OF PLAY

It is very important that you establish and maintain good working relationships with colleagues, so that a positive play environment is provided for children. A positive play environment has the following features:

* a caring environment that promotes respect and cooperation
* promotes child development through play
* works in partnership with parents for the benefit of the children

ACTIVITY: POLICIES AND PROCEDURES

Find out about your setting's policies and procedures for:
* health and safety

* child protection and bullying
* inclusion and anti-discriminatory practice.

Meadowfield Nursery

MANAGING ACCIDENTS & INCIDENTS POLICY

All accidents to children and adults must be recorded in the relevant Accident Report Book, as soon as possible.

ACCIDENTS TO CHILDREN

Record must include:

- ❑ name of child and date of birth
- ❑ date and time (this is particularly important in the case of head injuries)
- ❑ nature and cause of accident
- ❑ any visible signs of injury, e.g. bruising; state where marks are located; a check should be made during the session in case bruising occurs later, and the record added to
- ❑ treatment given
- ❑ how the child responded to the injury, e.g. upset, not concerned
- ❑ printed name and signature of member of staff dealing with injury; name and signature of witness
- ❑ details of how the child appears after, say, half an hour; in the case of head injuries the child should be monitored regularly throughout the session and behaviour noted.

At the end of the session the record must be read and signed by the parent/carer and a copy of the report should be handed to them.

In the case of an injury being caused by another child, that child's name should not be included in the report but referred to as 'another child'; an 'incident' report can be made for the offending child, if appropriate.

IN AN EMERGENCY

- ❑ The child must not be taken to hospital by car.
- ❑ If the child requires hospital admission an ambulance will be called – dial 999.
- ❑ Parents must be notified immediately.
- ❑ If parents are unavailable, notify emergency contact.
- ❑ Ensure all medical records are taken to the hospital.
- ❑ If necessary, arrange for additional adults to come into the group to maintain ratios.
- ❑ Keep other children distracted and reassured.

ACCIDENTS TO ADULTS

Record should include:

- ❑ name of injured person
- ❑ date of birth
- ❑ position held in nursery
- ❑ date and time of accident
- ❑ particulars of injury/accident
- ❑ activity at time of injury/accident
- ❑ place of injury/accident
- ❑ details of injury/accident
- ❑ first aid treatment given (if any) including if injured taken to hospital; if so which hospital?
- ❑ names of person(s) witnessing the injury/accident and signature(s)
- ❑ name of person(s) dealing with the injury/accident and signature(s).

IN AN EMERGENCY

If a member of staff has to be taken to hospital an ambulance should be called and they must be accompanied. Adequate cover must be maintained in the pre-school to comply with adult:child ratios. The next of kin of the staff member should be notified.

Fig 8.4. Sample Managing Accidents and Incident Policy

ACTIVITY: RESEARCH INTO PLAYWORK

Find out about the career of a **playworker**.

1. What is playwork?

2. What qualities do you need to become a playworker?

3. Where would you expect to find employment with a qualification in Playwork?

---

* provides a wide range of play opportunities appropriate to the individual play needs of each child.

(For more information on working with colleagues, see Unit 7.)

See the SkillsActive website for a list of courses: www.skillsactive.com.

HOW TO END A PLAY SESSION

You must be able to end each play session in a way that is appropriate to the children, their level of involvement and the requirements of your play setting. You can do this in the following ways.

* **Giving advance warning**: remember to warn the children 5 to 10 minutes in advance that the play session is about to end – so that they have a chance to finish what they are doing.
* **Asking for feedback**: give children the chance to give feedback on the play opportunities and environments, and note this feedback for future sessions; this can be done informally, by chatting to them about their experiences, or – with older children – using a questionnaire or suggestion box.
* **Ensuring child safety**: following your setting's procedures for ensuring the safety of the children on departure – for example, young children must be collected by a known adult.

* **Tidying up the play environment**: follow your setting's procedures for tidying up the play environment and dealing with resources.
* **Completing all required records**: such as attendance logs, notification slips, and so on.

Tidy-up time

The role of the adult is important at tidy-up time. This can be enjoyable if adults think of tidying up as part of the child's learning through play. Children love to sweep with dustpans and brooms with shortened handles, which can be made safe for the children to use. They enjoy wiping tables. If boxes have labels, pictures and words, they take pride in putting things away in the right box. If children have choices about taking things off shelves to use play materials, they know where to put them back when they have finished using them. Children will willingly help to water plants.

It is important to encourage both boys and girls to join in with tidying up. Knowing a child's interests helps adults to find something the child will enjoy tidying away. Children are eager to help put away large equipment in an outside shed. They will work as a team if encouraged.

Unit 9

Supporting Children with Additional Needs

Contents

Unit 9 is divided into three sections:

Section 1: Supporting children with additional needs and their families

Section 2: Planning to meet individual needs within the setting

Section 3: How to promote the participation of children with additional needs in activities and experiences

Section 1

Supporting children with additional needs and their families

WHAT ARE ADDITIONAL NEEDS?

Children with additional needs have needs that are 'in addition' to the general needs of children. Some children have a very obvious and well-researched **disability**, such as Down's syndrome or cerebral palsy; others may have a specific learning difficulty such as dyslexia or giftedness. What defines them as children with additional needs is the fact that they need *additional help* in some area of development, care or education compared with other children.

It is important to remember that children are more alike than they are different. *Every* child needs:

* to feel welcome
* to feel safe, both physically and emotionally
* to have friends and to feel as if they belong
* to be encouraged to live up to their potential
* to be celebrated for his or her uniqueness.

In other words, **children** are always **children first**; and the additional need is secondary.

Children with additional needs are often referred to as children with **special educational needs (SEN)**, and the current legislation in England and Wales reflects this; however, in Scotland, recent legislation emphasises children's need for additional support – to meet their additional needs.

What are additional needs?

Additional needs is a broad term to cover children and young people who need **extra support**, long term or temporarily. This might be because they have:

* a physical disability
* a learning disability
* sight and/or hearing problems
* specific behaviour problems
* some other disability condition that requires treatment over a long period.

It should also be noted that a child may also have only a *temporary* or short-term need; examples include: when a child's parent or sibling has died; when they are a victim of bullying or abuse; when they have a temporary hearing loss after a common cold.

CHILDREN WITH ADDITIONAL NEEDS: LEGAL REQUIREMENTS

Education is a lifelong process, but, in formal terms, it involves schooling between the ages of 4 or 5 and 16 years, with further options of attending colleges and universities, or training schemes with an employer. Until the 1950s in the UK, children born with an obvious disabling condition, such as Down's syndrome or cerebral palsy, would have been cared for within the family for the first few years of life. Then they would be admitted to a large mental handicap hospital where they may have spent the rest of their lives with no contact with mainstream educational institutions. Fortunately this is no longer the case.

The laws relating to special or additional needs

The term '**Special Educational Needs**', or SEN, has a legal definition. The Government's Department for Education and

Skills (DfES) defines children with SEN as having 'learning difficulties or disabilities which make it harder for them to learn or access education than most other children of the same age'.

A child with **special needs** may need extra or different help at school or home because of:

* physical difficulties or disability
* communication problems
* a visual or hearing impairment
* emotional, social and behavioural difficulties
* a serious medical condition
  or
* a combination of any of these.

The definition of special educational needs usually applies only to children and young people with particular types of **learning needs**. The new concept of **additional support needs** refers to any child or young person who, *for whatever reason*, requires additional support for learning.

The main **Acts** that have shaped the way in which children with special needs are cared for and educated today are:

* the Education Act 1996
* the Children Act 2004
* the Education (Additional Support for Learning) (Scotland) Act 2004
* the Disability Discrimination Act 2005
* the Special Needs and Disability Act (SENDA) 2001.

The **Education Act 1996** says that 'children have **special educational needs** if they have a **learning difficulty** which calls for special educational provision to be made for them'. Children have a learning difficulty if they:

* have a significantly greater difficulty in learning than the majority of children of the same age, or

* have a **disability** that prevents or hinders them from making use of educational facilities of a kind generally provided for children of the same age in schools within the area of the LEA
* are under compulsory school age and fall within the definitions above, or would do so if special educational provision were not made for them.

The **Children Act 2004** defines learning disability as 'a state of arrested or incomplete development of mind which induces significant impairment of intelligence and social functioning'.

The guidance to the **Education (Additional Support for Learning) (Scotland) Act 2004 (ASfL Act)** stresses that additional support needs are *not* the same as special needs. At any point in their lives children and young people may need extra help in school. This may be for any reason, at any time and for any length of time. This is often referred to as additional support for learning or having additional support needs. There are a number of reasons why a child or young person may need additional support in school. The ASfL Act outlines four broad categories that may give rise to **additional support needs**.

1. The **learning environment** is not appropriate for a child's needs.
   Examples: the child needs to be taught in a slightly different way; the classroom set-up is not suitable to the child's needs.
2. **Family circumstances** are affecting a child's ability to learn.
   Examples: The child may need support: to cope with a family breakdown; if they are a carer for another family member; if affected by homelessness; if looked after by the authority or if he or she has recently left care.
3. A child has a **disability or health need**.

Example: The child may: be affected by a physical or sensory disability; have a specific learning difficulty; be affected by autistic spectrum disorder; have a debilitating illness – or their mental health may impact on their learning.

4. A child is experiencing **social or emotional problems**.

Examples: The child may: have missed out in a lot of their education; need help coping with bereavement; have difficulties with behaviour; be involved in a bullying situation or subject to some form of discrimination.

The support provided will be tailored to the individual child and may include:

* extra time with a teacher or assistant, either alone or in a group
* help to come to school (e.g. a taxi, or child care if the child is a young parent)
* time with a therapist (e.g. a speech therapist who can help with speech and language)
* someone to help the child take medicine
* different work or homework to do
* someone to write for the child (a scribe)
* equipment (like a laptop)
* more time to do school work and exams
* a counselling buddy (older pupil who looks out for the child in the playground or helps them study).

The **Disability Discrimination Act 2005** placed new responsibilities on local authorities; these include the requirement to:

* eliminate unlawful discrimination against disabled children and adults
* eliminate harassment and bullying of disabled children and adults
* promote equality of opportunity and positive attitudes towards disabled children
* take steps to take account of disabled children's and adults' impairments, even if this results in more favourable treatment.

The **Special Needs and Disability Act (SENDA) 2001**

The Special Needs and Disability Act 2001 strengthened the right of children with disabilities to attend mainstream educational facilities. It was supported by the Code of Practice 2002 (see below).

Codes of practice and provision for children with special needs

The Special Educational Needs Code of Practice 2002

The **SEN Code** has the following general principles:

* a child with special needs should have his or her needs met
* the special needs of children will be met in **mainstream schools** – wherever possible
* the views of children should be sought and taken into account
* parents have a vital role to play in supporting their child's education – and must be seen as partners with Local Education Authorities (LEAs) and other agencies
* children with special educational needs should be offered full access to a broad, balanced and relevant education, including an appropriate curriculum for the Foundation Stage and the National Curriculum
* all early years settings have a **special educational needs policy** and follow the integrated team approach of the Foundation Stage Profile
* early identification, Early Years Action, Early Years Action Plus and for some children, statutory assessment.

According to the Code, every school must appoint a member of staff who takes responsibility for special education needs: the

Special Educational Needs Coordinator or SENCO.

Special educational needs policy

All schools must have a special educational needs policy. This should include information about:

* how they identify and make provision for children with special educational needs
* the facilities they have, including those that increase access for pupils who are disabled, including access to the curriculum
* how resources are allocated to and among pupils with special educational needs
* how they enable pupils with special educational needs to engage in activities of the school together with pupils with do not have additional needs
* how the governing body evaluates the success of the schools' work with pupils with special educational needs
* their arrangements for dealing with complaints from parents.

Schools should adopt a three-stage approach to identifying and providing for special educational needs. Records of this provision are usually held in schools by the Special Educational Needs Coordinator (SENCO).

1. **Stage 1 Early Years Action** or **School Action** should be initiated when a pupil is identified as having special educational needs that mean they need an adapted or differentiated curriculum and the teacher needs to use different strategies from those usually provided in the class.

2. **Stage 2 Early Years Action Plus** or **School Action Plus** may follow if a pupil is making inadequate progress at School Action level. Specialists, such as an educational psychologist or a therapist, or other external advisers will be involved, advising teachers and providing assessments and strategies.

3. **Stage 3 Statement of Special Educational Needs**. If a pupil is making inadequate progress despite intervention at School Action Plus, a request for a statutory assessment may be made to the local authority. Only a small proportion of pupils require a statutory assessment, and even fewer are provided with a statement.

THE ASSESSMENT PROCESS: THE STATEMENT OF SPECIAL EDUCATIONAL NEEDS

The **Statement of Special Educational Needs** is a legal document produced by LEAs following multi-professional assessment and contributions from parents or carers. It specifies the precise nature of the pupil's assessed difficulties and educational needs, and the special or additional provision that would be made in order to meet that pupil's needs. Statements must then be reviewed at least annually.

In the UK about 17 per cent of all schoolchildren have a special educational need. Most – around 60 per cent – are taught in **mainstream** schools, where they receive additional help from a range of services. Children with special educational needs but *without* a statement will have their needs met through **Early Years Action** or Early Years Action Plus. (When children reach school age these are called School Action and School Action Plus.)

THE EARLY SUPPORT PROGRAMME

The **Early Support programme** – started in 2002 – is the central government device for achieving better-coordinated, family-focused services for young disabled children and their families in England.

Features of Early Support include the following.

- It is for families with a baby or young child who has **additional support needs** because of a disability or an emerging special educational need. It is particularly relevant where families are in contact with a number of different agencies, because the programme facilitates better **coordination of support**.
- Each family is given a **Family File** – a family-held record that supports better coordination of services provided for a child and family, and more effective exchange of information between professionals working for different agencies.
- A range of **Information for Parents** booklets on particular conditions or disabilities are provided, which provide standard 'first step' information for families where a particular factor has been identified as significant for a child.
- Coordination/multi-agency support for families: families receive coordinated support through **key worker** systems, better sharing of information between agencies, family support plans and family-held records.
- **Partnership across agencies** and geographical boundaries: access to good services for families does not depend on where they live.

Where a child has severe or complex needs, Early Years Action and Early Years Action Plus will be bypassed.

An assessment must take account of the following five factors.

1. **Physical factors:** the child's particular illness or condition.
2. **Psychological and emotional factors:** the child's intellectual ability and levels of anxiety or depression will lead to different needs and priorities (e.g. severe anxiety may adversely affect all daily activities, and its alleviation will therefore assume top priority).
3. **Socio-cultural factors:** whether or not the child is part of a family, the family's background and the relationships within the family will all influence needs. Similarly, the individual's wider community and the social class to which they belong are also influential.
4. **Environmental factors:** a child living in a cold, damp house with an outside toilet will have different needs from someone who is more comfortably housed.
5. **Political and economic factors:** poverty or belonging to a disadvantaged group leads to less choice in day-to-day living.

Statutory support for children with additional needs and their families

Most families in an area use statutory services (i.e. the services provided by their local authority for *all* families and children, including **health**, **education** and **social services**). (See Unit 1 for the range of provision for children and their families.)

Local authorities provide some services directly – for example, benefits, schools and short break, or respite, schemes funded by social services.

Voluntary and independent support for children with additional needs and their families

In the independent sector, some services are provided by **charities** or commercial organisations with a particular interest in special needs or particular disabilities. Sometimes these services are funded by local authorities.

Example: Children with **autistic spectrum disorder (ASD)** might attend a nursery run by a local voluntary organisation with particular experience of supporting children with ASD, but with their local education authority or social services department paying for them to attend.

Problems occur when children are not recognised as having additional needs until their development begins to look different from that of other children. This is especially true for children with autistic spectrum disorder or ADHD (attention deficit hyperactivity disorder). Diagnosis of a disorder or disability is not always straightforward, and is often ambiguous.

Extra help or support in the pre-school years is provided at different levels, depending on how severe a child's need for extra help is, and on the approach taken by each individual local authority.

HOW TO ACCESS AVAILABLE INFORMATION TO SUPPORT CHILDREN AND THEIR FAMILIES

Parent partnership services

The Parent Partnership Scheme (PPS) is a statutory service that offers the following support:

* information, advice and support for parents of children and young people with special educational needs (SEN)
* putting parents in touch with other local organisations
* making sure that parents' views are heard and understood – and that these views inform local policy and practice.

Some parent partnerships are based in the voluntary sector, although the majority of them remain based in their LEA (Local Education Authority) or Children's Trust. All parent partnerships, wherever they are based, work separately and independently from the LEA; this means that they are able to provide impartial advice and support to parents.

For more information, visit the NPPN (National Parent Partnership Network) website at www.parentpartnership.org.uk.

The Every Disabled Child Matters (EDCM) campaign

The EDCM campaign was launched in September 2006 to get rights and justice for every disabled child. Every Disabled Child Matters wants:

* families with disabled children to have ordinary lives
* disabled children and their families to be fully included in society
* all disabled children and their families to get the right services and support – no matter where they live
* poverty among disabled children and their families to be cut by 50 per cent by 2010 and eliminated by 2020
* an education system that meets the needs of each child and enables them to reach their full potential.

Section 2

Planning to meet individual needs within the setting

THE IMPORTANCE OF INCLUSION

Inclusion is a term used within education to describe the process of ensuring **equality of learning opportunities** for all children and young people, whatever their disabilities or disadvantages. This means that all children have the right to have their needs met in the best way for them. They are seen as being part of the community, even if they need additional help to live a full life within that community.

Inclusion refers to *everyone*, no matter the additional support needs of an individual, their gender or sexual preference, religion, race or cultural background.

Inclusive practice in child settings is important because:

* it promotes an ethos of equality of opportunity and high achievement for all children, by encouraging the development of more flexible attitudes, policies and everyday practices
* it promotes community integration through understanding of and respect for others
* it recognises and celebrates diversity.

The government's aim is for all schools to become **inclusive schools**. These are schools that welcome all pupils, and develop values that promote pupils' educational, social and cultural development.

Despite the moves towards inclusion, there are arguments for keeping a minority of children in special schools. Inclusion is about much more than the *type* of setting that children attend – it is about the *quality* of

their experience and how they are welcomed, helped to learn and enabled to participate fully in the life of the school or setting.

Mainstream education

Children and young people with additional support needs have the right to be educated within a mainstream school alongside other children. Education authorities should provide education in mainstream school *unless:*

* education in a special school would better suit the ability or aptitude of a child with additional support needs
* mainstream education would not allow the other children in the classroom to get the most from their learning
* mainstream education for a child with additional support needs would result in unusually high public costs.

Special schools

Many special schools are developing their inclusive practice. They are educating children and young people directly, and they also share their expertise with mainstream schools; this promotes inclusion by making provision more flexible.

Ofsted (2001) states that, 'An educationally inclusive school is one in which the teaching and learning and the achievements, attitudes and well-being of every young person matter. Effective schools are educationally inclusive schools.'

The debate about inclusion is summarised in the box opposite.

HOW INCLUSION SHOULD WORK IN A RANGE OF SETTINGS

Under the Children Act 1989, all local authorities have to keep a register of local

THE INCLUSION DEBATE: THE LAST 30 YEARS

1. In 1978 Mary Warnock, an Oxford academic who headed a government commission into the education of 'handicapped' children, pioneered the concept of inclusion, arguing that children with special educational needs (SEN) should be taught in **mainstream schools**. She also invented the **'statement'** – a document that assessed and recorded the needs of pupils with SEN, which a local education authority then had to meet.

2. The inclusion agenda developed in the 1990s. Schools were given a legal requirement to meet the needs of children with learning difficulties. They also had to publish their SEN policies, meaning parents could see any discrepancies in standards across the country. The **Education Act 1996** said children with SEN should be taught in mainstream schools *unless it harmed the education of other children*.

3. Legislation in 2001 said inclusion should be pursued unless the parents did not want it. Many parents argue they cannot get their children into special schools despite wanting to.

4. Mary Warnock performed a dramatic U-turn in 2005: she declared that inclusion and statements were failures; that bullying of pupils with SEN was inevitable in mainstream schools, and that statements should only be passports to special schools. In other word, inclusion must be rethought.

5. In 2006, the government was criticised for barely mentioning SEN in its education bill. Two-thirds of children *excluded* from secondary school have SEN, but the section on discipline ignores this.

The debate continues . . .

---

disabled children. This is to help the local authority plan services more effectively. Registration is not compulsory and failure to register does not affect a child's right to services.

The professionals listed in Table 9.1 overleaf are all involved in the care and education of children with special needs. Many of them work in the community or in **special schools**; however, with the government's commitment to inclusive education, some are also involved in the education of children in mainstream settings.

THE ADVANTAGES AND DISADVANTAGES OF INCLUSION FOR THE CHILD

Each child will have individual needs, so the advantages and disadvantages of inclusion will vary according to these individual circumstances. Many parents of children with special needs believe that their child will benefit more from being in a 'special school.' Many teachers feel that trying to educate children with additional needs in a mainstream setting is demanding too much of the education system, and that the children *without* additional needs may find that *their* needs are not fully met.

The advantages of inclusion for the child

* The child gets the opportunity to be part of the bigger community – and not to feel marginalised.
* The child has peers on whom to model behaviour.
* The other children learn not to be scared of people who are different.

Family doctors (GPs)

Family doctors are independent professionals who are under contract to the National Health Service, but who are not employed by it. They are the most available of the medical profession, and are also able to refer carers on to specialist doctors and paramedical services.

Health visitors

Health visitors are qualified nurses who have done further training, including midwifery experience. They work exclusively in the community, and can be approached either directly or via the family doctor. They work primarily with children up to the age of 5 years; this obviously includes all children with disabilities, and they carry out a wide range of developmental checks.

Physiotherapists

The majority of 'physios' are employed in hospitals, but some work in special schools or residential facilities. Physiotherapists assess children's motor development and skills, and provide activities and exercises that parents and carers can use to encourage better mobility and coordination.

Paediatric occupational therapists

Paediatric occupational therapists (or OTs) specialise in working with children. They carry out assessments to see if children would benefit from using specialist equipment like adapted cups and cutlery, chairs or buggies, and provide advice on lifting and handling children safely. They also help children to improve daily living skills (e.g. eating and dressing).

They work in hospitals, schools and other residential care settings.

Community nurses

Most community nurses work closely with family doctors and provide nursing care in the home. They also advise the parent or carer on specialist techniques (e.g. on how to lift, catheter care).

School nurses

School nurses may visit a number of mainstream schools in their health district to monitor child health and development – by checking weight, height, eyesight and hearing, and by giving advice on common problems such as head lice. They may also be employed in special schools to supervise the routine medical care of disabled children.

Speech therapists

Speech therapists may be employed in schools, in hospitals or in the community. They assess a child's speech, tongue and mouth movements, and the effects of these on eating and swallowing. They also provide exercises and activities both to develop all aspects of children's expressive and receptive communication skills and to encourage language development.

Communication support worker

A communication support worker works alongside teachers to provide sign language for young deaf children in nursery or school.

Play specialists

Play specialists are employed in hospitals and are often qualified nursery nurses who have additional training. They may prepare a child for hospitalisation and provide play opportunities for children confined to bed or in a hospital playroom.

Play therapists

Play therapists also work in hospitals and have undertaken specialist training. They use play to enable children with special needs to feel more secure emotionally in potentially threatening situations.

Clinical psychologists

Clinical psychologists usually work in hospitals. They assess children's emotional, social and intellectual development and advise on appropriate activities to promote development.

Dieticians

Most dieticians work in hospitals and can advise on a range of special diets (e.g. for diabetics or those with cystic fibrosis or coeliac disease).

Social workers Most social workers now work in specialised teams dealing with a specific client group (e.g. a Disability and Learning Difficulties Team). They are employed by social services departments (called 'social work departments' in Scotland) and initially their role is to assess the needs of the child. They may refer the family to other departments, such as the Department of Social Security (DSS), the National Health Service (NHS) or voluntary organisations. A social worker may also act as an advocate on behalf of disabled children, ensuring that they receive all the benefits and services to which they are entitled.	**Technical officers** Technical officers usually work with people with specific disorders (e.g. audio technicians or audiologists monitor the level of hearing in children as a developmental check, and sign language interpreters translate speech into sign language for deaf and hearing-impaired people).
Nursery officers Nursery officers are trained nursery nurses who work in day nurseries and family centres. Such staff are involved in shift work, and they care for children under 5 years when it is not possible for those children to remain at home.	**Family aids** Family aids (or home care assistants) used to be called 'home helps'; they provide practical support for families in their own homes (e.g. shopping, cooking, looking after children).
The Special Educational Needs Coordinator (SENCO) The special educational needs coordinator liaises both with colleagues in special schools and with the parents of children with special needs. They are responsible for coordinating provision for children with special educational needs, for keeping the school's SEN register and for working with external agencies (e.g. educational psychology services, social service departments and voluntary organisations).	**Educational psychologists** Educational psychologists are involved in the educational assessment of children with special needs, and in preparing the statement of special educational needs. They act as advisers to professionals working directly with children with a range of special needs, particularly those with emotional and behavioural difficulties.
Portage worker Portage is an educational programme for children who have difficulty in learning basic skills due to either physical or behavioural problems. Home Portage Advisers are specially trained in understanding child development and come from a variety of professions, ranging from nurses or other health professionals to schoolteachers.	**Orthoptist** An orthoptist works with people who have visual problems and abnormal eye movements.
Special needs teachers Special needs teachers are qualified teachers with additional training and experience in teaching children with special needs. They are supported by: • **special needs support teachers** or **specialist teachers** who are often **peripatetic** (they visit disabled children in different mainstream schools) and who may specialise in a particular disorder (e.g. vision or hearing impairment) • **special needs support assistants** who may be qualified nursery nurses, and who often work with individual 'statemented' children under the direction of the specialist teacher.	**Educational welfare officers** As in mainstream education, educational welfare officers will be involved with children whose school attendance is irregular; they may also arrange school transport for disabled children.

Table 9.1: Professionals involved in the care and education of children with SEN

The disadvantages of inclusion for the child

* The child may disrupt the class and become resented both by other pupils and some staff.
* The child will not receive therapy as part of their school day – as they might in a special school.
* Teachers may not be experienced in teaching children with additional needs.
* The child may become isolated and feel different.
* There is often a risk of exclusion for a behaviourally challenged child.
* Bullying may be a problem.

ESTABLISHING AND MAINTAINING PARTNERSHIPS WITH PARENTS AND FAMILIES

Working in partnerships with families is particularly important when a child has additional support needs. Each parent should be made to feel welcome and valued as an expert on their child, and that they play a vital role in helping practitioners to enable their child to participate and learn.

Parents and families:

* have a unique knowledge and expertise regarding their children, and local authorities need this to help them to provide the best education possible
* should be encouraged to participate in the decisions that affect their children and their education
* should be provided with the information they need to be informed about changes to legislation and practice in education
* should be given a named contact person for more detailed information; this person will provide them with details of local and national organisations that can offer more help, if required.

Parents should also be able to choose the extent to which they are involved in their child's setting. Not all parents have the time or the confidence to become involved in activities within the setting.

PROVIDING SUPPORT FOR CHILDREN AND FAMILIES

Where factors that impact on a child's ability to learn and develop are just starting to become apparent, partnership working involving *all the adults* in a child's life becomes very important. The earlier a need for additional help is identified, the more likely it is that early intervention can prevent certain aspects of a child's development or behaviour developing into a persistent difficulty.

Information and advice

Parents find that getting a diagnosis for their child is important. Being given a name for their child's condition or special need enables them to discuss their child's development needs with health, social services and education professionals.

* **Shared experiences:** parents often find that the most helpful sources of information and advice are others with shared experiences. There are many organisations that exist to provide support and answer questions.

Examples: Contact a Family, the Down Syndrome Association, Mencap and the Royal Society for the Blind, but there are hundreds more – most with their own website and helpline.

* **Service provision:** getting information about what they and their children are entitled to, as early as possible, is very

important. This applies to the **benefits** they are entitled to as well as the services.

Communicating with parents

The principles of effective communication are discussed in Unit 5. One of the main purposes of communicating with parents is to provide and to share information about the child and about the setting – both about the care and education setting and the home. Practitioners need to build up a partnership with parents, and to do this they need to promote a feeling of trust.

Providing flexible support

* **Parents** want support that is flexible enough to respond to their particular families' needs, and that is both available in an emergency and can also be planned in advance.
* **Children and young people** want support that enables them to do the kinds of things their peers do; this can vary from going swimming with their siblings to spending time away from home with their friends.

The most popular services are generally those developed by parents themselves, or by local disability organisations.

THE IMPACT ON FAMILIES

Each family will respond in their own way when they find out that their child has a disability or a special need. Common reactions of parents to having a child with disabilities include the following.

* **A sense of tragedy:** parents who give birth to a child with a disability experience complex emotions. They may grieve for the loss of a 'normal' child, but they have not actually been

bereaved – they still have a child with a unique personality and identity of their own. Relatives and friends can be embarrassed if they do not know how to react to the event, and their awkward response can leave parents feeling very isolated at a time that is normally spent celebrating.

* **A fear of making mistakes:** sometimes there is an over-reliance on professional help. If the disability seems like the most important aspect of the child's personality parents may believe that only a medical expert can advise on the care of their child. The reality is that the parent almost always knows what is required for their child. A great deal of what the child needs is not related to their disability in any case.
* **Being over-protective:** a desire to cocoon the child can be counterproductive. The child needs to be equipped for life and can learn only by making mistakes. In addition, siblings may resent the disabled child who is seen as spoilt or never punished.
* **Exercising control:** parents may take freedom of choice away from the child, so disempowering them. Parents and carers often dictate where and with whom the child plays, thus depriving them of an opportunity for valuable social learning.

There are other factors that will have an impact on family life; these include:

* financial worries, especially when parents have to juggle work commitments with child care
* feeling guilty that other children in the family are missing out on family fun because of their child's special needs
* parents feeling tired and stressed because of the extra attention required by their child, especially during bouts of illness.

Section 3

How to promote the participation of children with additional needs in activities and experiences

HOW TO RECOGNISE AND PLAN FOR INDIVIDUAL NEEDS AND LEARNING OPPORTUNITIES

Practitioners should plan to meet the needs of:

* both boys and girls
* children with special educational needs
* children who are more able
* children with disabilities
* children with complex health needs
* children from all social, family, cultural and religious backgrounds
* looked-after children
* children of all ethnic groups, including traveller communities
* refugees and asylum seekers
* children from diverse linguistic backgrounds.

. . . in other words, every child in their care. This may seem a daunting task, but if you get used to focusing on each child as an individual, with their own needs and personalities, then it does not seem so difficult!

Practitioners need to:

* **be aware that all children have different experiences**, interests, skills and knowledge that affect their ability to develop and learn
* **provide a safe and supportive learning environment**, free from harassment, in which the contribution of all children and families is valued
* **challenge** all stereotypes and expressions of discrimination or prejudice
* **value the fact that families are all different** – that children may live with one or both parents, with other relatives or carers, with same-sex parents or in an extended family.

Planning for individual needs

Practitioners should work with parents to identify **learning needs** and respond quickly to any area of particular difficulty. In nurseries and schools, teachers and other staff **observe** and note children's ways of learning, and monitor their progress. They do this in many different ways, as shown in Fig. 9.1 below.

- **by talking with children**

- **by watching children when playing and working**

- **by checking and marking children's work**

- **by using different methods of assessment**

Fig 9.1. Adults identify learning needs. . .

Individual Education Plan (IEP)

Each child with special educational needs should have an **Individual Education Plan**. This IEP should detail the ways in which an individual child will be helped. For example:

* what special help is being given
* how often the child will receive the help
* who will provide the help
* what the targets for the child are
* how and when the child's progress will be checked
* what help parents can give their child at home.

The child's teacher is responsible for the planning and should discuss the IEP with the parents, and with their child whenever possible. IEPs are usually linked to the main areas of language, literacy, mathematics, and behaviour and social skills. Sometimes the school or early education setting will *not* write an IEP but will record how it is meeting the child's needs in a different way, perhaps as part of the whole-class lesson plans, and will record the child's progress in the same way as it does for all the other children.

In addition, practitioners should:

* assess how accessible the setting is for children who use wheelchairs or walking frames, or who are learning English as an additional language, and take appropriate action to include a wider range of children
* work together with professionals from other agencies, such as local and community health services, to provide the best learning opportunities for individual children.

Multi-agency approach

In order to provide inclusive care and education, settings and individual practitioners need to know when to call in help from outside and whom to approach when more specialist expertise and help is needed. **Specialist help** includes:

* specialist teachers for children who are learning English as an additional language
* traveller education service
* speech and language therapists
* occupational therapists
* physiotherapists
* paediatricians
* social workers
* nurses
* health visitors
* midwives
* educational psychologists
* child and adolescent mental health services
* specialist teachers working with children with visual or hearing impairments
* Portage services
* dieticians.

THE IMPORTANCE OF AVOIDING LABELLING AND STEREOTYPING

As we have seen in Units 1 and 7, stereotyping often leads to **discrimination**. It also matters a great deal how we 'label' people who are different from us. Many years ago, people who were obviously *different* – that is, they were perhaps unable to walk or talk or they seemed to be a bit simple-minded – were believed to be in some way evil; some were even burnt to death as witches. Today we are much more aware of individual differences and have much more knowledge about diverse needs and abilities. It is still very important that we do not apply labels to anyone.

Disabled children are often stereotyped and labelled. This *always* has a negative effect on the child and his or her family. Table 9.2 shows you which terms are appropriate to use and which should be avoided.

Avoid	Use instead
The handicapped	Disabled people
The disabled	Disabled people *or* people with an impairment
The deaf	Deaf people/hard of hearing people (depending on which group) *or* hearing impaired
The blind	Blind people *or* partially sighted people (depending on which group), or visually impaired
(Using the collective noun ('the . . .') implies that all disabled people have the same needs and issues, and reinforces their supposed separateness from the rest of society.)	
Deaf and dumb *or* deaf mute	A person who is deaf without speech *or* deaf sign language (or British Sign Language) user (BSL is a recognised language and for many deaf people it will be their first language)
Able-bodied, healthy, normal	Non-disabled
Handicapped, cripple, invalid	Disabled *or* disabled people/person, *or* if appropriate, a person with a mobility impairment
Victim of *or* suffering from	Has (an impairment), a person with, *and* avoid using medical labels that define people by their disability
Wheelchair bound *or* confined to a wheelchair	Wheelchair user *or* a person who uses a wheelchair
An epileptic	A person with epilepsy
A spastic	A person with cerebral palsy
Mentally ill, insane, crazy, psycho, schizo, etc.	A person with mental health problems
Mental handicap, retarded	A person with learning disabilities/learning difficulties
Dwarf *or* midget	Restricted growth *or* short stature
Fits, spells, attacks	Seizures

Table 9.2: Disabled children: terms to use and those to avoid

THE IMPORTANCE OF REALISTIC EXPECTATIONS OF CHILDREN'S DEVELOPMENT

Having positive, realistic expectations for children's achievements and behaviour is something both parents and practitioners should strive for. When expectations for children are set at the right level – not too high and not too low – then children can expect to have high self-esteem and also fulfil their potential.

A good understanding of child development is vital to your work with children. You need to be aware that every child varies as to when they pass through the normative stages of development described in Unit 2.

You – and the child's parents – need to have realistic expectations for each child – based on both the **child's stage of development** and his or her **temperament** and any **additional needs**.

You also need to take account of special or additional needs, where development may be very different from the norm.

It is very important to **promote the strengths** of the children as well as assisting with their difficulties. You can achieve this by choosing some of the activities that you know the child is good at. For example, Child A may have difficulties tying her shoelaces, but may be very skilled at cutting out shapes; therefore, do some cutting-out sessions and always offer plenty of praise and encouragement, both for **achievement** and for the **effort** the child has made.

HOW TO USE SPECIFIC METHODS OF COMMUNICATION

Most children with special educational needs have difficulties with language and communication. Many benefit from learning a 'sign language', such as Makaton, PECS, Signalong or British Sign Language/Signed English.

Makaton

The Makaton vocabulary is a list of over 400 items with corresponding signs and symbols, with an additional resource vocabulary for the UK National Curriculum. The signs are based on British Sign Language (BSL), but are used to support spoken English. The Makaton Project publishes a book of illustrations of the Makaton vocabulary. Most signs rely on movement, as well as position so you can't really learn the signs from the illustrations. Also in many signs *facial expression* is important. If a child at a school or nursery is learning Makaton, the parents should be invited to learn too. The Makaton Project will support schools and parents in this, as they know that everyone involved with the child must use the same signs.

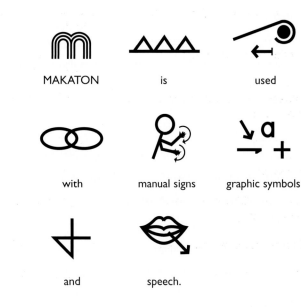

Fig 9.2. Makaton

TEMPER TANTRUMS

Temper tantrums in children usually occur from between 1 and 3 years of age and are a normal developmental stage that reflects a child's inner struggle to establish his own sense of self. (Temper tantrums are often called 'the terrible twos' and may involve crying, screaming, head-banging, breath-holding, breaking objects and/or jumping up and down.) However, if you were to see a colleague behaving in this way, you would be very alarmed! Your realistic expectations fit with the boisterous 2-year-old but not with an adult in their twenties.

Signalong

Signalong is a sign-supporting system, which is also based on British Sign Language; it is designed to help children and adults with communication difficulties – mostly associated with learning disabilities – that is user-friendly for easy access. The Signalong Group has researched and published the widest range of signs in Britain.

Picture Exchange Communication System (PECS)

PECS begins with teaching children to exchange a picture of an object that they want with a teacher, who immediately gives it to them. For example, if they want a drink, they will give a picture of 'drink' to an adult, who directly hands them a drink. Verbal prompts are not used; this encourages spontaneity and avoids children being dependent on the prompts. The system goes on to teach recognition of symbols and how to construct simple 'sentences'. Ideas for teaching language structures, such as asking and answering questions, are also incorporated. It has been reported that both pre-school and older children have begun to develop speech when using PECS. The system is often used as a communication aid for children and adults who have an **autistic spectrum disorder**.

THE BARRIERS TO PARTICIPATION FOR CHILDREN AND FAMILIES

There are certain potential barriers to participation – or **access to provision** – for children with additional needs and their families. These include the following.

* **Physical barriers:** this does not refer only to the more obvious physical barriers, such as not having any ramps nor sufficiently wide doors for wheelchair access; it also refers to such facilities as toilet and washing facilities, appropriate signage for people with visual impairments, etc.
* **Attitudes of staff:** settings may exclude children from participation in group activities because of their special needs; this exclusion can sometimes be justified on health and safety grounds, but usually could be remedied with some planning and communication with the child's family.
* **Poverty:** the cost of high-quality early years care is simply not affordable for those families living in poverty. Children are more likely to be living in poverty in:
  - families with one or more disabled persons
  - lone-parent households
  - inner-city areas.

The following activities show how early years settings can present barriers to equality of access for children and their families.

HOW TO REVIEW ACTIVITIES AND EXPERIENCES TO ENSURE AN INCLUSIVE APPROACH

Even when a setting has experience in providing inclusive care and education, it is still important that activities and experiences within the setting are regularly reviewed and evaluated. In order to ensure an inclusive approach, practitioners should:

* review the setting's policies, procedures and codes of practice on equality of opportunity
* review activities and trips away from the setting to determine whether the

ACTIVITY: EXCLUDED FROM AN OUTING

The nursery manager at a private nursery explains to a child's parents that their son, Thomas, will not be able to join the rest of his group on a visit to a local children's theatre production of 'The Gruffalo's Child'. Thomas has Down's syndrome and learning difficulties. The nursery staff had met to discuss the problem and had concluded that there was no point in Thomas going as he would not appreciate the show and would probably disrupt the other children. Thomas's mother is very unhappy with their decision and has accused the nursery of discriminating against Thomas on account of his disability.

Discuss the following questions in a group.

1. Do you think the nursery staff were justified in their decision?
2. Do you believe the nursery has discriminated against Thomas?
3. What could the nursery staff have done in order to enable Thomas to join the others?

ACTIVITY: A HEARING PROBLEM

Carla, a baby of 15 months, has just been diagnosed with a severe hearing impairment. When she has her nappy changed, Mary, the baby room supervisor, notices that Laura, one of the early years practitioners, changes her nappy in silence, although she always smiles, chats and plays with the other babies during nappy-changing routines. When Mary asked her why she doesn't do the same with Carla, Laura replied that she didn't see the point because Carla can't hear anything.

1. Why is Mary concerned about Laura's child care practice?
2. Discuss ways in which practitioners could promote Carla's development and meet her holistic needs.

practice is inclusive and that there was no discrimination against disabled children (or adults)

* be reflective in their practice – this means that you are constantly learning from experience, and learning how to improve your practice.

SPECIALIST AIDS AND EQUIPMENT

Many children with learning difficulties will have **personal priority needs** that are central to their learning and quality of life. Some children may need the provision of a specific **therapy** or may require paramedical care – for example, supervising medication.

Others need to have existing equipment or activities modified or adapted to suit their particular needs. This might involve:

* **minor adaptations** to the home, such as grab rails and temporary ramps
* **bathing, feeding and walking equipment**
* **major adaptations** including door widening for wheelchair access, lowering worktops, bathroom alterations and purpose-built extensions.
* **using specialist environments** – for example, ball pools, warm-water pools, light and sound stimulation or sensory rooms.
* **providing ramps** for wheelchair users

* **providing thick pencils and brushes** for children with poor fine motor skills
* **adapting standard equipment** – for example, by having a tray on the table so that objects stay on the table, and a child with a visual impairment does not 'lose' objects that fall off
* helping children to manage eating and drinking; there is a wide range of specialist aids for eating and drinking, such as angled spoons and suction plates
* promoting children's autonomy and independence through the use of specialist aids and equipment – for example, hearing aids, non-slip table mats and special 'standing' chairs.

Helping children without using special equipment

You can often meet children's additional needs without needing specialist aids and equipment. For example, by:

* positioning children so that they learn effectively – for example, by making sure the light falls on the adult's face, so that a child wearing a hearing aid is able to lip read and a child with a visual impairment can use any residual eyesight to see facial expressions
* providing the opportunity to learn sign languages – for example, Makaton or Signalong
* developing children's self-esteem (e.g. by encouraging and praising effort as well as achievement)
* allowing children's behaviour and alternative ways of communicating to be acknowledged and understood
* providing appropriate therapies – for example, speech and language, occupational or physiotherapy (support from health services is generally set out as non-educational provision in a child's **statement**); however, speech and language therapy may be regarded as either educational or non-educational provision)
* planning the use of music, art, drama or movement therapy – these therapies may play a complementary role in the curriculum for individual children and will need to be planned as part of the whole curriculum
* helping children to maintain good posture, appropriate muscle tone and ease of movement, and promoting skills in independent mobility
* promoting relaxation and support to help children manage stress and anxiety; some settings use a sensory room, but a quiet, comfortable area will benefit all children.

Safety when using aids and equipment

Using specialist aids and equipment safely is important – both for the children's health and your own safety. Some equipment should not be moved without taking certain precautions.

* All equipment and furniture must be installed correctly and maintained adequately.
* Children and adults must know how to use the equipment correctly and follow the manufacturer's instructions.
* Often the child – or the parents – can advise staff on how to best use the equipment.

Unit 10

Introduction to Children's Learning

Contents

Unit 10 is divided into three sections:

Section 1: The different frameworks for learning for children from birth to age 16 years

Section 2: How children learn

Section 3: Supporting and encouraging children's learning

Section 1

The different frameworks for learning for children from birth to age 16 years

Each country of the UK has a government department that deals with education curriculum requirements. These are:

* **England** – Department for Children, Schools and Families
* **Wales** – Education, Lifelong Learning and Skills Department within the Welsh Assembly
* **Scotland** – Education and Lifelong Learning Department within the Scottish Parliament
* **Northern Ireland** – Department of Education for Northern Ireland (DENI).

THE CURRICULUM FRAMEWORK IN ENGLAND

From birth to 5 years old: the Early Years Foundation Stage (EYFS)

The EYFS (2007/8) is a new single framework for care, learning and development for children in *all* registered early years settings and schools from birth to the end of the reception class (the academic year in which the child turns 5). The **EYFS**:

* builds on (and replaces) the existing statutory *Curriculum Guidance for the Foundation Stage*, the non-statutory *Birth to Three Matters framework*, and elements of regulatory frameworks in the *National Standards for Under 8s Day Care and Childminding*.

The EYFS is made up of six areas of Learning and Development. These areas are all equally important and interconnected (see Figure 10.1).

The English National Curriculum

The following stages make up the English National Curriculum:

* **Foundation Stage** (from 3 years to the end of the reception year)
* **Key Stage 1** (Years 1 and 2: 5–7 years)
* **Key Stage 2** (7–11 years)
* **Key Stage 3** (11–14 years)
* **Key Stage 4** (14–16 years).

Children are assessed through **Standard Assessment Tasks** (SATs) at the end of each Key Stage, with a **Foundation Profile** at the end of the Foundation Stage. Staff in early years settings are able to use the end of the Foundation Stage Profile assessment to:

* support and encourage a multilingual classroom
* identify children with special educational needs
* encourage a dialogue between home and school, perhaps building on a home visit which is made just before the child starts school.

The subjects in the English National Curriculum are:

* three core subjects – English, maths and science (soon to be four, including citizenship)
* foundation subjects – design and technology, information technology, history, geography, art, music, physical education and a modern language (from 11 years old).

The new secondary curriculum (2008)

The **Key Stage 3** curriculum consists of the following subjects:

* art and design
* citizenship
* design and technology

Age	England	Wales	Northern Ireland	Scotland
Birth to 5	Early Years Foundation Stage Nursery (non-compulsory)	Foundation Phase (3–7) Nursery (non-compulsory)	Curricular Guidance for Pre-school Education Nursery (non-compulsory)	Birth to Three & Curriculum Framework for Children 3–5 Nursery (non compulsory)
4–5	EYFS & Primary: Key Stage 1 Reception class	Framework for Children's Learning Reception Class Year 1 Year 2	Primary: Key Stage 1 Year 1	Curriculum Framework for Children 3–5 Nursery (non-compulsory)
5–6	Year 1		Year 2	Primary P1
6–7	Year 2		Year 3	P2
7–8	Key Stage 2 Year 3	Key Stage 2 Year 3	Key Stage 2 Year 4	P3
8–9	Year 4	Year 4	Year 5	P4
9–10	Year 5	Year 5	Year 6	P5
10–11	Year 6	Year 6	Year 7	P6
11–12	Secondary – Key Stage 3 Year 7	Secondary – Key Stage 3 Year 7	Secondary – Key Stage 3 Year 8	P7
12–13	Year 8	Year 8	Year 9	Secondary S1
13–14	Year 9	Year 9	Year 10	S2
14–15	Key Stage 4 Year 10	Key Stage 4 Year 10	Key Stage 4 Year 11	S3
15–16	Year 11	Year 11	Year 12	S4
END OF COMPULSORY SCHOOLING				
16–17	Year 12 (Lower Sixth)	Year 12 (Lower Sixth)	Year 13	S5
17–18	Year 13 (Upper Sixth)	Year 13 (Upper Sixth)	Year 14	S6

Notes: The Welsh National Curriculum includes Welsh as a core subject up to Key Stage 3.
Scotland is currently developing a generic framework for the curriculum: **The 3 to 18 framework: Excellence for all.**

Table 10.1: The different frameworks for learning in the UK

Fig 10.1. The Early Years Foundation Stage: areas of Learning and Development

* personal, social, health & economic education★
* English
* geography
* history
* ICT
* mathematics
* modern foreign languages
* music
* physical education
* religious education★
* science.

★ Denotes a non-statutory programme of study.

The **Key Stage 4** curriculum consists of the following subjects:

* citizenship
* personal, social, health & economic education★

* English
* ICT
* mathematics
* physical education
* religious education★
* science

★ Denotes a non-statutory programme of study.

THE CURRICULUM FRAMEWORK IN WALES

The Foundation Phase (3 to 7)

Between 2004 and 2008, 41 settings in Wales (The Learning Country) are being trialled as part of a pilot project integrating:

* desirable outcomes for children's learning before compulsory school age

* the programmes of study and focus statements in the current Key Stage 1 National Curriculum in Wales.

This is described as the draft **Framework for Children's Learning**.

There are seven areas of learning in the **Foundation Phase**, with an emphasis on experiential learning – that is, learning by *doing* and by solving real-life problems, both inside and outdoors:

1. Personal and Social Development and Wellbeing
2. Language, Literacy and Communication Skills
3. Mathematical Development
4. Bilingualism and Multicultural Understanding
5. Knowledge and Understanding of the World
6. Physical Development
7. Creative Development.

The Welsh National Curriculum

There are three or four core subjects, depending on whether Welsh is the first language of the child and on whether the child is being educated in a Welsh-medium school: English, maths, science and Welsh. Welsh is tested at the end of each Key Stage if it is a core subject, as are the other core subjects. Welsh is studied by all children up to Key Stage 3, but tests are optional if it is the child's second language. The other subjects are the same as for the English National Curriculum, except:

* at Key Stage 4, when modern language and technology are optional
* in art and music, where there is still a requirement to make and perform dances, music and art.

There will no longer be SATs at the end of Key Stage 1, and children will follow

an extension of the curriculum for 3–5 year olds.

THE CURRICULUM FRAMEWORK IN SCOTLAND

The curriculum in Scotland is different from those in the rest of the UK in that it is **non-statutory** – that is, it is not set by law. It is a flexible system, which places responsibility on individual education authorities and schools. National guidelines guide teachers by describing the subject areas that are to be covered. The key documents are *Birth to Three: Supporting Relationships, Responsive Care and Respect* and *A Curriculum Framework for Children 3 to 5*. (The curriculum is due to change in 2008 – becoming **A Curriculum for Excellence 3–18**.)

Birth to 3

The document is based on principles summarised as:

* the best interests of children
* the central importance of relationships
* the need for all children to feel included
* an understanding of the ways in which children learn.

There is also a strong emphasis on recognising and valuing the important role of parents. (This is so in all four countries of the UK.)

A curriculum framework for children 3 to 5

There are five key aspects of children's development and learning:

1. Emotional, Personal and Social Development

2. Communication and Language
3. Knowledge and Understanding of the World
4. Expressive and Aesthetic Development
5. Physical Development and Movement.

The framework:

* promotes effective learning – looking at the roles and responsibilities of adults in organising for children's learning; looking at the assessment and planning process; valuing observations that inform these; recording, reporting and evaluating
* sees each child as a unique individual – working together with homes and families, children with special educational needs, fostering equal opportunities, collaborating with other agencies and supporting transitions.

The Scottish Curriculum: A Curriculum for Excellence 3–18

Scotland is currently introducing A Curriculum for Excellence 3–18. It has been designed largely by practising teachers. Teachers decide when a child is ready to move to the next level. A sample of teacher assessments is monitored as a moderation exercise. This checks that all teachers are using the same criteria correctly. The results of the teacher assessments are shared with parents. (A total of 79 per cent of parents voted against SATs being introduced into the Scottish system.) The subject areas are also organised differently, with six different areas of learning. These are:

* English
* mathematics
* science
* design and technology
* creative and expressive studies
* language studies.

THE CURRICULUM FRAMEWORK IN NORTHERN IRELAND

Curricular Guidance for Pre-school Education

The document emphasises the importance of valuing the diverse experiences children bring to the early years setting, and building on this through providing a rich play environment. Children need to learn without experiencing a sense of failure. This requires:

* a stimulating environment, with adequate supervision, in which children are safe, secure and healthy
* an environment inside and outside the playroom with opportunities to investigate, satisfy curiosity, explore and extend their sense of wonder, experience success and develop a positive attitude towards learning
* appropriate periods of time for learning through sustained involvement in play
* adults who are sensitive and encouraging, with whom children feel secure in their relationships, knowing that adults are there to support them
* adults who treat children as individuals and participate in their play sensitively.

The curriculum framework needs to include opportunities, through play and other experiences, to develop the learning associated with:

* personal, social and emotional development
* physical development
* creative/aesthetic development
* language development
* early mathematical experiences

* early experiences in science and technology
* knowledge and appreciation of the environment.

The Northern Ireland Curriculum

In some ways, the Northern Ireland Curriculum is more like the Scottish Curriculum, with similar areas of study, although religious education lies outside these. In other ways, it is like the English National Curriculum in that it follows similar assessment procedures: children are tested at the end of each Key Stage.

The areas of study are:

* English – at Key Stage 1 (this includes drama and media studies)
* mathematics
* science
* design and technology – which may soon be combined with science
* environment and society – which includes geography and history, and may soon include home economics
* creative and expressive studies – which includes PE and dance, art and design, and music
* language studies – only at secondary level (when the Irish language is offered, another modern language must also be offered by the school).

THE PRINCIPLES AND APPROACHES OF COMPETING FRAMEWORKS FOR LEARNING

Early Years Foundation Stage (EYFS)

The overarching aim of the EYFS is to help young children achieve the five *Every Child Matters* outcomes to: **Be healthy**; **Stay safe**; **Enjoy and achieve**; **Make a positive contribution**; **Achieve economic well-being**.

The EYFS: themes and principles

The EYFS is based around four themes:

1. A Unique Child
2. Positive Relationships
3. Enabling Environments
4. Learning and Development.

Each theme is linked to an important **principle**, which is further broken down into four commitments. These describe how the principles are put into practice (see Table 10.2).

ALTERNATIVES TO MAINSTREAM EDUCATION

All children attending early years settings and schools must follow the appropriate curriculum for their age group and their location. A minority of children attend settings that offer an alternative approach and curriculum. Such schools and nurseries are usually – but not always – in the private sector, but are included within the relevant statutory inspection framework (e.g. Ofsted in England). These settings include those described below.

Montessori nurseries and schools

Maria Montessori (1870–1931) became the first female doctor in Italy and worked with children with learning difficulties. Montessori:

* used her observations of children to create new techniques of education that emphasised the unique development of each child

Theme and principle	Commitments
A unique child Every child is a competent learner from birth who can be resilient, capable, confident and self-assured.	1. **Child Development:** Babies and children develop in individual ways and at varying rates. Every area of development – physical, cognitive, linguistic, spiritual, social and emotional – is equally important. 2. **Inclusive Practice:** The diversity of individuals and communities is valued and respected. No child or family is discriminated against. 3. **Keeping Safe:** Young children are vulnerable. They develop resilience when their physical and psychological well-being is protected by adults. 4. **Health and Well-being:** Children's health is an integral part of their emotional, mental, social, environmental and spiritual well-being, and is supported by attention to these aspects.
Learning and development Children develop and learn in different ways and at different rates, and all areas of learning and development are equally important and interconnected.	1. **Respecting Each Other:** Every interaction is based on caring professional relationships and respectful acknowledgement of the feelings of children and their families. 2. **Parents as Partners:** Parents are children's first and most enduring educators. When parents and practitioners work together in early years settings, the results have a positive impact on children's development and learning. 3. **Supporting Learning:** Warm, trusting relationships with knowledgeable adults support children's learning more effectively than any amount of resources. 4. **Key Person:** A key person has special responsibilities for working with a small number of children, giving them the reassurance to feel safe and cared for, and building relationships with their parents.
Positive relationships Children learn to be strong and independent from a base of loving and secure relationships with parents and/or a key person.	1. **Observation, Assessment and Planning:** Babies and young children are individuals first, each with a unique profile of abilities. Schedules and routines should flow with the child's needs. All planning starts with observing children in order to understand and consider their current interests, development and learning. 2. **Supporting Every Child:** The environment supports every child's learning through planned experiences and activities that are challenging but achievable. 3. **The Learning Environment:** A rich and varied environment supports children's learning and development. It gives them the confidence to explore and learn in secure and safe, yet challenging, indoor and outdoor spaces. 4. **The Wider Context:** Working in partnership with other settings, other professionals and with individuals and groups in the community supports children's development and progress towards the outcomes of *Every Child Matters*: being healthy, staying safe, enjoying and achieving, making a positive contribution and economic well-being.
Enabling environments The environment plays a key role in supporting and extending children's development and learning.	1. **Play and Exploration:** Children's play reflects their wide-ranging and varied interests and preoccupations. In their play children learn at their highest level. Play with peers is important for children's development. 2. **Active Learning:** Children learn best through physical and mental challenges. Active learning involves other people, objects, ideas and events that engage and involve children for sustained periods. 3. **Creativity and Critical Thinking:** When children have opportunities to play with ideas in different situations and with a variety of resources, they discover connections and come to new and better understandings and ways of doing things. Adult support in this process enhances their ability to think critically and ask questions. 4. **Areas of Learning and Development:** The Early Years Foundation Stage (EYFS) is made up of six areas of Learning and Development. All areas of Learning and Development are connected to one another and are equally important. All areas of Learning and Development are underpinned by the Principles of the EYFS.

Table 10.2: The EYFS: themes and principles

THE PRINCIPLES UNDERPINNING A CURRICULUM FOR EXCELLENCE 3–18 (SCOTLAND)

- **Challenges and enjoyment:** young people should find their learning challenging, engaging and motivating. The curriculum should encourage high aspirations and ambitions for all. At all stages, learners of all aptitudes and abilities should experience an appropriate level of challenge, to enable each individual to achieve his or her potential. They should be active in their learning and have opportunities to develop and demonstrate their creativity. There should be support to enable young people to sustain their effort.
- **Breadth:** all young people should have opportunities for a broad, suitably weighted range of experiences. The curriculum should be organised so that they will learn and develop through a variety of contexts within both the classroom and other aspects of school life.
- **Progression:** young people should experience continuous progression in their learning from 3 to 18 within a single curriculum framework. Each stage should build upon earlier knowledge and achievements. Young people should be able to progress at a rate that meets their needs and aptitudes, and keep options open so that routes are not closed off too early.
- **Depth:** there should be opportunities for young people to develop their full capacity for different types of thinking and learning. As they progress, they should develop and apply increasing intellectual rigour, drawing different strands of learning together, and exploring and achieving more advanced levels of understanding.
- **Personalisation and choice:** the curriculum should respond to individual needs, and support particular aptitudes and talents. It should give each young person increasing opportunities for exercising responsible personal choice as they move through their school career. Once they have achieved suitable levels of attainment across a wide range of areas of learning, the choice should become as open as possible. There should be safeguards to ensure that choices are soundly based and lead to successful outcomes.
- **Coherence:** taken as a whole, children's learning activities should combine to form a coherent experience. There should be clear links between the different aspects of young people's learning, including opportunities for extended activities that draw different strands of learning together.
- **Relevance:** young people should understand the purposes of their activities. They should see the value of what they are learning and its relevance to their lives, present and future.

* created an environment in which the child is free to develop their own skills and abilities; **Practical Life** exercises develop gross and fine motor skills, concentration and responsibility in independently chosen activities
* designed a set of learning – or **didactic** – materials that encourage children to use their hands – developing a strong grasp of abstract concepts through concrete or 'hands on' experience
* believed that mixed age groups provide children with the opportunity to help and to be helped by other children, and to take part as both the youngest and oldest member

* thought that the highest moment in a child's learning was what she called the polarisation of the attention – the child is completely silent and absorbed in what they are doing.

Montessori teachers are specially trained to observe, to respond to the needs of each child and to **direct** the whole group. They do not teach in the traditional sense, but rather guide each child forward.

Steiner (Waldorf) nurseries and schools

Rudolf Steiner (1861–1925) believed (as did Froebel – see below) in the importance of the **community** and that children need a carefully planned environment in order to develop in a rounded way. Steiner schools are called **Waldorf** schools, and follow the principles outlined below.

* Children do not learn to read or write formally until they are around 7.
* The design of the environment emphasises warm colours, soft materials and rounded corners – and is without plastic toys.
* Outdoors the equipment is minimal, but logs and trunks are plentiful to encourage children's use of their own imagination.
* The use of televisions and computers with younger pupils is strongly discouraged.
* Pupils usually retain the same classmates throughout school and have the same class teacher from the age of 6 to 14.
* Festivals and seasons are given special attention so that pupils appreciate the rhythms of nature.

There are now about 40 Waldorf/Steiner schools in Great Britain and Ireland, which together make up the Steiner-Waldorf Schools Fellowship.

High/Scope

High/Scope is an educational programme originally designed for children in the USA in the 1960s. The High/Scope Approach is based on the following principles.

* **Active learning:** this involves the child having choice of a range of materials and activities. They are free to manipulate those materials, and encouraged to use their own language and have adult support.
* **Plan-Do-Review process:** children are encouraged to use a **Plan-Do-Review** process to give them the opportunity to use their initiative, to generate their own learning experiences and to reflect on those experiences.
* The environment includes four base areas: a book, a home, a construction and an art area. Other areas are added depending on the children's interests (e.g. computer, woodwork, gardening, office or shop). Materials are labelled and stored so that children can find, use and return the materials they need. Children's work is carefully displayed.
* The High/Scope Curriculum has been developed through extensive observations of young children learning, and supports the Early Years Foundation Stage in creating confident learners.

The Reggio Emilia approach

Loris Malaguzzi (1920–1994) founded the Reggio Emilia approach at a city in northern Italy called Reggio Emilia. Malaguzzi is often credited with inspiring the philosophical underpinning to the movement; however, the approach is also based on the ideas of both Piaget and Vygotsky. The main features of the approach are:

* the belief that children are capable of long-term, sustained learning when the topic is of interest to them
* teachers listen to and observe the children closely, ask questions and explore the children's ideas; they then provide experiences that stimulate children's thinking and learning
* the school environment is designed so that every part has its own purpose and identity, and spaces encourage communication through interaction; the *piazza* (communal areas) and *atelier* (art studios) are considered the core of the schools
* children are assisted in their discovery of ideas by both teachers and the *atelierista* (all pre-schools in Reggio have an artist based at the school)
* the 'hundred languages of children' – children should be free to express themselves in many different forms (e.g. painting, drawing, singing, puppetry, acting, dancing)
* parents provide ideas and skills that make them active partners in the children's learning through the interests of children.

The topics for study are derived from the talk of children, through community or family events, as well as the known interests of children (puddles, shadows, dinosaurs); they are then pursued in depth through projects. The role of the educators is not to answer questions for pupils or inform them if they are correct or not, but instead to help

children discover the answer for themselves and question further.

Home education

Elective home education is where parents or guardians decide to provide education for their children at home instead of sending them to school; they are entitled to do this under Section 7 of the Education Act 1996. Where parents opt for elective home education, the LEA needs to satisfy itself that the education being provided is 'efficient' and 'suitable'.

YOUR ROLE IN SUPPORTING DIFFERENT APPROACHES TO LEARNING IN A RANGE OF SETTINGS

You have a vital role to play in supporting children's learning. When planning for children's learning you should consider both the needs and achievements of the child, and the range of learning experiences that will help children to progress in different aspects of their learning and development.

Planning learning experiences

In order to plan learning experiences that will meet each individual child's needs it is important to find out as much as possible about the child and to build on this by:

* regularly observing children
* working together with parents and families
* taking account of special educational needs
* promoting equal opportunities
* collaborating with other agencies, when necessary, and
* supporting transitions.

Section 2
How children learn

THE STAGES AND SEQUENCE OF COGNITIVE DEVELOPMENT

(The normative stages and sequence of cognitive development are summarised in the charts in Unit 2.)

As is emphasised throughout this book, each child is unique. Just as children vary in the rate at which they grow and develop *physically*, so their cognitive development occurs at different rates and in different ways, with some children needing more attention at different stages than others.

Theories relating to cognitive development

Jean Piaget (1896–1990)

Jean Piaget, a Swiss psychologist, identified particular stages of cognitive development that continue to influence how we work with children. His stage theory stated that:

* children move through a series of stages, which are loosely related to age ranges
* children progress through the stages in a particular **sequence** (or order)
* no stage can be missed out or 'jumped over'
* basic concepts are formed early and are refined as children gain first-hand experiences
* very young children are 'egocentric' (i.e. they see things from their own viewpoint and have difficulty in putting themselves in another's place).

Schemas and cognitive development

Piaget uses the term **schema** to describe the skills and concepts that children acquire through the following processes.

* **Assimilation:** the child takes in information from their experiences and constructs a theory or schema.

Sensory motor stage (birth to approximately 2 years) *Main feature: the child begins to interact with the environment, using sensory and motor skills*	
0–6 months	Babies explore objects around them using their **senses** – squeezing, sucking, shaking, etc. They enjoy bright colours and can recognise familiar objects. They begin to differentiate familiar sounds, tastes and smells. They use their voices to produce a range of sounds. Their developing physical skills mean they can coordinate movements to help them explore their environment.
6–12 months	During this period babies learn that objects exist even when they cannot be seen – this is know as developing '**object permanence**'. They may repeat actions to watch cause and effect. They watch and imitate adults, and at this stage develop memory of events they have experienced. This helps them to understand familiar routines.
1–2 years	Increasing physical skills and mobility help children to play with a wider range of objects. They can understand the names of objects and can follow simple instructions. They continue to experiment by repeating actions and movements, and are developing early concepts linked to them. They begin **symbolic play** – using toys or objects to represent things in real life (e.g. a doll becomes a baby, a box becomes a car or television). They will also 'talk' to themselves and be aware of other children playing, although they will not necessarily play 'with' others.

Pre-operational stage (2 to 6 or 7 years)	
Main feature: the child begins to represent the world symbolically	
2–3 years	Manipulative skills develop and children are more able to control their movements to use tools and implements (e.g. hold a crayon and move it up and down, connect construction materials). They have some understanding of their own daily routine and are developing **memory skills**, which help their understanding of basic concepts. They can often match two (sometimes three) colours – usually yellow and red – and begin to name them. Children are still **egocentric** – that is, they are unable to see or understand things from another person's viewpoint. They are becoming able communicators. Play may involve 'looking on' at others and, sometimes, joining in, although they may still play alone or in parallel.
3–4 years	**Pincer grasp** is developed and helps them to use paintbrushes, pencils, beads (large) and other play materials with increasing control. They are developing independence in everyday tasks (e.g. toileting, hand washing, dressing). Play with a wide range of materials helps to develop their understanding of **concepts** (e.g. colour, weight, size, number – they may say the number sequence up to ten but with varying degrees of accuracy). They are becoming fluent speakers and beginning to use written symbols to represent an object or word ('pretend' writing). They can also recognise environmental print (e.g. road names, shop signs). Play may now involve cooperation with others, and they learn through trial and error and opportunities to solve relevant problems.
4–5 years	Physical skills help children to do up buttons, zips and other fastenings. They are becoming more independent in managing their own routines but still need adult help. They are **developing concepts** of time (day and night, sequence of their day), number (know number sequence to ten and may count reliably up to ten), colour (can name some accurately and sort objects by colour), size (can identify big and small when given two appropriate objects and begin to order by size), shape (can identify and name basic 2D shapes and some 3D shapes). They can remember and talk about their own experiences and are beginning to recognise letter shapes and associated sounds. Play is often cooperative and can involve taking on identified roles.
5–7+ years	Increasing independence through developing physical skills and ability to choose and make decisions. During this period they are usually able to **conserve** (see next stage). They are increasingly able to express their ideas and creativity in a variety of ways – through words (spoken and written), movement, music, pictures, models and other craft work. Their drawings include greater detail. **Concepts** are becoming more refined (e.g. time – understanding of seasons, months of the year, days of the week, hours in the day). They are able to play more complex games, and sustain interest and cooperation for longer periods of time. They are beginning to develop own research skills – knowing where to find information they are interested in.
Concrete operational stage (6 or 7 years to 11 or 12 years)	
Main feature: the child learns such rules as conservation	
7–12 years	Children are now less egocentric; they can increasingly see things from another's point of view – they **decentre** and are able to concentrate on more than one thing at a time. They understand the concept of **reversibility** – that both physical actions and mental operations can be reversed (e.g. a ball of play dough can be made into a cylinder shape and then be re-formed into a ball shape). They master **conservation** at about the age of 8 years: quantity, length or number of items is not related to the _arrangement_ or _appearance_ of the object or items. They also master **seriation**: the ability to arrange objects in an order according to size, shape or any other characteristic.

Formal operational stage (11 or 12 years to adulthood)	
Main feature: the adolescent can transcend the concrete (the 'here and now') and think about the future	
12 years – adulthood	Adolescents now begin to understand **abstract concepts** such as fairness, justice and peace. They use deductive logic; this means that they create rules that help them to test things out – to have a hypothesis and to solve problems.

Table 10.3: Piaget's stages of cognitive development

* **Accommodation:** the child has learnt from new experiences and has to adjust (or accommodate) the original schema to fit with the new information.
* **Adaptation:** the child now knows more about certain aspects of the world and can act upon this knowledge.

Piaget used the term **equilibrium** to describe the stage at which the child has successfully incorporated new understanding into an existing schema. He believed that the experience of **disequilibrium** was a crucial motivation to learning.

Lev Vygotsky (1896–1934)

Vygotsky believed it was very important for cognitive development that there be someone who knows more than the child to be available to help them to learn something that would be too difficult for them to learn on their own. He believed that 'what a child can do in cooperation today he can do alone tomorrow'.

The main features of Vygotsky's theory of child development are as follows.

* **The zone of proximal development (ZPD):** (proximal means 'next') also sometimes called the zone of *potential* development, the ZPD is defined as the difference between problem solving the child is capable of performing *independently*, and problem solving he or she is capable of performing with *guidance* or collaboration. Every child has a zone of proximal development, which is achievable only with help and encouragement from another person; this could be guidance from an adult, or collaboration with more competent peers. This 'expert intervention' can only enable learning if it is far enough ahead of the child's present level to be a challenge, but not so far ahead that it is beyond comprehension.

EXAMPLES OF ASSIMILATION AND ACCOMMODATION

1. A child believes that 'all furry four-legged animals are dogs'. One day he sees a breed of dog that he's never seen before and says, 'That's a dog.' The child recognises the similarities and makes the assumption. This is **assimilation**. Then the child sees a squirrel and the child says, 'That's a dog.' But his parents tell him it isn't a dog, it's a squirrel. The child alters his perception. This is **accommodation**.

2. A child learns that her father is called daddy, so she calls other males (e.g. the postman) daddy. This is **assimilation**. She is quickly told that the other man is *not* daddy, he is Harry, the postman. Again, the schema for daddy is modified. This is **accommodation**.

* **The importance of play:** play provides foundations for children's developing skills, which are essential to social, personal and professional activities. Children benefit from play as it allows them to do things *beyond* what they can do in 'real' life – such as pretend to drive a car. Play is another way through which children can reach their zone of proximal development.
* **Reconstruction:** children experience the same situations over and over again as they grow, but each time they can deal with them at a higher level and reconstruct them.
* **The importance of social interactions:** knowledge is not individually constructed, but co-constructed between two people. Remembering, problem solving, planning and abstract thinking have a social origin. What starts as a social function becomes *internalised*, so that it occurs within the child.

Jerome Bruner (1915–)

Bruner's work was influenced by both Piaget and Vygotsky. He claimed that children's learning moves through three stages: enactive, iconic and symbolic, in that order. Unlike Piaget's stages, Bruner did not state that these stages were necessarily age-dependent or inflexible. Bruner's theory has the following features.

* **Enactive stage:** we learn by enacting – or *doing* – things. This applies to adults as well: many adults can perform a variety of physical tasks (e.g. operating a lawn mower or learning to drive a car) that they would find difficult to describe in **iconic** (picture) or **symbolic** (word) form. Children need to have real, first-hand, direct experiences; this helps their thought processes to develop.

* **Iconic stage:** we learn by using visual images. This may explain why, when we are learning a new subject, it is often helpful to have diagrams or illustrations to accompany verbal information. Children need to be reminded of their prior experiences; books and interest tables with objects laid out on them are useful aids to this recall of prior experiences.
* **Symbolic stage:** we learn by making what we know into symbolic codes – languages, music, mathematics, drawing, painting, dance and play are all useful codes, which Bruner calls **symbolic thinking**.

Scaffolding

Bruner believed in the importance of 'scaffolding' in helping children to learn. Adults can help develop children's thinking by being like a piece of scaffolding on a building. At first, the building has a great deal of scaffolding (i.e. adult support of the child's learning), but gradually, as the children extend their competence and control of the situation, the scaffolding is progressively removed until it is no longer needed.

Scaffolding can be described as anything a teacher can provide in a learning environment that might help a student to learn. This includes anything that allows the student to grow in independence as a learner, such as:

* clues or hints
* reminders
* encouragement
* breaking a problem down into smaller steps
* providing an example.

The same scaffolding may be provided to all students, or teachers may offer customised scaffolding to individual learners.

THE FEATURES OF SCAFFOLDING

- **Recruitment:** the adult's first task is to engage the interest of the child and to encourage them to tackle the requirements of the task.
- **Reduction of degrees of freedom:** the adult has to simplify the task by reducing the number of actions required to reach a solution. The child needs to be able to see whether or not they have achieved a fit with the task requirements.
- **Direction maintenance:** the adult needs to maintain the child's motivation. At first, the child will be looking to the adult for encouragement; eventually, problem solving should become interesting in its own right.

- **Marking critical features:** the adult highlights features of the task that are relevant; this provides information about any inconsistencies between what the child has constructed and what they would perceive as a correct construction.
- **Demonstration:** modelling solutions to the task involves completion of a task or explanation of a solution already partly constructed by the child. The aim is that the child will imitate this back in an improved form.

Parents routinely act as teachers – or enablers – in the ways outlined above, through rituals and games, which are a part of normal adult–child interactions.

ACTIVITY: SCAFFOLDING AN ACTIVITY

Daniel and his father were out shopping. Daniel stopped walking and was obviously struggling to do up the zip on his jacket, but was becoming increasingly frustrated. His father stood behind him and – using his own hands to guide Daniel's – helped him to insert the end of the zip into the metal fitting. When Daniel had managed to slot it in, he was easily able to pull the zip up by himself and was delighted.

In class, think about the following scenarios and discuss how you could scaffold the child's learning:

1. Learning about the difference between weight and mass
2. Learning to ride a two-wheeled bike
3. Learning how to tie shoelaces.

Friedrich Froebel (1782–1852)

Froebel founded the first kindergarten in 1840 and his ideas have been very important in shaping the way early years services are integrated. He placed a great deal of emphasis on ideas, feeling and relationships. Froebel's theory has the following features.

* Children have inborn knowledge and skills and are innately **creative** beings.

* The curriculum consists of a set of special shaped wooden blocks – known as **Gifts** – and a set of craft projects known as **Occupations** (songs, movements and dancing, and crafts – such as modelling and drawing).

* There is a focus on mathematical and language skills, and on the adult–child relationship.

The critical (or sensitive) periods for learning

The human brain has a huge capacity to change; it is often referred to as being 'plastic', which means that it grows and develops all the time. *Critical* or *sensitive periods* are windows of opportunity in time, where a child is most receptive to learn with the least amount of effort.

There certainly seem to be critical periods – or sensitive times – when the brain develops in specific ways. For example:

* when in the womb, there is a critical time for brain development during the first three months of pregnancy
* during a baby's first few months, the **hearing** and **sight** pathways in the brain are particularly sensitive to stimulation.

Recent research in the field of neuroscience shows that – although there are certain 'sensitive' times when children are particularly receptive to learning – they are rarely so critical that a child cannot 'catch up' in their learning. For example, a child who has missed a lot of schooling through being in hospital for a series of operations will usually catch up when given the opportunity. He or she may find it more difficult once the sensitive period has passed, but will learn when certain skills are introduced with patience and sufficient time.

Studies of children who have been severely deprived, abused or neglected show that it is particularly difficult for them to catch up once the sensitive periods have been passed. The case study presented below shows how a young child was deprived of emotional, cognitive and social stimulation. There are many other sad cases of so-called 'feral' – or wild – children whose development has been severely delayed. The most famous documented case is that of Genie in the USA; another is that of Isabel Quaresma (see case study box below).

THE ROLE OF ACTIVE LEARNING AND THE IMPORTANCE OF PLAY IN A VARIETY OF SETTINGS

What is active learning?

Active learning is learning that engages and challenges children's thinking using real-life and imaginary situations. It takes full advantage of the opportunities for learning presented by:

* spontaneous play
* planned, purposeful play
* investigating and exploring

Case study: Confined to a hen coop

Isabel was born in 1970 in Tabua, Portugal, to a mentally deficient mother. Isabel was the only one of three children not fathered by a family member. When she was found in January 1980 at the age of 9, she had spent the previous eight years shut in a hen coop. Isabel's growth was seriously stunted, she was not toilet trained, and of course she couldn't talk. She held her arms in the position of hens' wings, and the palms of her hands were covered in hard, scaly patches – or calluses. She had been fed on scraps – the same food as the hens received. One eye was affected by a cataract and there was some speculation whether that had been caused by a hen scratch.

Eventually she was taken to an institution for handicapped children. Some 18 years later, Isabel had not grown much and had made little progress generally. She could understand simple orders, but if asked to fetch two items, would only understand one request and return with one item. Her mental age was estimated at about 2. Physically, she had learnt to walk, but she was unable to talk.

* events and life experiences
* focused learning and teaching.

These opportunities for learning are supported when necessary through sensitive intervention to support or extend learning. All areas of the curriculum can be enriched and developed through play.

The importance of play in active learning

As we have seen in Unit 4, well-planned play is important for the following reasons: It:

* helps children to think and make sense of the world around them
* develops and extends their linguistic skills
* enables them to be creative
* helps them to investigate and explore different materials, and
* provides them with opportunities to experiment and predict outcomes.

Children need opportunities to follow their own interests and ideas through free play. Children's learning is most effective when it arises from **first-hand experiences** (whether spontaneous or structured) and when they are given time to play without interruptions and to a satisfactory conclusion.

Play underlies a great deal of young children's active learning. In order to promote active learning through play, practitioners need to provide:

* a carefully planned and organised environment – with varied resources
* challenging and interesting play opportunities appropriate to children's needs, interests and abilities
* opportunities for creative play – intervening only when necessary to avoid repressing language or imagination
* enough time for children to develop their play

* opportunities for social interaction – promoting cooperation, turn-taking and sharing
* links between play activities and real-life situations (e.g. shop play linked with real shopping trips)
* opportunities to observe children's activities in order to plan for the future and to enable regular assessment.

THE FACTORS THAT CAN AFFECT THE CHILD'S ABILITY TO LEARN

Recently there have been many advances in the way we understand the brain and its functions – and particularly in our understanding of how children learn. It used to be accepted that the structure of our brains are fixed from birth – as a result of the genes we inherit from our parents. Neuroscientists now believe that while the *basic* brain structure is determined by our heredity, this serves only as a framework. Cognitive development is influenced by many factors; these include:

* **genetic factors** (e.g. sensory impairments, Down's syndrome)
* **physical factors** – general health, quality of nutrition, opportunities for physical activity, the development of physical skills (e.g. fine motor skills for hand–eye coordination)
* **environmental factors** – effects of poverty, provision for play and active learning
* **emotional factors** – self-esteem and confidence, effects of trauma (such as bereavement, abuse, a new baby in the family)
* **social factors** – role models, amount of opportunities to socialise, stability of relationship with adults
* **cultural factors** – different cultural experiences and expectations.

One factor may affect another. For example, physical factors such as a hearing impairment may affect a child socially and emotionally, which in turn may lead to lack of confidence and motivation. If children lack stimulation in their environment – in any area of development – they will miss out on important learning experiences that help in the formation of concepts.

The skills children need to learn effectively

In order to learn effectively, children need to develop skills in:

* thinking
* perception
* memory
* language and communication skills – reading and writing
* concentration
* reasoning and problem solving
* imagination and creativity
* understanding concepts.

The frameworks for learning for children from birth to 16 in the UK are designed to promote these skills, and to assess each child's skills throughout their schooling.

HOW TO ENCOURAGE CONCENTRATION AND ATTENTION IN CHILDREN

An important part of the learning process is being able to concentrate and to keep one's attention focused on one activity at a time, without being distracted by other things. We all use our attention and concentration skills every day, often without really noticing them. These skills help us to:

* **select and focus on what is important** (e.g. what the teacher is saying)

* **ignore irrelevant things** that we don't need to pay attention to (e.g. what you can hear going on outside)
* **maintain our effort or attention over time** (e.g. concentrate for the necessary amount of time).

Sometimes we need to pay attention more than one thing at a time; this may require certain skills – for example, copying work from the board while the teacher is explaining the information being given.

There are two types of concentration required in different situations:

1. **active concentration** – construction, creative activities, imaginative play, sand and water play, problem-solving in maths and science, and literacy activities.
2. **passive concentration** – watching television or videos, listening to stories, sitting in assembly, and so on.

Some children can concentrate passively for fairly long periods, while others are better able to concentrate actively when building a model or taking part in imaginative play.

Difficulties with attention and concentration

All children have times when they find it difficult to concentrate. This could be because they:

* are too tired or unwell
* are unable to focus in a busy environment (e.g. with other children talking to them or around them)
* are easily distracted by things going on around them
* are easily distracted by thoughts or feelings that are unrelated to the task at hand (daydreaming)

* are easily overwhelmed by large amounts of information
* are emotionally distressed
* have attention deficit hyperactivity disorder (ADHD).

How you can help

There are many ways in which you can help children to concentrate. These include the following.

* **Minimise distractions:** children need a quiet area for activities that require more concentration; carpets and rugs can be used to keep noise levels down.
* **Respond to individual needs**: some children react badly when they feel rushed in their learning – others become bored and may disrupt others if given too much time for one activity.
* **Time activities appropriately:** avoid situations where the students are passive listeners for long periods of time; keep activities brief, or structure them into short blocks; provide a clear beginning and end.
* **Provide children with hands-on activities:** for example, experiments, orienteering activities, projects.
* **Use children's names and make eye contact:** when giving instructions, get the child's attention by calling their name and making eye contact.
* **Use memory games** and encourage participation in classroom discussions and other collaborative activities.
* **Use songs and rhymes:** these will improve memory and concentration (see the information on **Sing Up** on page 267).
* **Use praise and positive feedback:** children benefit from having targets to improve their concentration, and incentives or rewards when they reach them.

Section 3

Supporting and encouraging children's learning

HOW TO SUPPORT THE DEVELOPMENT OF SKILLS FOR CHILDREN TO BECOME EFFECTIVE LEARNERS

Children need to learn to be capable and independent in order to learn new skills. The child who is self-reliant will be more active, independent and competent: he or she will have the confidence necessary to cope with situations on his/her own and to become an effective learner.

How to promote self-reliance

All children should be allowed and encouraged to do the things that they can do from an early age – and be praised and rewarded for their efforts.

Allow children to do things for themselves. Even very young children begin to show an interest in doing things for themselves.

* Encourage independence by letting children do things for themselves as soon as they express a desire to do so.
* Focus on the effort made by the child and avoid being critical of the 'end product'.
* Always praise children for doing things on their own. As children grow and mature, they will naturally want to do more and more for themselves.

Encourage children to help with challenging tasks. This helps to promote self-confidence.

* Encourage children to try to do new things and to face new challenges; this will promote self-confidence. Remember to choose tasks that children can accomplish.

Encourage children to make decisions. Children learn to make good choices by being given choices.

* At first, choices should be kept simple, like allowing children to choose what to wear out of two outfits. As children get older, encourage them to make more and more complex decisions.

Be a good role model for responsibility and independence. Children learn by watching adults.

* Let children see you making decisions without wavering, and also taking care of responsibilities in an appropriate manner.

Help and encourage children to solve their own problems. Problem solving is a skill that must be learned.

* Encourage children to come up with their own solutions to their problems. The ability to problem solve is a skill that will be useful throughout children's lives. It will also help in the development of confidence and independence.

Encourage children to take risks. Taking risks involves facing potential failure.

* Many parents – and other adults – try to shield children from the disappointment of failure. However, children need to take risks in order to grow. Children must experience failure in order to learn how to cope with it.

Be there to provide support, when needed. Even the most independent-minded children need adult support on certain occasions.

* Make an effort to be available to the children in your care and to provide

support when needed. Children who are secure in their relationships will have the confidence needed to explore the world.

Praise children. Children should receive praise when they display responsible and independent behaviour.

* Adults who praise such behaviour are letting children know that they notice and appreciate their efforts.

Give children responsibilities. One of the best ways for children to learn how to behave responsibly is to be given responsibilities.

* Make sure that the tasks assigned to the children match their capabilities. Take the time to show them how to do their assigned tasks properly. However, how well children perform a task is not as important as what they are learning about responsibility.

From birth, babies and children need to be encouraged to 'have a go' even if their early efforts are not always successful. You have an important role in helping to develop self-reliance at all stages of children's development (see Table 10.4).

HOW TO PROVIDE AN ENVIRONMENT THAT SUPPORTS AND ENCOURAGES CHILDREN'S LEARNING

Learning requires the active, constructive involvement of the learner. Learning in groups at school requires children:

* to pay attention and to concentrate
* to observe
* to memorise
* to understand
* to set goals
* to assume responsibility for their own learning.

Babies
• Encourage babies to cooperate when getting them dressed and undressed (e.g. by pushing their arms through sleeves and pulling off their socks) • Provide finger foods from about 8 months and tolerate mess when babies are feeding themselves • Set out a variety of toys to encourage them to make choices

Children aged 2–4 years
• Provide a range of activities – both indoors and outdoors • Encourage children to help tidy away toys • Allow children to have a free choice in their play • Encourage children in self-care skills – washing hands, brushing hair and getting dressed; be patient and provide them with adequate time • Build choice into routines such as meal and snack times • Encourage children to enjoy simple cooking activities

Children aged 5–8 years
• Provide activities that promote problem-solving skills, such as investigating volume and capacity in sand or water play • Allow children to take responsibility for set tasks (e.g. wiping the tables, caring for plants) • Encourage them to learn specific skills – such as using scissors and threading large needles • Allow children the opportunity to make choices, and encourage them to assess risks when supervised

Children 8–12 years
• Allow children to choose – for example, the choice of playing sports, musical instruments, a dance class, or nothing at all • Encourage them to set goals and work towards achieving them • Provide opportunities for them to plan and organise their own activities • Allow children to make mistakes and to learn from them • Encourage them to ask for support – but avoid taking over completely

Young people 13–16 years
• Allow them to take some control over their own learning, deciding what to learn and how • Assist them in creating learning goals that are consistent with their interests and future aspirations • Provide opportunities for them to demonstrate their skills and achievements (e.g. organising fundraising events or a display board)

Table 10.4: Promoting self-reliance skills throughout childhood

All children will flourish in a good learning atmosphere – or ethos – in which adults support and extend the development and learning of all the children. Every child needs full access to the curriculum in order to learn effectively. This applies to all children – regardless of their ethnic background, culture, gender, language, special educational (or additional) needs, or economic background.

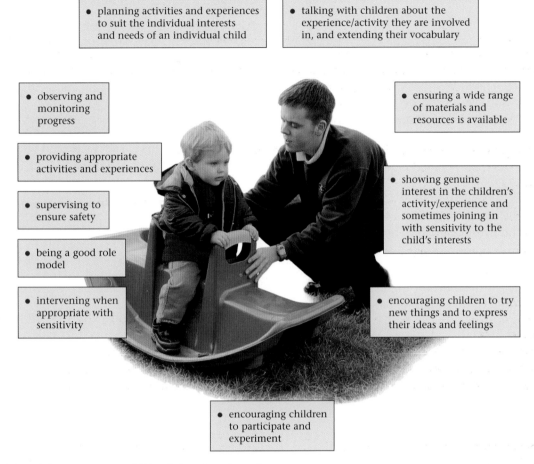

- planning activities and experiences to suit the individual interests and needs of an individual child
- talking with children about the experience/activity they are involved in, and extending their vocabulary
- observing and monitoring progress
- ensuring a wide range of materials and resources is available
- providing appropriate activities and experiences
- showing genuine interest in the children's activity/experience and sometimes joining in with sensitivity to the child's interests
- supervising to ensure safety
- being a good role model
- encouraging children to try new things and to express their ideas and feelings
- intervening when appropriate with sensitivity
- encouraging children to participate and experiment

Fig 10.2. Adults can support children's learning through. . .

THE DIFFERENT TYPES OF ACTIVITIES THAT MEET THE DIVERSE NEEDS OF CHILDREN

Planning activities to meet children's needs

When deciding what activities and experiences will be offered to children, staff in a work setting must consider safety, space, children's ages and stage of development, supervision and availability of resources. Most work settings plan activities around well-chosen themes or topics. In early years settings and primary schools, these are usually relevant to the children themselves

and, perhaps, the time of year – common ones are 'Ourselves', 'Autumn', 'Festivals' (e.g. Christmas, Diwali, Hanukkah, Chinese New Year), 'Growth' and 'Nursery Rhymes'.

Adult-led activities

These are planned, prepared and, often, initiated by adults. For example, a water activity might be planned that focuses particularly on 'force' or 'pressure'. The adult may have selected the equipment that lends itself to using water under pressure – squeezy bottles, thin plastic tubing, a water pump – and allowed children to use it in their own way, or played alongside the children, talking about what was happening and questioning them so that they express their ideas.

Even when an activity is adult-led it should always involve **active participation** by the children. Activities that have an 'end product' (e.g. a model or a special occasion card) must allow for children's experimentation and creativity so that each one is different and original. There is absolutely no value in directing every aspect of a task. You should not aim to have all the children's work looking the same or 'perfect' (i.e. your idea of what the finished article should look like). Ownership is very important: children need to feel that their work is their own. What children learn from doing the activity – practical skills, understanding of materials, textures, sounds, and so on – is far more important than the finished article. Young children should also be able to choose whether or not to make a card or a model.

Child-initiated activities

These occur when children make their own decisions, without suggestion or guidance from adults, about the way in which they use the equipment and resources provided for them. For example, although an adult may have chosen which construction materials to set out (e.g. wooden blocks) two children may decide to work together to build a castle for 'small world' figures or 'play people'. This, then, is a child-initiated activity.

Structured activities

These should be carefully planned to develop a particular aspect of understanding or skill. They are structured in that there are resources, carefully chosen, and usually a sequence of tasks, or steps, that may lead to a desired learning outcome or objective. An adult usually leads, supervises and monitors children's responses.

Example: a simple sorting activity

Aim: to find out if children can identify and sort all the blue objects from a selection of objects of different colours.

* Ask the children individually to find something blue and put it in the sorting 'ring' with other blue things – this ensures that all children participate, and enables the adult to find out if the child has understood the task and can carry it out.
* For this task the child has to know what 'blue' means and be able to distinguish objects of that colour from others.
* Some children may not realise that there are different shades of blue that are still 'blue'.
* Adults working with children on an activity such as this need to talk to them. Asking questions and enjoying a chat together helps adults check each child's understanding.

Spontaneous activities

These can be stimulated by natural events – a hailstorm, snow, a rainbow, puddles – or by an experience a child has had and wants to share with you (e.g. the arrival of a new baby, a new pet, a birthday). The excitement generated by such occurrences makes the learning opportunities too good to let pass without capitalising on them. Planned activities can be postponed to another time in order to make the most of spontaneity. Other spontaneous activities arise when children make their own decisions about how they use the play equipment – perhaps arranging chairs to pretend they are travelling on a bus.

The benefits of singing

Singing can meet all five outcomes of *Every Child Matters* and significantly contribute to all five Extended Schools Core Offer areas.

THE SING UP CAMPAIGN

Sing Up is the Music Manifesto's National Singing Programme, produced by Youth Music with AMV-BBDO, Faber Music and The Sage Gateshead, which was launched on 21st November 2007 by Government Minister Ed Balls. The campaign is being spearheaded by Howard Goodall, Singing Ambassador for the programme. The £40 million investment is part of a wider commitment to provide £332 million to support music-making in schools over the next three years.

The programme includes www.singup.org which hosts the national singing resource – a web-based songbook of new and traditional songs and all the resources that teachers need to integrate singing in their classroom activities. The website will be supported by a magazine and CD materials which are available free of charge to all primary schools.

A workforce development programme will build the confidence and expertise of teachers and other singing leaders, offering CPD and training to schools and singing leaders – 24 Area Leaders have been appointed to coordinate singing programmes across England, providing direct support for schools and organizing tailored training programmes.

For younger children: as part of the government's investment in singing, Youth Music has developed the Music Start pack to get pre-schoolers singing and making music at home with their parents. The pack is aimed at children aged between 2 and 5 and their parents; it contains an illustrated book, a selection of small, hand-held instruments, a CD of original music and suggestions to get parents doing some simple musical activities with their children at home.

* Singing can lead directly to whole-school improvement, particularly through creating a greater sense of community and increasing social cohesion within the school.
* Music lessons in school can help foster individuality, improve social skills and help create more positive attitudes in general. In studies, these effects have been particularly marked in low-ability, disaffected pupils.
* Singing can be used to prepare to start or finish routine activities such as settling down to take the register or signifying the end of the school day.
* Music can be used to reinforce mathematical development through the use of finger and counting games, and exploration of musical instruments and sound-makers through sequencing and patterning.
* Studies have shown that school music lessons can benefit reading and language skills. Very young children have been shown to increase the amount, quality and understanding of speech developed through singing activities.
* There are also many physical advantages to singing, such as increased blood flow and lung capacity. Combined with movement or dance, it can be used to help combat obesity and increase general physical fitness.

The adult role during an activity

The most obvious role is that of ensuring safety by supervising effectively. Regardless

ACTIVITY: PLANNING A SINGING ACTIVITY

1. Think about songs from your childhood, and discuss what makes them memorable.
2. How many mnemonics do you know? (A mnemonic is a short rhyme, phrase or other mental technique for making information easier to memorise –

e.g. the colours of the rainbow or the number of days in each month.)
3. In groups, plan a simple singing activity for a group of children aged 3 to 5 years. Include visual props and musical backing where appropriate.

---

of age and setting there are always some activities that must be supervised. These include:

* cooking
* tasting
* activities involving living things
* those involving equipment that could be dangerous if wrongly used
* physical – particularly those involving climbing frames and/or gymnastic equipment.

Another role is to encourage children to try new things and to express their ideas. This involves the adult showing genuine interest in the children's activities and talking with them about the activities they are involved in. It is important that children experiment themselves, explore the materials and use them in creative ways rather than follow an adult's directions. Asking 'open' questions (see the section on effective communication in Unit 5) encourages children to put their thoughts into words, and the adult can extend their vocabulary by offering the new words in context and at the right time.

When to intervene

You *must* intervene when:

* children are likely to harm themselves
* children could hurt others
* there is a risk of damage to property or equipment

* children are behaving unacceptably (e.g. showing discrimination by name-calling, physical aggression or spitefulness).

The important thing to remember is that children learn best by finding answers for themselves with encouragement and support. The adult role is *not* to take control of the activity away from the children and 'do the difficult bits' for them.

THE PRINCIPLES OF EFFECTIVE COMMUNICATION WHEN SUPPORTING CHILDREN'S LEARNING

(Unit 5 discusses the principles of effective communication with children.)

The importance of consulting the child when supporting children's learning

It is important to recognise that young people have a right to participate in the key decisions that affect their lives. Article 12 of the United Nations Convention on the Rights of the Child states that children and young people should have the opportunity to express their views on matters that concern them, and to have those views taken into account when decisions are made. It is

• ... **children become frustrated** – offer support to help them through the difficult stage and move them on to the next step, e.g. if they are having trouble joining two pieces of Lego assist them by calming them and then, perhaps, holding one piece firmly while they fit the other. DO NOT take both pieces and do it for them.

• ... **play is becoming rough or too boisterous** – sometimes just a look or a word will be enough to remind them of acceptable behaviour.

• ... **children are losing interest** – talk to them about the activity, ask questions that might prompt them to try something new or creative OR suggest they move to another activity.

• ... **children deserve praise** – for effort, acceptable behaviour, achievement.

• ... **some children appear to be excluded from an activity** – this may result from strong personalities 'taking over'. Just talking to the group and asking what each is doing may be enough to solve the problem.

• ... **you notice the children are experimenting and you see an opportunity to develop their understanding**, e.g. rolling toy cars down a slope and talking about which one is fastest. Questioning – 'Why do you think the blue one reached the carpet first?' encourages them to express their ideas – they may be on the wrong track 'because it's blue' or they might think of a reason that could be tested 'because it has more wheels than the red one' or 'because its wheels are bigger'.

• ... **children are experiencing difficulties** – this may result in them losing concentration and not managing to persevere with what they are trying to do. A little encouragement and praise for their efforts can give them the confidence to try again.

Fig 10.3. Adults may choose to intervene when. . .

generally agreed that participation by young people results in real benefits for themselves and for the organisations that consult them. These benefits include:

❋ skills development – communication, negotiation and teamwork
❋ educational experience
❋ promoting a sense of responsibility for oneself and others
❋ being enjoyable and sociable
❋ raising self-esteem.

Recent research into consultation with pupils found that children's learning experiences could be enhanced if tasks were more closely aligned with the social worlds in which they lived – both inside and outside the classroom. They said they found

it helpful when teachers used materials, objects and images that they were already familiar with.

Motivation to learn

Being able to make decisions about their activities is a very important aspect in children's active learning because it ensures that learning is matched to what they *want* to do and achieve. It also enables children to be in control and independent.

Unit 11

Supporting Children and Families

Contents

Unit 11 is divided into three sections

Section 1: The range of support available for children and families

Section 2: How to build positive relationships with children and their families

Section 3: The role of the adult when supporting children and their families in a social care setting

Section 1

The range of support available for children and families

FAMILY STRUCTURES

In today's society there are many different types of family structure and the children in a work setting are likely to come from a wide range of home backgrounds. Many children will live with parents who co-habit but are not legally married. They may have been given either (sometimes both) of the parents' surnames as their own.

There are many different types of family:

* the **nuclear family** – one that has a father, a mother and their 'joint' biological children
* the **reconstituted family** – one that has two parents, each of whom may have children from previous relationships, but has re-formed into a single unit
* the **extended family** – one that includes grandparents and/or aunts and uncles (usually living in the main family home)
* the **lone-parent family** – one in which there is only one parent living with the children – it is often assumed that this is the mother, but in many instances it is the father
* the **adoptive family** – one in which a child has been adopted, resulting in the parents have assumed legal responsibility for the child
* the **foster family** – one that is temporarily caring for a child and may or may not have 'parental responsibility' (see the information about the Children Act 1989 on page 276).

These represent patterns of family life that are commonly found, but within any of them there will be variations, as the following examples show.

* A **reconstituted family** may have not only step-parents and step-children but also children from the new adult partnership who become half-siblings (half-brothers or sisters) to the existing children.
* In **lone-parent families** the absent parent may remain in contact with, and have access to, the children but may have formed new relationships and had more children. This means that the original children are part of both a lone-parent family and a step-family.
* There is an increasing number of homosexual and lesbian couples who have children and live as family units.

Other family types, which are less common, include:

* the **nomadic family** – one that has no permanent town or village; a nomadic family may live in a 'mobile' home and travel to different sites, settling in any one place for only a short period of time
* the **communal family** – one in which children live in a commune where, in addition to their parent or parents, they are cared for by other people who share the home.

Regardless of family structure, all families develop their own customs and practices, even in small daily events such as mealtimes. For some it is always a 'sit at the table' affair, for others it is always 'eat on your lap', for many it is a mixture of formal and informal depending on the time and occasion. Similarly, some regular family activities, like walking the dog or going shopping, often follow a pattern, and a routine is developed that will be very different from another family's. Special occasions (such as birthday celebrations or other cultural festivals) often have highly developed routines that are followed every time; as they are passed down through families these routines become traditions, or even rituals.

There is no 'correct' model for a family structure, just as there is no 'best' way of bringing up children. However, certain things do seem to be important for all families. Always remember that each family is different from every other family.

THE NEEDS OF CHILDREN AND FAMILIES

All children and their families need:

* good-quality core **public services** such as health and education
* **safe places to play**

* **decent housing**
* **leisure opportunities**
* **an inclusive community** free of crime, anti-social behaviour and racial harassment.

SUPPORTING VULNERABLE CHILDREN AND FAMILIES THROUGH A MULTI-AGENCY APPROACH

Who are the vulnerable children and families?

Children in need

The **Children Act (1989)** defines '**children in need**' in broad and developmental terms as children:

ACTIVITY: GROUP DISCUSSION

Within the confidentiality of your group, find out the types of family structure that your own experiences reflect.

1. What can you identify as positive and negative aspects of them? Make two columns and write your ideas under the headings: positive aspects and negative aspects.

2. Look at the different types of family structure and choose one example to research and present to the group.

3. Identify any positive aspects a child in this situation might experience. How might staff in a work setting build on these?

GUIDELINES FOR WHAT ALL FAMILIES NEED TO GIVE CHILDREN

* **Primary needs:** children need to be fed, clothed and sheltered, and to have sleep. This fulfils their primary needs.
* **Nurture:** children need to feel loved and to learn to love. This means they need some reliable people in their lives to show them affection and warmth, and who enjoy receiving their love and warmth in return.

* **Culture:** families introduce children to their culture. This means that, through their family, children learn what people expect of them. The way this comes about varies in different parts of the world, and will be different in different families even within one culture.

* unlikely to achieve or maintain a reasonable standard of health and development without services
* whose health and development will be significantly impaired without services, or
* who are disabled.

In order to respond to the needs and aspirations of **children in need**, an assessment framework was developed that enables an increased understanding of what is happening to a child in relation to their parents and the wider context of family and community (Department of Health, 2000). The interaction of the three areas – the child's **developmental needs**, the **parenting capacity**, and the **family and environmental factors** – will have a direct impact on the current and long-term well-being of a child.

If a family has too little income to keep themselves, the Social Security Act 1986 provides a safety net and social security payments are made. Contributory benefits are available to those who have paid National Insurance during periods of employment. Non-contributory benefits are either:

* **available as of right** (Child Benefit is payable to all mothers, and Income Support is available to families provided there is no other source of income)
* **means tested** – your income is calculated and, if it is higher than a certain level, no benefit will be paid; because the forms are complicated to fill in and people feel anxious about the process, these benefits are often not claimed; examples of this type of benefit include help with rent for elderly people, or family tax credit for families where a parent is working full-time but the income falls below a certain level.

The Department for Works and Pensions is responsible for a range of benefits and services for families (its website address is: www.dwp.gov.uk).

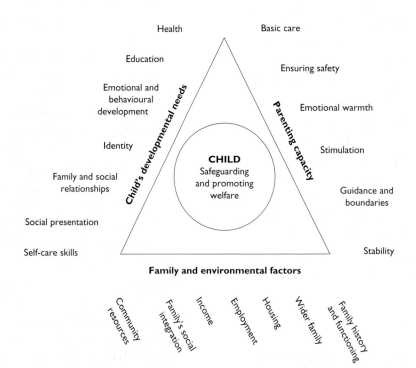

Fig 11.1. Framework assessment triangle

Children and families living in poverty

In the UK in 2007, there were estimated to be 1.3 million children living in **severe poverty**, with their families living on about £19 per week after housing costs. Overall, one in three children in the UK today are living in poverty.

Poverty causes a poor quality of life. It brings stress and sometimes also despair. These can affect social relationships and health.

Low educational achievement is strongly connected with poverty and disadvantage. For example:

* a young child in a comfortably off, 'professional' home will hear every day more than three times the number of words heard by a child with poor parents
* poor children start school less ready to learn, less able to understand the importance of learning and less able to benefit from the teaching they receive in school
* in many homes, there is nowhere quiet to study as the only warm room houses the TV; there is no table on which to work, no books, very few toys and certainly no computers
* almost one-quarter of children cannot afford to go on school trips.

Children in urban settings (located in the inner city rather than in the suburbs) are more likely to experience poverty, a lack of facilities for play, fewer swimming pools and parks, and poor school buildings. Because of the difficult conditions in many urban areas, teachers, doctors and other professionals do not always stay in their jobs for long and children experience a lack of continuity in their care.

Poverty of aspiration

Apart from poverty in wealth or income, children and their families also have a poverty of aspiration. This means that they have low self-esteem, often believing there is little point in making the effort to improve their education.

Housing

The welfare state made cheap, rentable council housing a priority. During the market forces approach of the 1980s, people were encouraged to buy their council houses, and local authorities have not been permitted to build more. This has meant that:

* government funding has supported **housing associations** (these are voluntary organisations) to develop alternatives to council housing (funding for these has, however, been reduced over recent years)
* there is less cheap **rented property** available
* nearly two-thirds of people have **mortgages** and are buying their own homes; this has led to increased homelessness through evictions when people cannot keep up mortgage payments
* some families rent in the **private sector** but may also be evicted if they cannot keep up with payments
* some families live with relatives in **overcrowded** circumstances
* some families have to move into **temporary housing**; constant moves mean a lack of stability for children
* some families are unsuitably placed in **bed and breakfast accommodation**, with inadequate space for basic cooking and washing facilities.

Different problems exist in rural and urban areas respectively. In the UK, fewer children live in the country, but the children of low-paid casual farm workers often grow up in poverty. They are also often lonely and isolated.

* they broaden the range and play experience for the child
* families can save money
* they are particularly useful for children with disabilities as it can be much more difficult to predict what the child will enjoy – parents can experiment
* they help parents to see how pre-structured toys are less interesting to children than toys that can be used in a variety of ways; so-called educational toys, generally quite expensive, are often narrowly pre-structured.

Leisure libraries were pioneered in the UK in 1988, evolving from toy libraries for **children with special needs**. They are often run by groups of parents and by the users themselves, with the support of Social Services. They provide facilities, advice, equipment to borrow and a social meeting place for adults with learning difficulties and their families.

Book libraries and activity packs

These help parents to provide opportunities for early language and literacy, maths and science experiences in the family home, at no – or low – cost. They encourage parents to enjoy books and educational activities with their children.

THE RANGE OF CHALLENGES EXPERIENCED BY CHILDREN AND THEIR FAMILIES

Every family undergoes periods of strain or difficulty from time to time. For some it is short term, while for others it is prolonged and may give rise to tensions and problems that affect children's daily lives. When working with children and their families you need to be understanding of the needs of individuals as well as the whole family unit in order to support them effectively.

Many families experiencing any of the factors listed in Figure 11.2 will cope well with the difficulties, finding support among relatives and friends and other organisations. Indeed, some of the factors (particularly those marked with an asterisk: ★) can have very definite positive aspects to them.

Case study: A young family

Samantha is 19 and lives in a first-floor flat in a large inner-city area. She has one child, Jamie, who is 2 years old. Jamie's father, Kevin, lived with Samantha until Jamie was 2 years old but has now returned to his mother's home because he felt he couldn't cope with all the arguments over money and child care. Kevin's mother dislikes Samantha and feels that she 'trapped' her son by becoming pregnant. Samantha is very close to her own parents, who live around the corner. Her mother has a full-time job but helps out by baby-sitting. Samantha has the opportunity to return to study to take GCSEs. Kevin has offered to look after Jamie for one day a week and will take him to the college nursery the following morning. Samantha is excited by the prospect of this new opportunity but anxious about Kevin caring for Jamie overnight because of his mother's feelings.

1. Identify some of the difficulties that each person may have.

2. How can the staff at the nursery support Jamie and all the family members involved in his care?

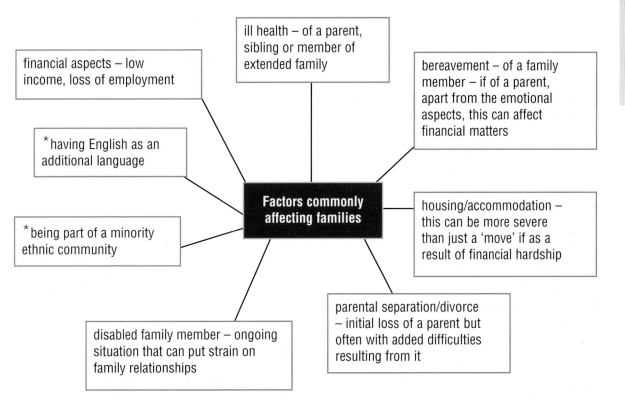

Fig 11.2. Factors commonly affecting families

ACTIVITY: FACTORS COMMONLY AFFECTING FAMILIES

1. In pairs, choose one factor from those detailed in Figure 11.2 and create an imagined situation for a family with a young child in a work setting. Try to use different-aged children for each factor. Then identify:
   - the different ways in which staff might know about the situation
   - what extra provision might be needed for the child
   - how staff might approach the parent(s) to talk about how the child is behaving or progressing
   - what other support would be available to them from state or voluntary organisations.
2. Present the results of your discussions and research to the rest of your group.

Section 2

How to build positive relationships with children and their families

Positive relationships are relationships that help and support children by improving their ability to participate in and benefit from the setting. Working with parents is an essential aspect of work with children. Parents are the first and primary educators of their children. You can strengthen and build on this responsibility so that parents experience an increase in enjoyment of their children and an understanding of child development. Remember that it takes time and regular communication to build good relationships with parents that are founded on mutual trust and respect.

STARTING THE RELATIONSHIP: MAKING PARENTS WELCOME IN THE SETTING

Parents start off in an unequal relationship with child care staff. Some parents may feel very anxious, as they are not familiar with the building, the staff or the rules and relationships within the setting. Other factors may increase their uncertainty and feelings of helplessness. For example:

* they may speak a different language from that spoken in the setting
* they may be under emotional pressure about leaving their child
* they may have other worries (e.g. about getting to work, financial problems).

You need to be able to see things from a parent's point of view and to do everything possible to make them welcome in the setting. Some useful ideas include the following.

* **Names accurately recorded:** first of all, make sure that you have the parents' names accurately recorded. Find out how they want to be addressed – do not assume that their surnames will necessarily be the same as the child's.
* **Greeting:** make a point of greeting parents and smiling at them.
* **Name badges:** these are useful so that parents know to whom they are talking and who their children are talking about.
* **Photos:** a board with staff names and regularly updated photos could be put in the reception area and in newsletters.
* **Key person:** parents need to know which staff member will be working most closely with their child. Most nursery settings have an identified key

person, who will be responsible for keeping notes and records of progress for a small number of children; these key workers will be the main point of contact for the families of those children.

In many nursery settings the children are cared for in groups according to age and/or stage of development and there may be one supervisor for each group. The manager or supervisor of a nursery, or the head teacher in an infant school, would still retain overall responsibility.

The importance of effective communication

Ongoing communication with parents is essential if children's needs are to be met. For many parents there can be regular and informal communication when children are brought to, or collected from, the work setting. However, it is unusual for both parents to perform this task and, therefore, it is often the same parent who has contact. The methods below can usually work for both parents and care workers.

* **Regular contact with the same person:** always meet and greet parents when they arrive. At the start, it is very important that parents meet the same care worker – preferably their child's teacher or key person/worker – on a daily basis.
* **A meeting place for parents:** ideally, there should be a room that parents can use to have a drink and a chat together.

Finding ways to communicate with parents can sometimes be difficult, especially when staff may not feel confident themselves.

Exchanging routine written information

Information that applies in the longer term should, ideally, be given in writing – for example, information concerning food allergies or medical conditions, such as asthma or eczema. As well as telling staff, notices may need also to be attached to a child's own equipment or lunchbox, or displayed in particular areas (e.g. food preparation, nappy-changing). In a school setting the class teacher should ensure that any other adults involved in the child's care receive information as appropriate.

Copies of all letters received and sent, and a record of all communication should be kept for future reference.

Verbal information

Routine information can be – and often is – exchanged verbally. This usually happens at the start and end of the session, when parents and their child's key worker chat informally.

* **Talking with parents:** always let parents know about their child's positive behaviour, and take the opportunity to praise the child in front of their parents. Then, if you need to share a concern with them, they will already understand that you are interested in their child's

Written information	How and when it is used
Formal letter	Welcome letter prior to admission to the setting To give information about parents' evenings or meetings To alert parents to the presence of an infectious disease within the setting To advise parents about any change of policy or staff changes
Newsletter	To give information about future events (e.g. fundraising fairs, open forums and visiting speakers)
Notice board	To give general information about the setting, local events for parents, support group contact numbers, health and safety information, daily menus, and so on
Activity slip	To inform parents about what their child has been doing
Admission form	All parents fill in an admission form when registering their child (see the sample in Figure 11.3); this is confidential information and must be kept in a safe place where only staff have access to it
Home book	To record information from both staff and parents Home books travel between the setting and the home, and record details of the child's progress, any medication given, how well they have eaten and slept, and so on
Accident slip	To record information when a child has been ill or is injured while at the setting
Suggestion box	Some settings have a suggestion box where parents can contribute their own ideas for improving the service
Policy and procedure documents	These official documents should be openly available, and parents should be able to discuss them with staff if they have any concerns

Table 11.1: Exchanging routine written information

Greenfield Day Nursery

ADMISSIONS FORM

Child's name:

Date of birth: Sex:

Child's first language:

Religion: Ethnic origin:

Disabled? Y/N   Access requirements:

Address:

Telephone number:

Mother's name: Occupation:

Name and address of workplace:

Telephone number:

Father's name: Occupation:

Name and address of workplace:

Telephone number:

In an emergency, please contact:

Name:

Relationship to child: Telephone number:

People authorised to pick up child:

Name:

Relationship to child: Telephone number:

Sessions required:

Required starting date:

Signed: Date:

Fig 11.3. Admissions form

welfare and are not being judgemental. (Many adults associate being called in to see the person in charge with their own experiences of a 'telling off'.)

* **Recording information and passing on messages:** you will need to record some information the parent has talked to you about – especially if you are likely to forget it! You should always write down a verbal message that affects the child's welfare, so that it can be passed on to other members of staff – for example, if someone else is collecting the child, if a favourite comfort object has been left at home, or if the child has experienced a restless night. The person delivering the message also needs confirmation that it will be acted upon. Where there are shift systems in operation a strict procedure for passing on messages needs to be established.

* **Telephone calls:** information received or delivered by telephone should be noted in a diary so that action can be taken.

Barriers to communication: how you can help

* **Time constraints:** there may be several children arriving at the same time, which puts pressure on staff at a busy time. Parents may be in a rush to get away when bringing their children. It is important that you do not interpret this as a lack of interest. Greet them with a friendly nod and pass on any information as briefly as possible.

* **Not seeing parents regularly:** when someone other than the parents brings and fetches the child, staff will need to find other ways to maintain regular communication.

* **Body language and non-verbal communication:** be aware of how parents may be feeling at a particular time, even when they do not mention anything specific; for example, if a parent does not make eye contact, it may be that they are depressed.

* **Written communication:** unless sent in the post, there is a chance that some letters and other written notes may not reach the parent. Also, some parents might have difficulty reading and writing, and may not want to seek help. The **notice board** can also be used to display a general letter sent to all parents.

* **Making messages clear:** remember that we understand messages not only from what is said but also from *how* it is said – our tone of voice, gestures and facial expressions can change the meaning of a message. The person on the receiving end of a written message has no such clues. It is important to give careful consideration to the wording of any letter and try to make sure that it cannot be misinterpreted.

* **When English is not the parent's first language:** you can help by signing or – where possible – by involving bilingual staff or translators. Notice boards can display signs in picture form – for example, showing the activities their child will be doing during the session. Having written information in a number of different languages is also helpful.

ACTIVITY: COMMUNICATING WITH PARENTS

* The parents of 3-year-old Thomas have been anxious about their son's appetite since he was ill with a virus. The staff at the day nursery have been observing Thomas, keeping written records and taking photographs, at snack and mealtimes over a period of a week. They have made sure the food is attractively presented, includes some of Thomas's favourite items and offered in small portions. They have noticed a great improvement and want to share their findings with his parents and discuss how he is at home.

* Charlotte, who is 5, has recently become withdrawn, both from adults and other children. For the past week or so she has needed encouragement to complete work tasks that are within her capability, and when she has had free-choice activity she has tended to sit alone in the home corner with a soft toy. This represents a change in Charlotte's behaviour and the teacher wants to discuss her concerns with Charlotte's parents.

1. In each case, what method would you use to contact the parents?

2. Explain what you would say/write and what you would arrange in order to deal with each situation.

ACTIVITY: DESIGNING A NEWSLETTER

Design a newsletter for parents of a reception class child. It should include information about the topic being studied for the forthcoming half-term, suggest what items the children might like to bring in, what parents could do to support the topic or get involved in school. Include some reminders about days when children need their PE kit and any school fundraising events coming up.

WORKING IN PARTNERSHIP WITH CHILDREN AND THEIR FAMILIES

Practices in child-rearing vary around the world, and many cultures have strong traditions as to the role of each parent and in relation to discipline. Whatever the children's backgrounds, the parents are their earliest educators. While some parents will have looked at many different care and education settings before deciding which suits them and their child best, others will have had little choice. It is likely that they will have read the prospectus or brochure, which explains the aims and ethos of the work setting, but that does not necessarily mean that they share *all* those views and attitudes.

Managing sensitive situations

It is not the job of staff in a work setting to tell parents how to raise their children. They can, however, offer suggestions and support, when appropriate, in the best interests of the child. To be able to do this effectively a good, trusting relationship between parents and staff needs to be established. Parents need to feel able to express anxieties and difficulties in confidence and without feeling their parenting skills are being judged.

Confidentiality

In order to establish a relationship of mutual trust and respect, you must ensure that you practise confidentiality at all times. Information about the children in your care

Case study: A conflict between school and home

An infant school clearly states in its prospectus that there is a uniform and gives reasons why it wishes pupils to wear it. Ryan, who is 4, has just started in the reception class and his parents believe that:

- uniforms prevent children from being seen as individuals, and
- wearing uniforms is inappropriate for very young children.

Ryan's teacher believes that Ryan has noticed that he is the only child in the class not in a school sweatshirt and he keeps asking when he will be given his own sweatshirt.

In your group, think about and discuss the following questions.

1. What reasons might the school have for wanting its pupils to wear a uniform?

2. What should the teacher's first step be?

3. How can the situation be resolved to everyone's satisfaction?

4. What are your views about uniforms, generally, and why?

5. List the advantages and disadvantages of having a school uniform.

is confidential and should be kept in a safe place where only staff members may have access to it. The supervisor or manager must check that all staff members are aware of medical conditions or cultural issues that affect the day-to-day care of a child. It is also important to ensure that these details are updated regularly. Most settings have a Confidentiality Policy.

Settling-in policies

Most work settings will have a settling-in policy to make the transition from home to day care, nursery or school, or from one care setting to another, as smooth as possible. Unit 2, Section 5, deals with these in considering the children and their needs; here we need to think about them from the viewpoint of the parents.

Helping a distressed or concerned parent to separate from their equally unhappy child is one of the main issues in nursery settings. This particular age group (under 4 years) finds it particularly hard to separate. This is not helped by a system of often irregular attendance, which makes continuity of settling difficult. Some children sail through this process – however, many do not.

Good practice in settling-in procedures

* **Training:** training should be provided to enable staff to gain skills in interacting with and settling babies and children for whom they are not the key person.
* **Arrival and greeting:** a child's key person should greet parents each time their child attends and leaves the setting. The key person should always ensure time is allowed for two-way communication to take place with each parent on these occasions.

* **Key worker or key person:** parents need to meet and get to know the adults who will be caring for their child. They need to know that their anxieties will be taken seriously and that they can trust staff to support them.
* **Policies, procedures and routines:** parents should be given full information about how the nursery or other setting operates when they apply for a place, both verbally and in booklet form. The policies and procedures should be openly available and parents should be able to discuss them with staff if they have any concerns.
* **Child's preferences:** parents should be given the opportunity to explain their child's likes and dislikes, routines, and so on, so that the work setting may take them into account. Ideally, there will be a home visit made by the setting's staff prior to the child attending. Encourage parents to provide the child's favourite teddy or comfort object.
* **Parental preferences:** it is important to find out, in the event of the child becoming upset, whether the parents would prefer to be called immediately or would be happy for staff to persist for a bit longer with trying to settle her. Find out how and when parents can be contacted if there is a problem with settling in.
* **Communicating with parents:** the needs of parents whose first language is not English should ideally be met through translation services, interpreters and staff language skills. The local Early Years Development and Childcare Partnership (EYDCP) can offer useful advice.
* **Supporting parents:** staff should also be skilled in identifying ways in which all parents, including those with disabilities or learning difficulties, can be

supported in their contribution to their child's learning and development.

* **Keeping parents informed:** parents need to be reassured that they will be told about their child's day and progress, with the opportunity to check that she or he has settled. This is particularly important in the early stages of settling in.

Understanding and respecting the needs of parents

You need to be aware of the wide variety of parenting and family approaches.

* **Full-time employment:** some parents, who are in full-time employment, may have a different attitude towards their child settling in from those who have chosen to place their child in a nursery or playgroup on a part-time basis to widen the child's experience.
* **Individual needs:** every situation and family must be treated individually and its needs met through a flexible approach. For example, parents who are dealing with a large family or with disabled family members will have different priorities from a lone-parent family with one child.
* **Transition to school:** schools often have to deal with children who have had no experience of early childhood education or nursery care, as well as with those who have been in day nurseries from a few months old. Some parents whose children have been in full-time day care find the school's 'staggered' intake – when children attend on a part-time basis at first – both unnecessary and inconvenient, especially if they work. However, most children take time to adapt to a full school day – as this includes a long lunchtime period with less supervision than they are used to and no facilities for an afternoon rest.

* **Referral by Social Services:** when children have been placed in a child care setting on the advice of a social worker, there may be some resentment from parents. They may feel that their rights and responsibilities have been overridden. It is important that a positive relationship between the parents and the setting is established as soon as possible, with a clear understanding that the interest of the child is everyone's main concern. In these situations there will usually be regular meetings involving parents, staff and other professionals to discuss the child's progress.

The role of the key person or worker

A key person is a designated member of staff who is responsible for the care of one or more children within the nursery. Their responsibilities might include:

* planning the child's day
* monitoring and recording the child's development
* liaising with the child's parents
* welcoming and settling in the child and returning the child to the parent at the end of a session.

The key person system helps children to cope with separation and change; it also enables the key person and the child to form an **attachment**. Parents who have to work full-time may not be able to spend time settling their children in to the nursery, and the key person needs to adapt their practice to fit in with parents' needs.

The value of involving parents in the work setting

There are many reasons why it is valuable to involve parents or carers in the work setting.

* Parents know their children better than anyone else.

* Children benefit from the extra attention, particularly one-to-one help.
* A range of different skills can be brought to the work setting (e.g. music, sewing, drawing, cooking).
* Parents who do not share the same language or culture as the work setting can extend the awareness and knowledge of both staff and children about the way other people live, cook and communicate.
* Parents and carers can help by sharing lots of books with children from an early age, and by hearing and helping their child read when they start school.
* Involving parents in the play and learning experiences of their children can help to counteract any negative feelings parents may have about education systems, arising perhaps from memories of their own school days.

Reasons why parents may not want to become involved

Many parents will want to become involved in their child's setting, especially if there is an open, welcoming atmosphere and a place to meet other parents. There will always be some parents who do not want to participate. There could be a number of reasons for this reluctance. These include:

* working full-time or having other daytime commitments
* feeling that they have nothing of value to contribute
* not being interested in spending time with other people's children
* lacking confidence or feeling shy.

It is important that parents do not feel pressured into becoming involved. You should always respect parents' decisions and not assume that this shows a lack of interest in their children.

Some early years settings have a drop-in facility for parents, which helps support those feeling isolated and experiencing problems, while a family support group, with a skilled family worker on hand, can help people with parenting skills and other issues.

In most instances you will be working under the supervision of others and it is likely that parents will pass confidential information directly to a staff member. However, there may be occasions on which you are given information and asked to pass it on, or that you may hear or be told confidential information in the course of the daily routine. This issue is dealt with in the section on confidentiality in Unit 5, and as long as you follow the guidelines, procedures and practices that apply to the work setting you will not go far wrong.

Remember that there are lines of management in place in most work settings and you should follow them if you need to check your understanding or to ask advice. Try to be aware of the ways in which staff members relate to, and communicate with, parents, and try to identify which methods seem to be most effective.

Section 3

The role of the adult when supporting children and their families in a social care setting

Communities throughout the UK provide a range of services that are available to help children and families who are in need of support. **Social workers** help children and families in the following ways. They:

* provide counselling – listening to families and young people in crisis

* put people in touch with other helping agencies
* ensure children, young people and families have access to the most appropriate services available
* provide access to services for children with disabilities and their families
* provide access to support for young carers
* provide access to support for private foster carers
* provide accommodation support to homeless young people
* provide a service to the courts.

STATUTORY CHILD CARE SETTINGS

Social Services provides a range of care and support for children and families, including families where children are assessed as being in need (including disabled children), children who may be suffering 'significant harm', children who require looking after by the local authority (through fostering or residential care) and children who are placed for adoption.

Sure Start Children's Centres

Sure Start Children's Centres are a focal point within each community for parents and carers of children up to age 5:

* they pull together everything families need – from midwives, health visitors and early years provision (integrated day care and early learning) to parenting support, skills training and help to find employment
* they perform **outreach work** to those in the community who are most isolated; they also offer a base for childminder networks and links to other day care provision, out-of-school clubs and extended schools (for more information see Unit 1).

Residential children's homes

Children's homes exist to ensure that the needs of children are met when they cannot live with their own family. They offer a safe place for children to develop and grow, as well as providing food, shelter, and space for play and leisure in a caring environment. Generally, when children and young people need to live away from their families, they will stay with foster carers. It is only when foster care is either not possible or not desirable that residential care is chosen.

Children and young people have to live away from their own families for all sorts of reasons. These include:

* their parents are unwell
* they have problems with their family and need to spend some time away from home (e.g. behaviour problems or educational difficulties)
* they may have a disability and need a break from living with their families
* they are in the care of local authority subject to a Court Order or Voluntary Agreement.

All children and young people who come to live in a Children's Home must have a **Care Plan**. Their Care Plan states:

* why a child is living in a home
* what is supposed to happen while they are living there
* what is supposed to happen at the end of their stay.

Most children *will* go home, but a few go to live with other families and some go to live in other homes. Older children who are not planning to return home are given help to prepare them for living on their own; this is called the **16+ Careleavers Service** (formerly Aftercare).

* Children go to their own school if they have a school place, or social workers help to get them back into school.
* Some young people still attend resources in the community – for example, school or college.
* It is considered very important that children and young people stay in touch with their family and friends. It is only when they might be hurt, or a Court Order says that contact is not allowed, that some children will not be able to have visits from their family or will not be able to visit them.

Foster Care

Foster care is also social care; it is arranged through local social services departments or through **independent** fostering agencies. There are different types of foster care depending on the needs of both the child and their family. These include short-term care for just a few days or weeks, or longer-term placements, as well as care for disabled children or children with behavioural problems.

The main categories of foster care are as follows.

* **Emergency:** when children need somewhere safe to stay for a few nights.
* **Short-term:** when carers look after children for a few weeks or months, while plans are made for the child's future.
* **Short breaks:** when disabled children, children with special needs or children with behavioural difficulties regularly stay for a short time with a family, so that their parents or usual foster carers can have a break.
* **Remand:** when young people are remanded by a court to the care of a specially trained foster carer.
* **Long-term:** not all children who need to permanently live away from their birth family want to be adopted, so instead they go into long-term foster care until they are adults.
* **'Family and friends'** or **'kinship'**: a child who is the responsibility of the local authority goes to live with someone they already know, which usually means family members such as grandparents, aunts and uncles or their brother or sister.
* **Specialist therapeutic:** for children and young people with very complex needs and/or challenging behaviour.

Anyone can apply to be a foster carer, so long as they have the qualities needed to look after children who cannot live with their parents. There is no maximum age limit for being a foster carer.

PRIVATE, INDEPENDENT AND VOLUNTARY CHILD CARE SETTINGS

Some private and voluntary settings provide child care in children's centres, neighbourhood nurseries and extended schools. These programmes are founded on partnerships between local authorities, schools and providers. Others provide care within their own privately managed settings: nurseries, crèches, day nurseries and playgroups.

Childminding

Childminders are often the child care of choice for working parents. Childminders can:

* provide consistent one-to-one care, tailored to the individual needs of a child
* form a stable ongoing relationship with the child, continuing from infancy through to when they need care around schooling

* provide care for siblings together
* be very flexible over the hours of care provided, and can pick up or deliver children to and from other forms of care
* provide care in a home that can include involvement in activities such as cooking, shopping, gardening and family mealtimes.

A **registered childminder** works in their own home, and is registered and inspected by Ofsted, demonstrating the quality and standards of their care. Ofsted ensures that every registered childminder meets the national standards, such as:

* ensuring that they are suitable to be with children
* checking that they provide a safe, stimulating and caring environment, giving children opportunities for learning and play
* making sure they work in partnership with parents and carers.

In addition, in order to become registered, a childminder must undertake police and health checks, have a regular inspection of their home, and take an introductory childminding course and first aid training. Registered childminders can look after only a certain number of children at any one time, which allows them to focus more on each child.

The importance of **working in a team** and providing feedback to colleagues is covered in Unit 1.

YOUR PERSONAL ROLE AND RESPONSIBILITIES IN A SOCIAL CARE SETTING

Your specific role and responsibilities will be governed by the area in which you work.

You should always act in a professional manner and be prepared to ask for guidance when new to the job. (Unit 5 covers the professional skills required when working with children, young people and their families.) Generally, when working in a social care setting, you will need to have a thorough understanding of child development and behaviour. You will also need to know how to promote and maintain:

* a family-centred (not only a child-centred) approach
* multi-agency working – including agencies such as housing, leisure and the benefits agency
* health and safety
* confidence and self-esteem
* diversity and understanding of heritage
* appropriate family contacts.

If you work in a residential children's home, you will be required to undertake a special induction programme within six weeks of starting work. This applies to *all* children's home staff, including any agency, temporary, volunteer and student staff). The induction programme teaches you how to follow procedures relating to:

* emergencies
* health and safety
* child protection (prevention of abuse, recognition of abuse – including its recognition in non-verbal children – dealing with disclosures or suspicions of abuse) and notification of incidents.

ACTIVITY: YOUR ROLE IN RELATION TO CHILDREN AND THEIR PARENTS

1. (a) For each of the following settings, and *working in pairs*, make a list of the *main concerns* parents might have about their baby or child starting and settling into the setting:
   - day care setting
   - nursery class
   - school setting.

   (b) Compare your list with that of another pair, and discuss any similarities and/or differences.

2. Working in small groups, choose *one* of the settings and write a list of the ways in which the setting would welcome a baby or child and parents, and how the settling-in period can be eased. (Note: try to use your own practical experiences in placement to help you – for example, what information do parents provide about their child? Is there a key-worker system?)

3. The amount of parental involvement varies from setting to setting and depends on the age of the children concerned. Thinking about your answers to questions 1 and 2, and using the same setting you chose for question 2, explain how a parent will be involved in the settling-in process.

4. Complete a chart, as in the example below, to show the role of the practitioner during the settling-in process in relation to the child and to the parent(s).

Role in relation to child	Role in relation to parent
Learn child's name quickly	Greet by name
Always welcome child by name	Make time to discuss any concerns
Be ready to give reassurance and attention etc. . . .	etc. . . .

5. A strong partnership between parents and carers helps a child to develop and to make good progress. Most settings provide parents with information about various policies (for example, discipline or behaviour), explain why they have certain procedures and how they will care for, and educate, the children. As a member of staff (in the setting chosen in question 2) some parents have asked you what they should be doing to ensure their child's care and education progresses well, and how they can support you and your work.

   Create a leaflet to give to parents, identifying their role. It must suggest what they can do to support different areas of your work (for example, feeding or mealtimes, behaviour, politeness, getting enough sleep), and explain how it helps the child, the parents and you!

Glossary

additional needs a term which acknowledges that some children have additional individual needs such as those resulting from a disability or a specific learning difficulty, or may have a continuing health condition that affects their life

ADHD (attention deficit hyperactivity disorder) a developmental disorder which can cause overactive behaviour (hyperactivity), impulsive behaviour and difficulties in concentrating

ageism discrimination against an individual or group on account of their age

anti-discriminatory practice involves valuing children, protecting them from discrimination, challenging discriminatory practices, and providing positive models and images for children from a young age

attachment a close relationship − at first with their parents − which babies usually develop with those who care for them

autism a rare developmental disorder which impairs children's understanding of their environment

benefit system benefits are the statutory amounts of money that are issued and distributed via the Benefits Agency to those members of society who need this support

benefits agency the agency within the Department for Work and Pensions (DWP) which is responsible for the assessment and payment of social security benefits

body language the language of non-verbal communication, body language also covers the way the body, face, eyes and hands look and move

calorie unit of energy obtained from foods

code of practice a document which states how a policy (e.g. Equal Opportunities Policy) is put into place

cognitive/intellectual development these words both refer to the ideas and thinking of the child − cognition emphasises that children are aware, active learners, and that

understanding is an important part of intellectual life; intelligence is about the ability to profit from experience

colic an attack of acute abdominal pain caused by spasms in the intestines as food is being digested; sometimes called '3-month colic'

convulsions uncontrolled movements of the muscles, which may be accompanied by loss of consciousness

dehydration the loss of fluid or water from the body

disablism discrimination against an individual or group on account of their disability

discrimination treating a person or group unfairly, usually because of a negative view of certain of their characteristics

Down's syndrome a genetic disorder resulting from the presence of an extra chromosome; children with Down's syndrome usually, but not always, have learning difficulties

eczema a skin condition which can give rise to cracked and sore patches of skin

egocentric self-centred, or viewing things from one's own standpoint

equality of opportunity the principle that all people should be provided with an equal opportunity to succeed, irrespective of their age, sex, ethnic or religious group, physical abilities or sexual orientation

ethos characteristics/beliefs and attitudes of a community (in this case, work setting)

fine motor skills these use the smaller muscles, and include manipulative skills involving precision in finger and hand movements

first-hand experience one which is 'lived' through personally rather than experienced by someone else and seen or heard about

gene unit of the chromosome containing a pattern that is passed on through generations (genes influence hair and eye colour, blood group, etc.)

Glossary

gross motor skills these use the large muscles in the body, as in, say, walking, climbing, running

gross pay the pay you receive before any deductions, such as tax or National Insurance, are made

hearing impairment a loss of hearing ranging from slight, through moderate and severe to profound, because of damage to the nerve endings of the inner ear

holistic seeing a child in the round, as a whole person emotionally, socially, intellectually, physically, morally, healthily, culturally and spiritually

implement to carry out or put into effect; to execute a plan

inclusion refers to the principle of the SEN Code of Practice (2001), which states that children with SEN will usually have their needs met in a mainstream school or early education setting

jaundice yellow coloration of the skin and the whites of the eye caused by the interference with the production of bile

key person or key worker a member of staff (usually in a nursery setting) who spends more time with a small number of identified children, builds a close relationship with them and is the main contact person for their families

learning difficulty a learning difficulty may be moderate to severe, and often leads to low attainment and/or poorly developed social and mobility skills

motherese when adults (often mothers) talk to babies in a high-pitched tone about what is happening

nature/nurture nature = the features, characteristics, abilities one is born with; nurture = one's upbringing, including health, emotional, social and educational factors

non-verbal communication everything that is not actual words; can include body language, posture, tone of voice, etc.

nutrient essential dietary factors, such as carbohydrates, proteins, certain fats, vitamins and minerals

open-ended materials there are many possible ways to use such materials (e.g. clay, wooden blocks)

parallel play children playing along side each other but quite separately and without communicating with each other

pejorative insulting or derogatory

plaque a rough, sticky coating on the teeth that consists of saliva, food debris and bacteria

policy document a document which covers areas of ethical concern and good practice (e.g. health and safety policy)

posseting when a baby regularly vomits small amounts of her feeds but has no sign of illness; usually caused by a weakness of the muscle at the opening of the stomach

practitioner adult who works with young children and their families in any one of a number of settings – for example a childminder in the home environment

prejudice to prejudge somebody on the basis of their membership of a particular category or group

private sector independent from local authority services (e.g. a private nursery)

provision resources and materials provided by adults to support the development and learning of babies and children

pulse in musical terms this is the regular, underlying beat of a tune or rhythm

racism discrimination against an individual or group on account of their race or ethnic group

reconstituted family a family unit which is made up of members of two or more 'original' families

reflective practice involves adults thinking about their work with children, and planning

Glossary

and implementing the curriculum to best support the children's interests and strengths; observing, listening and discussing with colleagues are key components of reflective practice

representing keeping hold of an experience by bringing it back to the mind and making it into some kind of product (e.g. drawing, painting, dance, music)

rhythm the pattern of beats or sounds of varying lengths; when clapping to 'Baa Baa Black Sheep' there is a steady underlying beat as follows – '**Baa** Baa **Black** Sheep, **Have** you any **Wool**?'

role model an individual whose behaviour may be copied or aspired to

scaffolding a process by which adults support and guide children's learning, enabling them to reach to the next level of ability, beyond their own personal capability at that time; the term was coined by Bruner, building on Vygotsky's work

schemas Piaget calls early concepts schemas; they are patterns of linked behaviour that the child can generate and use in a variety of situations

self-esteem the way you feel about yourself – good or bad – leads to high or low self-esteem

self-image/self-concept how you see yourself, and how you think others see you

sexism discrimination against an individual or a group on account of their biological sex

sibling term for a brother or sister

social skills the ability to be with others in a pair or in a group; knowing the appropriate

behaviour for particular situations or activities

socialisation the lifelong process by which we learn about ourselves, others and the world around us

solitary play play which is undertaken alone, sometimes through choice and at other times because the child finds it hard to join in, or because of his/her developmental stage

statementing a formal process of negotiation between an education authority and parents; it aims to identify the child's needs and to specify the educational provision required

statutory services central government services and local government services (e.g. the NHS, Social Services, Local Education Authority)

stereotyping the process whereby individuals or groups are characterised in simple and often pejorative terms, so that all members within the category are seen in one particular way

transition movement between different environments, rooms, settings

voluntary organisation an association or society that has been created by its members rather than by the state (e.g. a charity)

welfare state a society in which the state (i.e. the government) accepts responsibility for ensuring a minimum standard of living for all people; it was set up in 1948 following the Beveridge Report and is supported by a benefit system

Bibliography

Bee, H. (1992) *The Developing Child*. New York: HarperCollins.

Bruce, T. (2004) *Cultivating Creativity in Babies, Toddlers and Young Children*. London: Hodder Education.

Bruce, T. (2004) *Developing Learning in Early Childhood*. London: Paul Chapman Publishing Ltd.

Bruce, T. (2005) *Early Childhood Education* (3rd edn). London: Hodder Education.

Bruce, T. and Meggitt, C. (2007) *CACHE Level 3 Award/Certificate/Diploma in Child Care and Education*. London: Hodder Education.

Cole, M. and Cole, S.R. (1993) *The Development of Children*. New York: Scientific American.

Einon, D. (1985) *Creative Play*. Harmondsworth: Penguin.

Flanagan, C. (1996) *Applying Psychology to Child Development*. London: Hodder Education.

Meggitt, C. (2001) *Baby and Child Health*. Oxford: Heinemann.

Meggitt, C. (2006) *An Illustrated Guide to Child Development* (2nd edn). Oxford: Heinemann.

Nolte, D.L. (1998) *Children Learn What They Live*. New York: Workman Publishing Company, Inc.

Nutbrown, C. (2005) *Key Concepts in Early Childhood Education and Care*. London: Sage Publications Ltd.

Thomson, H. and Meggitt, C. (1997) *Human Growth and Development*. London: Hodder Education.

USEFUL WEBSITES

Action for Sick Children
www.actionforsickchildren.org

Advisory Centre for Education (ACE)
www.ace-ed.org.uk

Bookstart
(aims to promote the enjoyment of books and the pleasure of reading)
www.bookstart.co.uk

British Institute of Learning Disabilities
www.bild.org.uk

CACHE (Council for Awards in Children's Care and Education)
www.cache.org.uk

Child Growth Foundation
www.childgrowthfoundation.org

Children's Information Services (CIS)
www.childcarelink.gov.uk

Commission for Racial Equality
www.cre.gov.uk

Contact a Family
(helps families who care for children with any disability or special need)
www.cafamily.org.uk

Daycare Trust
(the national childcare campaign)
www.daycaretrust.org.uk

Down's Syndrome Association
www.downs-syndrome.org.uk

Dyslexia Action
www.dyslexiaaction.org.uk

Food Standards Agency
www.eatwell.gov.uk

Home-Start UK
(Home-Start schemes offer friendship, support and practical advice to families in difficulties with children under 5 in their homes)
www.home-start.org.uk

I CAN
(I CAN helps children with a communication disability)
www.ican.org.uk

Mencap
www.mencap.org.uk

National Asthma Campaign
www.asthma.org.uk

National Autistic Society
www.nas.org.uk

National Childminding Association
www.ncma.org.uk

National Children's Bureau
www.ncb.org.uk

National Deaf Children's Society (NDCS)
www.ndcs.org.uk

National Eczema Society (NES)
www.eczema.org

Pre-School Learning Alliance
www.pre-school.org.uk

Royal Institute for the Blind (RNIB)
www.rnib.org.uk

Scope
(the association for people with cerebral palsy)
www.scope.org.uk

Social, Emotional and Behavioural Difficulties Association
www.sebda.org

Sure Start
www.surestart.gov.uk

Appendix

MULTIPLE-CHOICE QUESTIONS

1. When a baby begins to sit unaided this is an expected stage of:
   (a) language development
   (b) physical development
   (c) emotional development
   (d) intellectual development

2. When babies show distress when their mother leaves this is an expected stage of:
   (a) physical development
   (b) intellectual development
   (c) communication development
   (d) emotional development

3. A child of 3 can match two or three primary colours; this is an expected stage of:
   (a) language development
   (b) physical development
   (c) emotional development
   (d) intellectual development

4. Children's gross motor skills can BEST be stimulated by:
   (a) playing with wooden bricks
   (b) catching balls
   (c) jumping from a low bench
   (d) threading beads onto a lace

5. Which of the following activities will BEST promote fine manipulative skills in a child of 3 years?
   (a) threading beads
   (b) playing with water
   (c) playing with sand
   (d) pushing a truck

6. Sam can kick a ball hard, stand and walk on tiptoe, walk upstairs with one foot to a step and ride a tricycle using the pedals. Sam is aged:
   (a) 18 months
   (b) 2 years 6 months
   (c) 3 years
   (d) 2 years

7. Between which years are children characteristically possessive and tend to extreme swings of mood and behaviour?
   (a) 1 and 2 years
   (b) 2 and 3 years
   (c) 3 and 4 years
   (d) 4 and 5 years

8. An early years practitioner who is trying to promote self-help skills and independence in young children will be more successful if she or he says:
   (a) 'Come on, you're a big boy now; you can do it by yourself'
   (b) 'See – everyone else has done it. You can do it too'
   (c) 'You'll have a present if you do it all by yourself'
   (d) 'That's clever. Shall I help you with this bit if you can't manage?'

9. Most children will be able to tie their own shoelaces by the age of:
   (a) 3 years
   (b) 4 years
   (c) 5 years
   (d) 6 years

10. At 3 years of age, most children are able to:
    (a) build a tower of nine or ten bricks, cut with scissors, copy a circle
    (b) build three steps with six bricks, thread small beads, copy a square
    (c) catch a ball, draw recognisable pictures, thread a needle
    (d) draw a diamond shape, sew neatly with needle and thread, tie shoelaces

11. How can an early years worker BEST use a 'home area' to promote language development in a group of 3-year-old children?
    - (a) sit in the home corner and talk to one of the children
    - (b) dress up in a hat and take the part of a visitor
    - (c) leave the children alone to develop their play
    - (d) join in the play and direct questions to the children

12. Which of the following activities is most likely to promote communication skills in a 3-year-old child?
    - (a) a varied messy play area
    - (b) a variety of good construction toys
    - (c) discussion and review time
    - (d) jigsaw puzzles

13. Physical development in adolescent boys and girls involves physical, hormonal and sexual changes. This is a stage of development known as:
    - (a) puberty
    - (b) menstruation
    - (c) menopause
    - (d) growth spurt

14. Children aged 8 and 9 years form friendships quite casually and tend to have friends of the same gender. This is an expected stage of:
    - (a) intellectual development
    - (b) social development
    - (c) communication development
    - (d) physical development

15. Isabel's key worker has decided to observe and record Isabel's behaviour over a period of one week. Which method of observation would be the MOST appropriate?
    - (a) narrative – free description
    - (b) tick chart
    - (c) event sample
    - (d) flow diagram

16. Which method of observation involves making a series of short observations at regular intervals over a fairly long period?
    - (a) event sample
    - (b) narrative – free description
    - (c) tick chart
    - (d) time sample

17. When helping a child to settle in a new nursery setting, which of the following should you do:
    1. keep the child away from the door at arrival and departure times
    2. encourage parents to stay with their child until the child asks them to leave
    3. allow the child to bring a comforter, e.g. a blanket or a teddy bear, to the nursery
    4. let the child play in the home area
    - (a) 1, 2
    - (b) 2, 3
    - (c) 1, 3
    - (d) 3, 4

18. It is important to maintain **confidentiality** when recording observations of children. You can best maintain confidentiality by doing which of the following:
    1. ensuring you have signed permission for making an observation
    2. using codes rather than names to refer to the individuals involved
    3. understanding and abiding by policies and procedures in the setting
    4. never discussing children or staff from your work setting in a public place

Appendix

(a) 1, 2, 4

(b) 1, 3, 4

(c) 1, 2, 3, 4

(d) 1, 2, 3

19. Any written records about children and their families should be:

(a) stored securely and confidentiality maintained

(b) available to the head teacher or nursery manager only

(c) freely available to all the staff

(d) kept in the office, to which only staff have access

20. When separated from his main carer, a 2-year-old child will benefit MOST from nursery care that includes:

(a) a group of children of a wide variety of ages

(b) a set routine that is applied equally to all the children in the nursery

(c) a large, lively stimulating group of children

(d) a key person/worker system that has a high ratio of carers to children

For answers, see opposite.

Appendix

ANSWERS TO MULTIPLE-CHOICE QUESTIONS

1	b
2	d
3	d
4	b
5	a
6	c
7	b
8	d
9	d
10	a
11	b
12	c
13	a
14	b
15	c
16	d
17	b
18	c
19	a
20	d

Index

Index

Index

coughing 88
Council for Voluntary Service 6
counting 218
crawling 33–4, 127
creativity 213–14, 250, 258, 266, 268
  creative development 144, 146–7, 149, 151–2, 154
crèches 2
critical periods of development 258–9
critical thinking 250
criticism 172
culture 260, 273
Curricular Guidance for Pre-school Education 248–9
Curriculum for Excellence, A 247, 248, 251
Curriculum framework 244–9
  England 244–7
  Northern Ireland 248–9
  Scotland 247–8, 251
  Wales 246–7
curriculum vitae (CV) 177–8, 179
cuts 89, 95–6, 107
CWDC see Children's Workforce Development Council
cystic fibrosis 60

dairy foods 55
dairy-free diets 68
Day Care and Childminding Regulations 2003 219
day nurseries 2
  key workers 83, 84–5
  settling into 83–4
Daycare Trust 176
deafness without speech 238
  see also hearing impairment
decentring 255
decision making 263
dental care 75, 80
dental caries 51
Department for Children, Schools and Families 244
Department of Education for Northern Ireland (DENI) 244
Department for Education and Skills (DfES) 4, 5, 224–5
Department for Works and Pensions 274
departure times 107
depression 53
deprivation 259
depth perception 42
development see child development
diabetes mellitus 60
diarrhoea 77, 90
didactic (learning) materials 251
diet 54–69, 124
  for babies 63–9
  balanced 57
  and child development 51–2

drinks 54, 57–8
eating habits 58
energy-rich 54
feeding charts 69, 70
guidelines 59
information sharing on 62
meals 56, 57, 59, 80, 124, 216, 272
multicultural influences on 61–2
nutrients 54–5
and parental preferences 69
portion sizes 54–5, 56, 59
snacks 56, 57, 80
social and educational role 62
special 58–60, 62, 68, 218, 219
variety 59
see also food hygiene; food safety
dieticians 232
digging patches 142, 150
Directgov 176
Disability Discrimination Act 2005 225, 226
disabled people 109, 224, 224–6, 228, 229, 238
disablism 18, 19, 196, 197
disapproval 116
discrimination 18, 118, 195–8
  anti-discriminatory play 140
  challenging 15, 197–8
  defining 195
  direct 196
  effects on children's development 196–7
  indirect 196
  institutionalised 196
  and special educational needs children 236, 237
  types of 195–6
disequilibrium 256
disorientation 82
displays 188, 191–2, 199
  interactive 192
  mobiles/hanging 192
  table-top 192
  wall 191
  window 191–2
disputes, handling 17
disruptive behaviour 116
distraction techniques 99, 115
distractions 261, 262
distress 83–4
diversity, encouraging 198–9
divorce 82, 276
dolls 213
domestic abuse 54, 109
dominoes 208
dough play 150, 152–3, 190
Down's syndrome 69
drama 132, 213, 242
drawing 153–5
dreams 69, 70
dress codes 9, 207

dressing-up clothes 101, 148–50, 213
dressings 96, 97, 98
drinks 54, 57–8
drowning 89
drug addiction 19
dummies 66, 75–6
Dunn, Judy 46
dyslexia 24

Early Support programme 169–70, 228
Early Years Action 226, 227, 228
Early Years Action Plus 226, 227, 228
Early Years First Aid 91
Early Years Foundation Stage (EYFS) 142, 244–6, 249–50, 252
Early Years Services 5
echolalia 39
economic factors 228
EDCM (Every Disabled Child Matters) campaign 229
education 4
  achievement 275
  and poverty 52, 275
  travellers and 276
  see also learning; special educational needs children
Education Act 1996 225, 231, 253
Education (Additional Support for Learning) (Scotland) Act 2004 225
Education and Lifelong Learning Department within the Scottish Parliament 244
Education, Lifelong Learning and Skills Department within the Welsh Assembly 244
educational psychologists 118, 233
Educational Visit Coordinators 106
educational welfare officers 233
egocentrism 254, 255
electric shocks 89
electric sockets 188
emergency procedures 91–7, 220, 221
emergency services see ambulances, calling
emotional contagion 42
emotional control/regulation 165
emotional development 31, 44–6
  impairments 77
  and play 53, 133–4, 144, 146–7, 149, 151–2, 154
emotional factors 260
emotional problems 77, 226, 228
empathic listening 163
empathy 12
employers, local 176
employment opportunities 174–80
enabling environments 249, 250

Index

Index

home education 253
home environment 186–7
Home Learning Environment
    (HLE) 4, 186
homosexual parents 272
hopping 127–8
hopping trails 215
hospitals 83, 140
housing 5, 273, 275
    and child development 52
    damp 52
    moving home 82
    overcrowded 52, 275
    temporary 275
housing associations 275
hygiene 124
    equipment 76
    food 88, 105–6, 216, 216–17, 219
    routines for children 72–8, 80–1,
      192
    toy 100
hypoglycaemia (low blood sugar)
    60

iconic stage 257
ideas 125–6, 133–4, 218
identity
    sense of 45
    sexual 46
IEPs (Individual Education Plans)
    237
illnesses
    care worker 100
    infectious 52, 88, 100, 102
    reporting of 90
imitation 115
immunisations 52
inclusion 18, 230–4, 240–1, 250,
    273
    advantages 231–2
    disadvantages 231, 234
    importance 230
    in play 156–7, 206, 207
    schools and 230
    working with children from birth
      to 5 years 195–9
independence 203, 218, 242, 262,
    269
independent care 289–90
independent schools 4, 249, 251–3
Individual Education Plans (IEPs)
    237
individual learning plans 173
infant schools 4, 6, 186
information access, for special
    educational needs 229, 234–5
Information for Parents booklets
    228
information sharing 170
    about behaviour 113
    on diet 62
    and observations 50
information sources 6–7

initiative 16
inspections 90
institutionalised discrimination 196
integrated provision 4–5
intellectual/cognitive development
    and play 125–6, 131–4
    stages and sequences of 254–9
    theories of 254–8
    see also thinking
intellectual/cognitive impairment
    77
interest, showing 161
interest tables 190
internet 25
interpersonal interaction 12,
    160–70
    group 160
    one-to-one 160
intervention 268
interviews 162, 178, 180
iron, dietary 56, 59–60
Ital foods 61–2

Jewish people 62
job applications 177–8, 179–80
Jobcentres 176
journals 175
jumping 127, 128

key issues 25
key persons 85, 107, 250
    and parents 194, 280, 286
    and play 157
    role 193–4
    second 194
    and settling-in policies 285
    working with children from birth
      to 5 years 193–4
Key Stages 244–6, 247, 249
key workers 83, 84–5
    Early Support 170
    role 193–4
    and settling-in policies 285
    and special educational needs
      228
    working with children from birth
      to 5 years 193–4
    working with parents 286
kindergartens 123, 258
kitchen safety 106
knowledge 12
kosher food 62

labelling/labels 15, 18–19, 167,
    196–7, 237–8
lactose intolerance 68
language development 31, 38–41,
    62, 163–5
    and play 133–4, 144, 146–7, 149,
      151–2, 154
language(s)
    additional 167, 198, 199, 283
    appropriate use 14

expressive 168
impairment 77
receptive 168
sign 188, 198, 239–40, 242
unacceptable 117–18
laundry 79
lead poisoning 53
learned helplessness 81
learning 243–69
    active 137, 250, 252, 259–60
    activities 202, 265–8
    and communication 268–9
    and concentration 261–2
    and development 250
    experiential 12
    frameworks 244–53
    how children learn 254–62
    influences on 260–1
    motivation 269
    nature of 30–1
    needs 174, 236, 265–8
    planning 253
    and play 124–5, 133, 165–7, 202,
      257
    scaffolding the 125
    skills 261, 262–3
    support 262–9
    through play 165–7
    see also education
learning disabilities 24, 219, 224–6
learning environment 250
learning resources 191
learning strategies 21–7
learning styles 19–21, 22
    auditory 20, 21, 22
    tactile (kinaesthetic) 20, 21, 22
    visual 20, 21, 22
learning support 250
leisure activities and recreation
    services 5
leisure libraries 278
leisure opportunities 273
lesbian parents 272
letters
    of application 178, 180
    to parents 280–1
libraries
    book 7, 24–5, 278
    leisure 278
    toy 277–8
lifting 189
lighting 187–8, 242
limb elevation 97
lines of reporting 194
listening activities, in group settings
    167–9
listening skills 12, 160, 161–2, 163,
    166, 173
living conditions, unsafe 53–4
living things 190
local authorities 3, 5–6, 228
Local Authority (Council)
    Information Service 7

Index

Index

Index

Index

Index

Index